ROBERT LOUIS STEVENSON

Vol. XIII

VIRGINIBUS PUERISQUE

MEMORIES AND PORTRAITS

THE TRAVELS AND ESSAYS OF ROBERT LOUIS STEVENSON

VIRGINIBUS PUERISQUE MEMORIES AND PORTRAITS

PUBLISHED IN NEW YORK BY CHARLES SCRIBNER'S SONS 1896

CONTENTS

VIRGINIBUS PUERISQUE

CONTENTS

MEMORIES AND PORTRAITS

VIRGINIBUS PUERISQUE

AND OTHER PAPERS

My dear William Ernest Henley,

We are all busy in this world building Towers of Babel; and the child of our imaginations is always a changeling when it comes from nurse. This is not only true in the greatest, as of wars and folios, but in the least also, like the trifling volume in your hand. Thus I began to write these papers with a definite end: I was to be the *Advocatus,* not I hope *Diaboli,* but *Juventutis;* I was to state temperately the beliefs of youth as opposed to the contentions of age; to go over all the field where the two differ, and produce at last a little volume of special pleadings which I might call, without misnomer, *Life at Twenty-five.* But times kept changing, and I shared in the change. I clung hard to that entrancing age; but, with the best will, no man can be twenty-five for ever. The old, ruddy convictions deserted me, and, along with them, the style that fits their presentation and defence. I saw, and indeed my friends informed me, that the game was up. A good part of the volume would answer to the long-projected title; but the shadows of the prison-house are on the rest.

It is good to have been young in youth and, as years go on, to grow older. Many are already old before they are through their teens; but to travel deliberately through one's ages is to get the heart out of a liberal education. Times change, opinions vary to their opposite, and still this world appears a brave gymnasium, full of sea-bathing, and horse exercise, and bracing, manly virtues; and what can be more encouraging than to find the friend who was welcome at one age, still welcome at another? Our affections and beliefs are wiser than we; the best that is in us is better than we can understand; for it is grounded beyond experience, and guides us, blindfold but safe, from one age on to another.

These papers are like milestones on the wayside of my life; and as I look back in memory, there is hardly a stage of that distance but I see you present with advice, reproof, or praise. Meanwhile, many things have changed, you and I among the rest; but I hope that our sympathy, founded on the love of our art, and nourished by mutual assistance, shall survive these little revolutions undiminished, and, with God's help, unite us to the end.

R. L. S.

Davos Platz, 1881.

I

WITH the single exception of Falstaff, all Shakespeare's characters are what we call marrying men. Mercutio, as he was own cousin to Benedick and Biron, would have come to the same end in the long run. Even Iago had a wife, and, what is far stranger, he was jealous. People like Jacques and the Fool in *Lear,* although we can hardly imagine they would ever marry, kept single out of a cynical humour or for a broken heart, and not, as we do nowadays, from a spirit of incredulity and preference for the single state. For that matter, if you turn to George Sand's French version of *As You Like It* (and I think I can promise you will like it but little), you will find Jacques marries Celia just as Orlando marries Rosalind.

At least there seems to have been much less hesitation over marriage in Shakespeare's days; and what hesitation there was was of a laughing sort, and not much more serious, one way or the other, than that of Panurge. In modern comedies the heroes are mostly of Benedick's way of thinking, but twice as much in earnest, and not one quarter so confident. And I take this diffidence as a proof of how sincere their terror is. They know they are only human after all; they know what

3

gins and pitfalls lie about their feet; and how the shadow of matrimony waits, resolute and awful, at the cross-roads. They would wish to keep their liberty; but if that may not be, why, God's will be done! "What, are you afraid of marriage ?" asks Cécile, in *Maître Guerin*. "Oh, mon Dieu, non!" replies Arthur; "I should take chloroform." They look forward to marriage much in the same way as they prepare themselves for death : each seems inevitable; each is a great Perhaps, and a leap into the dark, for which, when a man is in the blue devils, he has specially to harden his heart. That splendid scoundrel, Maxime de Trailles, took the news of marriages much as an old man hears the deaths of his contemporaries. "C'est désespérant," he cried, throwing himself down in the arm-chair at Madame Schontz's; "c'est désespérant, nous nous marions tous!" Every marriage was like another gray hair on his head; and the jolly church bells seemed to taunt him with his fifty years and fair round belly.

The fact is, we are much more afraid of life than our ancestors, and cannot find it in our hearts either to marry or not to marry. Marriage is terrifying, but so is a cold and forlorn old age. The friendships of men are vastly agreeable, but they are insecure. You know all the time that one friend will marry and put you to the door; a second accept a situation in China, and become no more to you than a name, a reminiscence, and an occasional crossed letter, very laborious to read; a third will take up with some religious crotchet and treat you to sour looks thenceforward. So, in one way or another, life forces men apart and breaks up the goodly fellowships for ever. The very flexibility and ease which make men's friendships so agreeable while they endure, make them the easier to destroy and forget. And a man who has a few friends, or one who has a dozen (if there be any one so wealthy on this earth), cannot forget on how precarious a base his happiness reposes; and how by a stroke or two of fate — a death, a few light words, a piece of stamped paper, a woman's bright eyes — he may be left, in a month, destitute of all. Marriage is certainly a perilous remedy. Instead of on two or three, you stake your happiness on one life only. But still, as the bargain is more explicit and complete on your part, it is more so on the other; and you have not to fear so many contingencies; it is not every wind that can blow you from your anchorage; and so long as Death withholds his sickle, you will always have a friend at home. People who share a cell in the Bastille, or are thrown together on an uninhabited island, if they do not immediately fall to fisticuffs, will find some possible ground of compromise. They will learn each other's ways and humours, so as to know where they must go warily, and where they may lean their whole weight. The discretion of the first years becomes the settled habit of the last; and so, with wisdom and patience, two lives may grow indissolubly into one.

But marriage, if comfortable, is not at all heroic. It certainly narrows and damps the spirits of generous men. In marriage, a man becomes slack and selfish, and undergoes a fatty degeneration of his moral being. It is not only when Lydgate misallies himself with Rosamond Vincy, but when Ladislaw marries above him with Dorothea, that this may be exemplified. The air of the fireside withers out all the fine wildings of the husband's heart. He is so comfortable and happy that he begins to prefer comfort and happiness to everything else on earth, his wife included. Yesterday he would have shared his last shilling; to-day "his first duty is to his family," and is fulfilled in large measure by laying down vintages and husbanding the health of an invaluable parent. Twenty years ago this man was equally capable of crime or heroism; now he is fit for neither. His soul is asleep, and you may speak without constraint; you will not wake him. It is not for nothing that Don Quixote was a bachelor and Marcus Aurelius married ill. For women, there is less of this danger. Marriage is of so much use to a woman, opens out to her so much more of life, and puts her in the way of so much more freedom and usefulness, that, whether she marry ill or well, she can hardly miss some benefit. It is true, however, that some of the merriest and most genuine of women are old maids; and that those old maids, and wives who are unhappily married, have often most of the true motherly touch. And this would seem to show, even for women, some narrowing influence in comfortable married life. But the rule is none the less certain: if you wish the pick of men and women, take a good bachelor and a good wife.

I am often filled with wonder that so many marriages are passably successful, and so few come to open failure, the more so as I fail to understand the principle on which people regulate their choice. I see women marrying indiscriminately with staring burgesses and ferret-faced, white-eyed boys, and men dwelling in contentment with noisy scullions, or taking into their lives acidulous vestals. It is a common answer to say the good people

6

marry because they fall in love; and of course you may use and misuse a word as much as you please, if you have the world along with you. But love is at least a somewhat hyperbolical expression for such lukewarm preference. It is not here, anyway, that Love employs his golden shafts; he cannot be said, with any fitness of language, to reign here and revel. Indeed, if this be love at all, it is plain the poets have been fooling with mankind since the foundation of the world. And you have only to look these happy couples in the face, to see they have never been in love, or in hate, or in any other high passion, all their days. When you see a dish of fruit at dessert, you sometimes set your affections upon one particular peach or nectarine, watch it with some anxiety as it comes round the table, and feel quite a sensible disappointment when it is taken by some one else. I have used the phrase "high passion." Well, I should say this was about as high a passion as generally leads to marriage. One husband hears after marriage that some poor fellow is dying of his wife's love. "What a pity!" he exclaims; "you know I could so easily have got another!" And yet that is a very happy union. Or again: A young man was telling me the sweet story of his loves. "I like it well enough as long as her sisters are there," said this amorous swain; "but I don't know what to do when we're alone." Once more: A married lady was debating the subject with another lady. "You know, dear," said the first, "after ten years of marriage, if he is nothing else, your husband is always an old friend." "I have many old friends," returned the other, "but I prefer them to be nothing more." "Oh, perhaps I might *prefer* that also!" There

7

is a common note in these three illustrations of the modern idyll; and it must be owned the god goes among us with a limping gait and blear eyes. You wonder whether it was so always; whether desire was always equally dull and spiritless, and possession equally cold. I cannot help fancying most people make, ere they marry, some such table of recommendations as Hannah Godwin wrote to her brother William anent her friend, Miss Gay. It is so charmingly comical, and so pat to the occasion, that I must quote a few phrases. "The young lady is in every sense formed to make one of your disposition really happy. She has a pleasing voice, with which she accompanies her musical instrument with judgment. She has an easy politeness in her manners, neither free nor reserved. She is a good housekeeper and a good economist, and yet of a generous disposition. As to her internal accomplishments, I have reason to speak still more highly of them: good sense without vanity, a penetrating judgment without a disposition to satire, with about as much religion as my William likes, struck me with a wish that she was my William's wife." That is about the tune: pleasing voice, moderate good looks, unimpeachable internal accomplishments after the style of the copy-book, with about as much religion as my William likes; and then, with all speed, to church.

To deal plainly, if they only married when they fell in love, most people would die unwed; and among the others, there would be not a few tumultuous households. The Lion is the King of Beasts, but he is scarcely suitable for a domestic pet. In the same way, I suspect love is rather too violent a passion to make, in all cases,

8

a good domestic sentiment. Like other violent excitements, it throws up not only what is best, but what is worst and smallest, in men's characters. Just as some people are malicious in drink, or brawling and virulent under the influence of religious feeling, some are moody, jealous, and exacting when they are in love, who are honest, downright, good-hearted fellows enough in the everyday affairs and humours of the world.

How then, seeing we are driven to the hypothesis that people choose in comparatively cold blood, how is it they choose so well ? One is almost tempted to hint that it does not much matter whom you marry; that, in fact, marriage is a subjective affection, and if you have made up your mind to it, and once talked yourself fairly over, you could "pull it through" with anybody. But even if we take matrimony at its lowest, even if we regard it as no more than a sort of friendship recognised by the police, there must be degrees in the freedom and sympathy realised, and some principle to guide simple folk in their selection. Now what should this principle be? Are there no more definite rules than are to be found in the Prayer-book? Law and religion forbid the bans on the ground of propinquity or consanguinity; society steps in to separate classes; and in all this most critical matter, has common sense, has wisdom, never a word to say? In the absence of more magisterial teaching, let us talk it over between friends : even a few guesses may be of interest to youths and maidens.

In all that concerns eating and drinking, company, climate, and ways of life, community of taste is to be sought for. It would be trying, for instance, to keep bed and board with an early riser or a vegetarian. In

matters of art and intellect, I believe it is of no consequence. Certainly it is of none in the companionships
of men, who will dine more readily with one who has
a good heart, a good cellar, and a humorous tongue,
than with another who shares all their favourite hobbies
and is melancholy withal. If your wife likes Tupper,
that is no reason why you should hang your head.
She thinks with the majority, and has the courage of
her opinions. I have always suspected public taste to
be a mongrel product out of affectation by dogmatism;
and felt sure, if you could only find an honest man of
no special literary bent, he would tell you he thought
much of Shakespeare bombastic and most absurd, and
all of him written in very obscure English and wearisome to read. And not long ago I was able to lay by
my lantern in content, for I found the honest man. He
was a fellow of parts, quick, humorous, a clever painter,
and with an eye for certain poetical effects of sea and
ships. I am not much of a judge of that kind of thing,
but a sketch of his comes before me sometimes at night.
How strong, supple, and living the ship seems upon the
billows! With what a dip and rake she shears the flying sea! I cannot fancy the man who saw this effect,
and took it on the wing with so much force and spirit,
was what you call commonplace in the last recesses of
the heart. And yet he thought, and was not ashamed
to have it known of him, that Ouida was better in every
way than William Shakespeare. If there were more
people of his honesty, this would be about the staple of
lay criticism. It is not taste that is plentiful, but courage that is rare. And what have we in place? How
many, who think no otherwise than the young painter,

have we not heard disbursing second-hand hyperboles ?
Have you never turned sick at heart, O best of critics!
when some of your own sweet adjectives were returned
on you before a gaping audience ? Enthusiasm about
art is become a function of the average female being,
which she performs with precision and a sort of haunting sprightliness, like an ingenious and well-regulated
machine. Sometimes, alas! the calmest man is carried
away in the torrent, bandies adjectives with the best,
and out-Herods Herod for some shameful moments.
When you remember that, you will be tempted to put
things strongly, and say you will marry no one who is
not like George the Second, and cannot state openly a
distaste for poetry and painting.

The word "facts" is, in some ways, crucial. I have
spoken with Jesuits and Plymouth Brethren, mathema-
ticians and poets, dogmatic republicans and dear old
gentlemen in bird's-eye neckcloths ; and each understood the word "facts" in an occult sense of his own.
Try as I might, I could get no nearer the principle of
their division. What was essential to them, seemed to
me trivial or untrue. We could come to no compromise
as to what was, or what was not, important in the life
of man. Turn as we pleased, we all stood back to back
in a big ring, and saw another quarter of the heavens,
with different mountain-tops along the sky-line and different constellations overhead. We had each of us some
whimsy in the brain, which we believed more than anything else, and which discoloured all experience to its
own shade. How would you have people agree, when
one is deaf and the other blind ? Now this is where
there should be community between man and wife.

They should be agreed on their catchword in "*facts of religion,*" or "*facts of science,*" or "*society, my dear*"; for without such an agreement all intercourse is a painful strain upon the mind. "About as much religion as my William likes," in short, that is what is necessary to make a happy couple of any William and his spouse. For there are differences which no habit nor affection can reconcile, and the Bohemian must not intermarry with the Pharisee. Imagine Consuelo as Mrs. Samuel Budget, the wife of the successful merchant ! The best of men and the best of women may sometimes live together all their lives, and, for want of some consent on fundamental questions, hold each other lost spirits to the end.

A certain sort of talent is almost indispensable for people who would spend years together and not bore themselves to death. But the talent, like the agreement, must be for and about life. To dwell happily together, they should be versed in the niceties of the heart, and born with a faculty for willing compromise. The woman must be talented as a woman, and it will not much matter although she is talented in nothing else. She must know her *métier de femme,* and have a fine touch for the affections. And it is more important that a person should be a good gossip, and talk pleasantly and smartly of common friends and the thousand and one nothings of the day and hour, than that she should speak with the tongues of men and angels; for a while together by the fire, happens more frequently in marriage than the presence of a distinguished foreigner to dinner. That people should laugh over the same sort of jests, and have many a story of "grouse in the gun-room," many an old joke between them which time cannot wither

nor custom stale, is a better preparation for life, by your
leave, than many other things higher and better sounding in the world's ears. You could read Kant by yourself, if you wanted; but you must share a joke with
some one else. You can forgive people who do not follow you through a philosophical disquisition; but to find
your wife laughing when you had tears in your eyes,
or staring when you were in a fit of laughter, would go
some way towards a dissolution of the marriage.

I know a woman who, from some distaste or disabil-
ity, could never so much as understand the meaning of
the word *politics,* and has given up trying to distinguish
Whigs from Tories; but take her on her own politics,
ask her about other men or women and the chicanery
of everyday existence — the rubs, the tricks, the vanities on which life turns — and you will not find many
more shrewd, trenchant, and humorous. Nay, to make
plainer what I have in mind, this same woman has a
share of the higher and more poetical understanding,
frank interest in things for their own sake, and enduring
astonishment at the most common. She is not to be
deceived by custom, or made to think a mystery solved
when it is repeated. I have heard her say she could
wonder herself crazy over the human eyebrow. Now
in a world where most of us walk very contentedly in
the little lit circle of their own reason, and have to be
reminded of what lies without by specious and clamant
exceptions — earthquakes, eruptions of Vesuvius, banjos
floating in mid-air at a *séance,* and the like — a mind so
fresh and unsophisticated is no despicable gift. I will
own I think it a better sort of mind than goes necessarily with the clearest views on public business. It will

wash. It will find something to say at an odd moment. It has in it the spring of pleasant and quaint fancies. Whereas I can imagine myself yawning all night long until my jaws ached and the tears came into my eyes, although my companion on the other side of the hearth held the most enlightened opinions on the franchise or the ballot.

The question of professions, in as far as they regard marriage, was only interesting to women until of late days, but it touches all of us now. Certainly, if I could help it, I would never marry a wife who wrote. The practice of letters is miserably harassing to the mind; and after an hour or two's work, all the more human portion of the author is extinct; he will bully, backbite, and speak daggers. Music, I hear, is not much better. But painting, on the contrary, is often highly sedative; because so much of the labour, after your picture is once begun, is almost entirely manual, and of that skilled sort of manual labour which offers a continual series of successes, and so tickles a man, through his vanity, into good humour. Alas! in letters there is nothing of this sort. You may write as beautiful a hand as you will, you have always something else to think of, and cannot pause to notice your loops and flourishes; they are beside the mark, and the first law stationer could put you to the blush. Rousseau, indeed, made some account of penmanship, even made it a source of livelihood, when he copied out the *Héloïse* for *dilettante* ladies; and therein showed that strange eccentric prudence which guided him among so many thousand follies and insanities. It would be well for all of the *genus irritabile* thus to add something of skilled labour to intangible brain-work. To find the right word is so doubtful a success and lies so near to failure, that there is no satisfaction in a year of it; but we all know when we have formed a letter perfectly; and a stupid artist, right or wrong, is almost equally certain he has found a right tone or a right colour, or made a dexterous stroke with his brush. And, again, painters may work out of doors; and the fresh air, the deliberate seasons, and the "tranquillising influence" of the green earth, counterbalance the fever of thought, and keep them cool, placable, and prosaic.

A ship captain is a good man to marry if it is a marriage of love, for absences are a good influence in love and keep it bright and delicate; but he is just the worst man if the feeling is more pedestrian, as habit is too frequently torn open and the solder has never time to set. Men who fish, botanise, work with the turning-lathe, or gather sea-weeds, will make admirable husbands; and a little amateur painting in water-colour shows the innocent and quiet mind. Those who have a few intimates are to be avoided; while those who swim loose, who have their hat in their hand all along the street, who can number an infinity of acquaintances and are not chargeable with any one friend, promise an easy disposition and no rival to the wife's influence. I will not say they are the best of men, but they are the stuff out of which adroit and capable women manufacture the best of husbands. It is to be noticed that those who have loved once or twice already are so much the better educated to a woman's hand; the bright boy of fiction is an odd and most uncomfortable mixture of shyness and coarseness, and needs a deal of civilising. Lastly (and this is, perhaps, the golden rule), no woman should marry a teeto-

taller, or a man who does not smoke. It is not for nothing that this "ignoble tabagie," as Michelet calls it,
spreads over all the world. Michelet rails against it because it renders you happy apart from thought or work;
to provident women this will seem no evil influence in
married life. Whatever keeps a man in the front garden,
whatever checks wandering fancy and all inordinate
ambition, whatever makes for lounging and contentment, makes just so surely for domestic happiness.

These notes, if they amuse the reader at all, will probably amuse him more when he differs than when he
agrees with them; at least they will do no harm, for
nobody will follow my advice. But the last word is of
more concern. Marriage is a step so grave and decisive
that it attracts light-headed, variable men by its very
awfulness. They have been so tried among the inconstant squalls and currents, so often sailed for islands in
the air or lain becalmed with burning heart, that they
will risk all for solid ground below their feet. Desperate pilots, they run their sea-sick, weary bark upon the
dashing rocks. It seems as if marriage were the royal
road through life, and realised, on the instant, what we
have all dreamed on summer Sundays when the bells
ring, or at night when we cannot sleep for the desire of
living. They think it will sober and change them.
Like those who join a brotherhood, they fancy it needs
but an act to be out of the coil and clamour for ever.
But this is a wile of the devil's. To the end, spring
winds will sow disquietude, passing faces leave a regret
behind them, and the whole world keep calling and
calling in their ears. For marriage is like life in this —
that it is a field of battle, and not a bed of roses.

"VIRGINIBUS PUERISQUE"

II

HOPE, they say, deserts us at no period of our existence. From first to last, and in the face of smarting
disillusions, we continue to expect good fortune, better
health, and better conduct; and that so confidently, that
we judge it needless to deserve them. I think it improbable that I shall ever write like Shakespeare, conduct an army like Hannibal, or distinguish myself like
Marcus Aurelius in the paths of virtue; and yet I have
my by-days, hope prompting, when I am very ready to
believe that I shall combine all these various excellences
in my own person, and go marching down to posterity
with divine honours. There is nothing so monstrous
but we can believe it of ourselves. About ourselves,
about our aspirations and delinquencies, we have dwelt
by choice in a delicious vagueness from our boyhood
up. No one will have forgotten Tom Sawyer's aspiration: "Ah, if he could only die *temporarily!*" Or, perhaps, better still, the inward resolution of the two pirates, that "so long as they remained in that business,
their piracies should not again be sullied with the crime
of stealing." Here we recognise the thoughts of our
boyhood; and our boyhood ceased — well, when ? —
not, I think, at twenty; nor, perhaps, altogether at
twenty-five; nor yet at thirty; and possibly, to be quite

17

frank, we are still in the thick of that Arcadian period. For as the race of man, after centuries of civilisation, still keeps some traits of their barbarian fathers, so man the individual is not altogether quit of youth, when he is already old and honoured, and Lord Chancellor of England. We advance in years somewhat in the manner of an invading army in a barren land; the age that we have reached, as the phrase goes, we but hold with an outpost, and still keep open our communications with the extreme rear and first beginnings of the march. There is our true base; that is not only the beginning, but the perennial spring of our faculties; and grandfather William can retire upon occasion into the green enchanted forest of his boyhood.

The unfading boyishness of hope and its vigorous irrationality are nowhere better displayed than in questions of conduct. There is a character in the *Pilgrim's Progress,* one Mr. *Linger-after-Lust,* with whom I fancy we are all on speaking terms; one famous among the famous for ingenuity of hope up to and beyond the moment of defeat; one who, after eighty years of contrary experience, will believe it possible to continue in the business of piracy and yet avoid the guilt of theft. Every sin is our last; every 1st of January a remarkable turning-point in our career. Any overt act, above all, is felt to be alchemic in its power to change. A drunkard takes the pledge; it will be strange if that does not help him. For how many years did Mr. Pepys continue to make and break his little vows? And yet I have not heard that he was discouraged in the end. By such steps we think to fix a momentary resolution; as a timid fellow hies him to the dentist's while the tooth is stinging.

But, alas, by planting a stake at the top of flood, you can neither prevent nor delay the inevitable ebb. There is no hocus-pocus in morality; and even the "sanctimonious ceremony" of marriage leaves the man unchanged. This is a hard saying, and has an air of paradox. For there is something in marriage so natural and inviting, that the step has an air of great simplicity and ease; it offers to bury for ever many aching preoccupations; it is to afford us unfailing and familiar company through life; it opens up a smiling prospect of the blest and passive kind of love, rather than the blessing and active; it is approached not only through the delights of courtship, but by a public performance and repeated legal signatures. A man naturally thinks it will go hard with him if he cannot be good and fortunate and happy within such august circumvallations.

And yet there is probably no other act in a man's life so hot-headed and foolhardy as this one of marriage. For years, let us suppose, you have been making the most indifferent business of your career. Your experience has not, we may dare to say, been more encouraging than Paul's or Horace's; like them, you have seen and desired the good that you were not able to accomplish; like them, you have done the evil that you loathed. You have waked at night in a hot or a cold sweat, according to your habit of body, remembering, with dismal surprise, your own unpardonable acts and sayings. You have been sometimes tempted to withdraw entirely from this game of life; as a man who makes nothing but misses withdraws from that less dangerous one of billiards. You have fallen back upon the thought that you yourself most sharply smarted for your misde-

meanours, or, in the old, plaintive phrase, that you were
nobody's enemy but your own. And then you have
been made aware of what was beautiful and amiable,
wise and kind, in the other part of your behaviour; and
it seemed as if nothing could reconcile the contradiction,
as indeed nothing can. If you are a man, you have shut
your mouth hard and said nothing; and if you are only
a man in the making, you have recognised that yours
was quite a special case, and you yourself not guilty of
your own pestiferous career.

Granted, and with all my heart. Let us accept these
apologies; let us agree that you are nobody's enemy
but your own; let us agree that you are a sort of moral
cripple, impotent for good; and let us regard you with
the unmingled pity due to such a fate. But there is
one thing to which, on these terms, we can never agree:
— we can never agree to have you marry. What! you
have had one life to manage, and have failed so strangely,
and now can see nothing wiser than to conjoin with it
the management of some one else's? Because you have
been unfaithful in a very little, you propose yourself to
be a ruler over ten cities. You strip yourself by such a
step of all remaining consolations and excuses. You
are no longer content to be your own enemy; you must
be your wife's also. You have been hitherto in a mere
subaltern attitude; dealing cruel blows about you in
life, yet only half responsible, since you came there by
no choice or movement of your own. Now, it appears,
you must take things on your own authority: God made
you, but you marry yourself; and for all that your wife
suffers, no one is responsible but you. A man must
be very certain of his knowledge ere he undertake to

guide a ticket-of-leave man through a dangerous pass;
you have eternally missed your way in life, with consequences that you still deplore, and yet you masterfully
seize your wife's hand, and, blindfold, drag her after
you to ruin. And it is your wife, you observe, whom
you select. She, whose happiness you most desire, you
choose to be your victim. You would earnestly warn
her from a tottering bridge or bad investment. If she
were to marry some one else, how you would tremble
for her fate! If she were only your sister, and you
thought half as much of her, how doubtfully would you
entrust her future to a man no better than yourself!

Times are changed with him who marries; there are
no more by-path meadows, where you may innocently
linger, but the road lies long and straight and dusty to
the grave. Idleness, which is often becoming and even
wise in the bachelor, begins to wear a different aspect
when you have a wife to support. Suppose, after you
are married, one of those little slips were to befall you.
What happened last November might surely happen
February next. They may have annoyed you at the
time, because they were not what you had meant; but
how will they annoy you in the future, and how will
they shake the fabric of your wife's confidence and
peace! A thousand things unpleasing went on in the
chiaroscuro of a life that you shrank from too particularly realising; you did not care, in those days, to make
a fetish of your conscience; you would recognise your
failures with a nod, and so, good day. But the time
for these reserves is over. You have wilfully introduced
a witness into your life, the scene of these defeats, and
can no longer close the mind's eye upon uncomely pas-

sages, but must stand up straight and put a name upon your actions. And your witness is not only the judge, but the victim of your sins; not only can she condemn you to the sharpest penalties, but she must herself share feelingly in their endurance. And observe, once more, with what temerity you have chosen precisely *her* to be your spy, whose esteem you value highest, and whom you have already taught to think you better than you are. You may think you had a conscience, and believed in God; but what is a conscience to a wife? Wise men of yore erected statues of their deities, and consciously performed their part in life before those marble eyes. A god watched them at the board, and stood by their bed-side in the morning when they woke; and all about their ancient cities, where they bought and sold, or where they piped and wrestled, there would stand some symbol of the things that are outside of man. These were lessons, delivered in the quiet dialect of art, which told their story faithfully, but gently. It is the same lesson, if you will — but how harrowingly taught! — when the woman you respect shall weep from your un-kindness or blush with shame at your misconduct. Poor girls in Italy turn their painted Madonnas to the wall: you cannot set aside your wife. To marry is to domesticate the Recording Angel. Once you are married, there is nothing left for you, not even suicide, but to be good.

And goodness in marriage is a more intricate problem than mere single virtue; for in marriage there are two ideals to be realised. A girl, it is true, has always lived in a glass house among reproving relatives, whose word was law; she has been bred up to sacrifice her judg-ments and take the key submissively from dear papa;

22

and it is wonderful how swiftly she can change her tune into the husband's. Her morality has been, too often, an affair of precept and conformity. But in the case of a bachelor who has enjoyed some measure both of privacy and freedom, his moral judgments have been passed in some accordance with his nature. His sins were always sins in his own sight; he could then only sin when he did some act against his clear conviction; the light that he walked by was obscure, but it was single. Now, when two people of any grit and spirit put their fortunes into one, there succeeds to this comparative certainty a huge welter of competing jurisdictions. It no longer matters so much how life appears to one; one must consult another: one, who may be strong, must not offend the other, who is weak. The only weak brother I am willing to consider is (to make a bull for once) my wife. For her, and for her only, I must waive my righteous judgments, and go crookedly about my life. How, then, in such an atmosphere of compromise, to keep honour bright and abstain from base capitulations? How are you to put aside love's pleadings? How are you, the apostle of laxity, to turn suddenly about into the rabbi of precision; and after these years of ragged practice, pose for a hero to the lackey who has found you out? In this temptation to mutual indulgence lies the particular peril to morality in married life. Daily they drop a little lower from the first ideal, and for a while continue to accept these changelings with a gross complacency. At last Love wakes and looks about him; finds his hero sunk into a stout old brute, intent on brandy pawnee; finds his heroine divested of her angel brightness; and in the flash of that first disenchantment, flees for ever.

Again, the husband, in these unions, is usually a man, and the wife commonly enough a woman; and when this is the case, although it makes the firmer marriage, a thick additional veil of misconception hangs above the doubtful business. Women, I believe, are somewhat rarer than men; but then, if I were a woman myself, I daresay I should hold the reverse; and at least we all enter more or less wholly into one or other of these camps. A man who delights women by his feminine perceptions will often scatter his admirers by a chance explosion of the under side of man; and the most masculine and direct of women will some day, to your dire surprise, draw out like a telescope into successive lengths of personation. Alas! for the man, knowing her to be at heart more candid than himself, who shall flounder, panting, through these mazes in the quest for truth. The proper qualities of each sex are, indeed, eternally surprising to the other. Between the Latin and the Teuton races there are similar divergences, not to be bridged by the most liberal sympathy. And in the good, plain, cut-and-dry explanations of this life, which pass current among us as the wisdom of the elders, this difficulty has been turned with the aid of pious lies. Thus, when a young lady has angelic features, eats nothing to speak of, plays all day long on the piano, and sings ravishingly in church, it requires a rough infidelity, falsely called cynicism, to believe that she may be a little devil after all. Yet so it is: she may be a tale-bearer, a liar, and a thief; she may have a taste for brandy, and no heart. My compliments to George Eliot for her Rosamond Vincy; the ugly work of satire she has transmuted to the ends of art, by the companion

figure of Lydgate; and the satire was much wanted for
the education of young men. That doctrine of the excellence of women, however chivalrous, is cowardly as
well as false. It is better to face the fact, and know,
when you marry, that you take into your life a creature
of equal, if of unlike, frailties; whose weak human heart
beats no more tunefully than yours.

But it is the object of a liberal education not only to
obscure the knowledge of one sex by another, but to
magnify the natural differences between the two. Man
is a creature who lives not upon bread alone, but prin-
cipally by catchwords; and the little rift between the
sexes is astonishingly widened by simply teaching one
set of catchwords to the girls and another to the boys.
To the first, there is shown but a very small field of experience, and taught a very trenchant principle for judgment and action; to the other, the world of life is more
largely displayed, and their rule of conduct is proportionally widened. They are taught to follow different
virtues, to hate different vices, to place their ideal, even
for each other, in different achievements. What should
be the result of such a course? When a horse has run
away, and the two flustered people in the gig have each
possessed themselves of a rein, we know the end of
that conveyance will be in the ditch. So, when I see a
raw youth and a green girl, fluted and fiddled in a danc-
ing measure into that most serious contract, and setting
out upon life's journey with ideas so monstrously divergent, I am not surprised that some make shipwreck,
but that any come to port. What the boy does almost
proudly, as a manly peccadillo, the girl will shudder at as
a debasing vice; what is to her the mere common sense

of tactics, he will spit out of his mouth as shameful. Through such a sea of contrarieties must this green couple steer their way; and contrive to love each other; and to respect, forsooth; and be ready, when the time arrives, to educate the little men and women who shall succeed to their places and perplexities.

And yet, when all has been said, the man who should hold back from marriage is in the same case with him who runs away from battle. To avoid an occasion for our virtues is a worse degree of failure than to push forward pluckily and make a fall. It is lawful to pray God that we be not led into temptation; but not lawful to skulk from those that come to us. The noblest passage in one of the noblest books of this century, is where the old pope glories in the trial, nay, in the partial fall and but imperfect triumph, of the younger hero.[1] Without some such manly note, it were perhaps better to have no conscience at all. But there is a vast difference between teaching flight, and showing points of peril that a man may march the more warily. And the true conclusion of this paper is to turn our back on apprehensions, and embrace that shining and courageous virtue, Faith. Hope is the boy, a blind, headlong, pleasant fellow, good to chase swallows with the salt; Faith is the grave, experienced, yet smiling man. Hope lives on ignorance; open-eyed Faith is built upon a knowledge of our life, of the tyranny of circumstance and the frailty of human resolution. Hope looks for unqualified success; but Faith counts certainly on failure, and takes honourable defeat to be a form of victory. Hope is a kind old pagan; but Faith grew up in Christian days,

[1]Browning's *Ring and Book.*

and early learnt humility. In the one temper, a man is indignant that he cannot spring up in a clap to heights of elegance and virtue; in the other, out of a sense of his infirmities, he is filled with confidence because a year has come and gone, and he has still preserved some rags of honour. In the first, he expects an angel for a wife; in the last, he knows that she is like himself — erring, thoughtless, and untrue; but like himself also, filled with a struggling radiancy of better things, and adorned with ineffective qualities. You may safely go to school with hope; but ere you marry, should have learned the mingled lesson of the world: that dolls are stuffed with sawdust, and yet are excellent playthings; that hope and love address themselves to a perfection never realised, and yet, firmly held, become the salt and staff of life; that you yourself are compacted of infirmities, perfect, you might say, in imperfection, and yet you have a something in you lovable and worth preserving; and that, while the mass of mankind lies under this scurvy condemnation, you will scarce find one but, by some generous reading, will become to you a lesson, a model, and a noble spouse through life. So thinking, you will constantly support your own unworthiness, and easily forgive the failings of your friend. Nay, you will be wisely glad that you retain the sense of blemishes; for the faults of married people continually spur up each of them, hour by hour, to do better and to meet and love upon a higher ground. And ever, between the failures, there will come glimpses of kind virtues to encourage and console.

III. — ON FALLING IN LOVE

"Lord, what fools these mortals be!"

THERE is only one event in life which really astonishes a man and startles him out of his prepared opinions. Everything else befalls him very much as he expected. Event succeeds to event, with an agreeable variety indeed, but with little that is either startling or intense; they form together no more than a sort of background, or running accompaniment to the man's own reflections; and he falls naturally into a cool, curious, and smiling habit of mind, and builds himself up in a conception of life which expects to-morrow to be after the pattern of to-day and yesterday. He may be accustomed to the vagaries of his friends and acquaintances under the influence of love. He may sometimes look forward to it for himself with an incomprehensible expectation. But it is a subject in which neither intuition nor the behaviour of others will help the philosopher to the truth. There is probably nothing rightly thought or rightly written on this matter of love that is not a piece of the person's experience. I remember an anecdote of a well-known French theorist, who was debating a point eagerly in his *cénacle*. It was objected against him that he had never experienced love. Whereupon he arose, left the society, and made it a point not to return to it until he considered that he had supplied the defect. "Now," he remarked, on entering, "now I am in a position to continue the discussion." Perhaps he had not penetrated very deeply into the subject after all; but the story indicates right thinking, and may serve as an apologue to readers of this essay.

When at last the scales fall from his eyes, it is not without something of the nature of dismay that the man finds himself in such changed conditions. He has to deal with commanding emotions instead of the easy dislikes and preferences in which he has hitherto passed his days; and he recognises capabilities for pain and pleasure of which he had not yet suspected the existence. Falling in love is the one illogical adventure, the one thing of which we are tempted to think as supernatural, in our trite and reasonable world. The effect is out of all proportion with the cause. Two persons, neither of them, it may be, very amiable or very beautiful, meet, speak a little, and look a little into each other's eyes. That has been done a dozen or so of times in the experience of either with no great result. But on this occasion all is different. They fall at once into that state in which another person becomes to us the very gist and centrepoint of God's creation, and demolishes our laborious theories with a smile; in which our ideas are so bound up with the one master-thought that even the trivial cares of our own person become so many acts of devotion, and the love of life itself is translated into a wish to remain in the same world with so precious and desirable a fellow-creature. And all the while their acquaintances look on in stupor, and ask each other, with almost passionate emphasis, what so-and-so can see in that woman, or such-an-one in that man? I am sure, gentlemen, I cannot tell you. For my part, I cannot think what the women mean. It might be very well, if the Apollo Belvedere should suddenly glow all over into life, and step forward from the pedestal with that godlike air of his. But of the misbegotten changelings who call themselves men, and prate intolerably over dinner-tables, I never saw one who seemed worthy to inspire love — no, nor read of any, except Leonardo da Vinci, and perhaps Goethe in his youth. About women I entertain a somewhat different opinion; but there, I have the misfortune to be a man.

There are many matters in which you may waylay Destiny, and bid him stand and deliver. Hard work, high thinking, adventurous excitement, and a great deal more that forms a part of this or the other person's spiritual bill of fare, are within the reach of almost any one who can dare a little and be patient. But it is by no means in the way of every one to fall in love. You know the difficulty Shakespeare was put into when Queen Elizabeth asked him to show Falstaff in love. I do not believe that Henry Fielding was ever in love. Scott, if it were not for a passage or two in *Rob Roy,* would give me very much the same effect. These are great names and (what is more to the purpose) strong, healthy, high-strung, and generous natures, of whom the reverse might have been expected. As for the innumerable army of anæmic and tailorish persons who occupy the face of this planet with so much propriety, it is palpably absurd to imagine them in any such situation as a love-affair. A wet rag goes safely by the fire; and if a man is blind, he cannot expect to be much impressed by romantic scenery. Apart from all this, many lovable people miss each other in the world, or meet under some unfavourable star. There is the nice and critical moment of declaration to be got over. From timidity or lack of opportunity a good half of possible love cases never get so far, and at least another quarter do there cease and determine. A very adroit person, to be sure, manages to prepare the way and out with his declaration in the nick of time. And then there is a fine solid sort of man, who goes on from snub to snub; and if he has to declare forty times, will continue imperturbably declaring, amid the astonished consideration of men and angels, until he has a favourable answer. I daresay, if one were a woman, one would like to marry a man who was capable of doing this, but not quite one who had done so. It is just a little bit abject, and somehow just a little bit gross; and marriages in which one of the parties has been thus battered into consent scarcely form agreeable subjects for meditation. Love should run out to meet love with open arms. Indeed, the ideal story is that of two people who go into love step for step, with a fluttered consciousness, like a pair of children venturing together into a dark room. From the first moment when they see each other, with a pang of curiosity, through stage after stage of growing pleasure and embarrassment, they can read the expression of their own trouble in each other's eyes. There is here no declaration properly so called; the feeling is so plainly shared, that as soon as the man knows what it is in his own heart, he is sure of what it is in the woman's.

This simple accident of falling in love is as beneficial as it is astonishing. It arrests the petrifying influence of years, disproves cold-blooded and cynical conclusions, and awakens dormant sensibilities. Hitherto the man had found it a good policy to disbelieve the existence of any enjoyment which was out of his reach; and thus he turned his back upon the strong sunny parts of nature, and accustomed himself to look exclusively on what was common and dull. He accepted a prose ideal, let himself go blind of many sympathies by disuse; and if he were young and witty, or beautiful, wilfully forewent these advantages. He joined himself to the following of what, in the old mythology of love, was prettily called *nonchaloir ;* and in an odd mixture of feelings, a fling of self-respect, a preference for selfish liberty, and a great dash of that fear with which honest people regard serious interests, kept himself back from the straightforward course of life among certain selected activities. And now, all of a sudden, he is unhorsed, like St. Paul, from his infidel affectation. His heart, which has been ticking accurate seconds for the last year, gives a bound and begins to beat high and irregularly in his breast. It seems as if he had never heard or felt or seen until that moment; and by the report of his memory, he must have lived his past life between sleep or waking, or with the preoccupied attention of a brown study. He is practically incommoded by the generosity of his feelings, smiles much when he is alone, and develops a habit of looking rather blankly upon the moon and stars. But it is not at all within the province of a prose essayist to give a picture of this hyperbolical frame of mind; and the thing has been done already, and that to admiration. In *Adelaide,* in Tennyson's *Maud,* and in some of Heine's songs, you get the absolute expression of this midsum-

32

mer spirit. Romeo and Juliet were very much in love ; although they tell me some German critics are of a different opinion, probably the same who would have us think Mercutio a dull fellow. Poor Antony was in love, and no mistake. That lay figure Marius, in *Les Misérables*, is also a genuine case in his own way, and worth observation. A good many of George Sand's people are thoroughly in love; and so are a good many of George Meredith's. Altogether, there is plenty to read on the subject. If the root of the matter be in him, and if he has the requisite chords to set in vibration, a young man may occasionally enter, with the key of art, into that land of Beulah which is upon the borders of Heaven and within sight of the City of Love. There let him sit awhile to hatch delightful hopes and perilous illusions.

One thing that accompanies the passion in its first blush is certainly difficult to explain. It comes (I do not quite see how) that from having a very supreme sense of pleasure in all parts of life — in lying down to sleep, in waking, in motion, in breathing, in continuing to be — the lover begins to regard his happiness as beneficial for the rest of the world and highly meritorious in himself. Our race has never been able contentedly to suppose that the noise of its wars, conducted by a few young gentlemen in a corner of an inconsiderable star, does not re-echo among the courts of Heaven with quite a formidable effect. In much the same taste, when people find a great to-do in their own breasts, they imagine it must have some influence in their neighbourhood. The presence of the two lovers is so enchanting to each other that it seems as if it must be the best thing possible for everybody else. They are half inclined to fancy it is because of them and their love that the sky is blue and the sun shines. And certainly the weather is usually fine while people are courting. . . . In point of fact, although the happy man feels very kindly towards others of his own sex, there is apt to be something too much of the magnifico in his demeanour. If people grow presuming and self-important over such matters as a dukedom or the Holy See, they will scarcely support the dizziest elevation in life without some suspicion of a strut; and the dizziest elevation is to love and be loved in return. Consequently, accepted lovers are a trifle condescending in their address to other men. An overweening sense of the passion and importance of life hardly conduces to simplicity of manner. To women, they feel very nobly, very purely, and very generously, as if they were so many Joan-of-Arc's; but this does not come out in their behaviour; and they treat them to Grandisonian airs marked with a suspicion of fatuity. I am not quite certain that women do not like this sort of thing; but really, after having bemused myself over *Daniel Deronda,* I have given up trying to understand what they like.

If it did nothing else, this sublime and ridiculous superstition, that the pleasure of the pair is somehow blessed to others, and everybody is made happier in their happiness, would serve at least to keep love generous and great-hearted. Nor is it quite a baseless superstition after all. Other lovers are hugely interested. They strike the nicest balance between pity and approval, when they see people aping the greatness of their own sentiments. It is an understood thing in the play, that while

34

the young gentlefolk are courting on the terrace, a rough
flirtation is being carried on, and a light, trivial sort of
love is growing up, between the footman and the singing chambermaid.   As people are generally cast for the
leading parts in their own imaginations, the reader can
apply the parallel to real life without much chance of
going wrong.   In short, they are quite sure this other
love-affair is not so deep-seated as their own, but they
like dearly to see it going forward.   And love, considered as a spectacle, must have attractions for many who
are not of the confraternity.   The sentimental old maid
is a commonplace of the novelists; and he must be rather
a poor sort of human being, to be sure, who can look on
at this pretty madness without indulgence and sympathy.   For nature commends itself to people with a
most insinuating art; the busiest is now and again arrested by a great sunset; and you may be as pacific or
as cold-blooded as you will, but you cannot help some
emotion when you read of well-disputed battles, or meet
a pair of lovers in the lane.

Certainly, whatever it may be with regard to the world
at large, this idea of beneficent pleasure is true as between
the sweethearts.   To do good and communicate is the
lover's grand intention.   It is the happiness of the other
that makes his own most intense gratification.   It is not
possible to disentangle the different emotions, the pride,
humility, pity and passion, which are excited by a look
of happy love or an unexpected caress.   To make one's
self beautiful, to dress the hair, to excel in talk, to do anything and all things that puff out the character and attributes and make them imposing in the eyes of others, is
not only to magnify one's self, but to offer the most del-

icate homage at the same time. And it is in this latter
intention that they are done by lovers; for the essence
of love is kindness; and indeed it may be best defined
as passionate kindness: kindness, so to speak, run mad
and become importunate and violent. Vanity in a merely
personal sense exists no longer. The lover takes a perilous pleasure in privately displaying his weak points
and having them, one after another, accepted and con-
doned. He wishes to be assured that he is not loved
for this or that good quality, but for himself, or something as like himself as he can contrive to set forward.
For, although it may have been a very difficult thing to
paint the marriage of Cana, or write the fourth act of
Antony and Cleopatra, there is a more difficult piece of
art before every one in this world who cares to set about
explaining his own character to others. Words and acts
are easily wrenched from their true significance; and
they are all the language we have to come and go upon.
A pitiful job we make of it, as a rule. For better or
worse, people mistake our meaning and take our emotions at a wrong valuation. And generally we rest pretty
content with our failures; we are content to be misap-
prehended by cackling flirts; but when once a man is
moonstruck with this affection of love, he makes it a point
of honour to clear such dubieties away. He cannot have
the Best of her Sex misled upon a point of this importance; and his pride revolts at being loved in a mistake.

He discovers a great reluctance to return on former
periods of his life. To all that has not been shared with
her, rights and duties, bygone fortunes and dispositions,
he can look back only by a difficult and repugnant effort
of the will. That he should have wasted some years in

ignorance of what alone was really important, that he may have entertained the thought of other women with any show of complacency, is a burthen almost too heavy for his self-respect. But it is the thought of another past that rankles in his spirit like a poisoned wound. That he himself made a fashion of being alive in the bald, beggarly days before a certain meeting, is deplorable enough in all good conscience. But that She should have permitted herself the same liberty seems inconsistent with a Divine providence.

A great many people run down jealousy, on the score that it is an artificial feeling, as well as practically inconvenient. This is scarcely fair; for the feeling on which it merely attends, like an ill-humoured courtier, is itself artificial in exactly the same sense and to the same degree. I suppose what is meant by that objection is that jealousy has not always been a character of man; formed no part of that very modest kit of sentiments with which he is supposed to have begun the world; but waited to make its appearance in better days and among richer natures. And this is equally true of love, and friendship, and love of country, and delight in what they call the beauties of nature, and most other things worth having. Love, in particular, will not endure any historical scrutiny: to all who have fallen across it, it is one of the most incontestable facts in the world; but if you begin to ask what it was in other periods and countries, in Greece for instance, the strangest doubts begin to spring up, and everything seems so vague and changing that a dream is logical in comparison. Jealousy, at any rate, is one of the consequences of love; you may like it or not, at pleasure; but there it is.

37

It is not exactly jealousy, however, that we feel when we reflect on the past of those we love. A bundle of letters found after years of happy union creates no sense of insecurity in the present; and yet it will pain a man sharply. The two people entertain no vulgar doubt of each other: but this pre-existence of both occurs to the mind as something indelicate. To be altogether right, they should have had twin birth together, at the same moment with the feeling that unites them. Then indeed it would be simple and perfect and without reserve or afterthought. Then they would understand each other with a fulness impossible otherwise. There would be no barrier between them of associations that cannot be imparted. They would be led into none of those comparisons that send the blood back to the heart. And they would know that there had been no time lost, and they had been together as much as was possible. For besides terror for the separation that must follow some time or other in the future, men feel anger, and something like remorse, when they think of that other separation which endured until they met. Some one has written that love makes people believe in immortality, because there seems not to be room enough in life for so great a tenderness, and it is inconceivable that the most masterful of our emotions should have no more than the spare moments of a few years. Indeed, it seems strange; but if we call to mind analogies, we can hardly regard it as impossible.

"The blind bow-boy," who smiles upon us from the end of terraces in old Dutch gardens, laughingly hails his bird-bolts among a fleeting generation. But for as fast as ever he shoots, the game dissolves and disappears into eternity from under his falling arrows; this one is gone ere he is struck; the other has but time to make one gesture and give one passionate cry; and they are all the things of a moment. When the generation is gone, when the play is over, when the thirty years' panorama has been withdrawn in tatters from the stage of the world, we may ask what has become of these great, weighty, and undying loves, and the sweethearts who despised mortal conditions in a fine credulity; and they can only show us a few songs in a bygone taste, a few actions worth remembering, and a few children who have retained some happy stamp from the disposition of their parents.

IV.—TRUTH OF INTERCOURSE

AMONG sayings that have a currency in spite of being wholly false upon the face of them for the sake of a half-truth upon another subject which is accidentally combined with the error, one of the grossest and broadest conveys the monstrous proposition that it is easy to tell the truth and hard to tell a lie. I wish heartily it were. But the truth is one; it has first to be discovered, then justly and exactly uttered. Even with instruments specially contrived for such a purpose — with a foot rule, a level, or a theodolite — it is not easy to be exact; it is easier, alas! to be inexact. From those who mark the divisions on a scale to those who measure the boundaries of empires or the distance of the heavenly stars, it is by careful method and minute, unwearying attention that men rise even to material exactness or to sure knowledge even of external and constant things. But it is easier to draw the outline of a mountain than the changing appearance of a face; and truth in human relations is of this more intangible and dubious order: hard to seize, harder to communicate. Veracity to facts in a loose, colloquial sense — not to say that I have been in Malabar when as a matter of fact I was never out of England, not to say that I have read Cervantes in the original when as a

40

matter of fact I know not one syllable of Spanish — this, indeed, is easy and to the same degree unimportant in itself. Lies of this sort, according to circumstances, may or may not be important; in a certain sense even they may or may not be false. The habitual liar may be a very honest fellow, and live truly with his wife and friends; while another man who never told a formal falsehood in his life may yet be himself one lie — heart and face, from top to bottom. This is the kind of lie which poisons intimacy. And, *vice versa*, veracity to sentiment, truth in a relation, truth to your own heart and your friends, never to feign or falsify emotion — that is the truth which makes love possible and mankind happy.

L'art de bien dire is but a drawing-room accomplishment unless it be pressed into the service of the truth. The difficulty of literature is not to write, but to write what you mean; not to affect your reader, but to affect him precisely as you wish. This is commonly understood in the case of books or set orations; even in making your will, or writing an explicit letter, some difficulty is admitted by the world. But one thing you can never make Philistine natures understand; one thing, which yet lies on the surface, remains as unseizable to their wits as a high flight of metaphysics — namely, that the business of life is mainly carried on by means of this difficult art of literature, and according to a man's proficiency in that art shall be the freedom and the fulness of his intercourse with other men. Anybody, it is supposed, can say what he means; and, in spite of their notorious experience to the contrary, people so continue to suppose. Now, I simply open the last book I have been reading — Mr. Leland's captivating *English Gipsies*. "It is said," I find on p. 7, "that those who can converse with Irish peasants in their own native tongue form far higher opinions of their appreciation of the beautiful, and of *the elements of humour and pathos in their hearts*, than do those who know their thoughts only through the medium of English. I know from my own observations that this is quite the case with the Indians of North America, and it is unquestionably so with the gipsy." In short, where a man has not a full possession of the language, the most important, because the most amiable, qualities of his nature have to lie buried and fallow; for the pleasure of comradeship, and the intellectual part of love, rest upon these very "elements of humour and pathos." Here is a man opulent in both, and for lack of a medium he can put none of it out to interest in the market of affection! But what is thus made plain to our apprehensions in the case of a foreign language is partially true even with the tongue we learned in childhood. Indeed, we all speak different dialects; one shall be copious and exact, another loose and meagre; but the speech of the ideal talker shall correspond and fit upon the truth of fact — not clumsily, obscuring lineaments, like a mantle, but cleanly adhering, like an athlete's skin. And what is the result? That the one can open himself more clearly to his friends, and can enjoy more of what makes life truly valuable — intimacy with those he loves. An orator makes a false step; he employs some trivial, some absurd, some vulgar phrase; in the turn of a sentence he insults, by a side wind, those whom he is labouring to charm; in speaking to one sentiment he unconsciously ruffles another in parenthesis; and you are not surprised, for you know his task to be delicate and filled with per-

ils. "O frivolous mind of man, light ignorance!" As
if yourself, when you seek to explain some misunderstanding or excuse some apparent fault, speaking swiftly
and addressing a mind still recently incensed, were not
harnessing for a more perilous adventure; as if yourself
required less tact and eloquence; as if an angry friend or
a suspicious lover were not more easy to offend than a
meeting of indifferent politicians! Nay, and the orator
treads in a beaten round; the matters he discusses have
been discussed a thousand times before; language is
ready-shaped to his purpose; he speaks out of a cut and
dry vocabulary. But you — may it not be that your defence reposes on some subtlety of feeling, not so much as
touched upon in Shakespeare, to express which, like a
pioneer, you must venture forth into zones of thought
still unsurveyed, and become yourself a literary inno-
vator? For even in love there are unlovely humours;
ambiguous acts, unpardonable words, may yet have
sprung from a kind sentiment. If the injured one could
read your heart, you may be sure that he would understand and pardon; but, alas! the heart cannot be shown
— it has to be demonstrated in words. Do you think it
is a hard thing to write poetry? Why, that is to write
poetry, and of a high, if not the highest, order.

I should even more admire "the lifelong and heroic
literary labours" of my fellow-men, patiently clearing
up in words their loves and their contentions, and speaking their autobiography daily to their wives, were it not
for a circumstance which lessens their difficulty and my
admiration by equal parts. For life, though largely, is
not entirely carried on by literature. We are subject to
physical passions and contortions; the voice breaks and

changes, and speaks by unconscious and winning inflections; we have legible countenances, like an open book; things that cannot be said look eloquently through the eyes; and the soul, not locked into the body as a dungeon, dwells ever on the threshold with appealing signals. Groans and tears, looks and gestures, a flush or a paleness, are often the most clear reporters of the heart, and speak more directly to the hearts of others. The message flies by these interpreters in the least space of time, and the misunderstanding is averted in the moment of its birth. To explain in words takes time and a just and patient hearing; and in the critical epochs of a close relation, patience and justice are not qualities on which we can rely. But the look or the gesture explains things in a breath; they tell their message without ambiguity; unlike speech, they cannot stumble, by the way, on a reproach or an allusion that should steel your friend against the truth; and then they have a higher authority, for they are the direct expression of the heart, not yet transmitted through the unfaithful and sophisticating brain. Not long ago I wrote a letter to a friend which came near involving us in quarrel; but we met, and in personal talk I repeated the worst of what I had written, and added worse to that; and with the commentary of the body it seemed not unfriendly either to hear or say. Indeed, letters are in vain for the purposes of intimacy; an absence is a dead break in the relation; yet two who know each other fully and are bent on perpetuity in love, may so preserve the attitude of their affections that they may meet on the same terms as they had parted.

Pitiful is the case of the blind, who cannot read the

face; pitiful that of the deaf, who cannot follow the changes of the voice. And there are others also to be pitied; for there are some of an inert, uneloquent nature, who have been denied all the symbols of communication, who have neither a lively play of facial expression, nor speaking gestures, nor a responsive voice, nor yet the gift of frank, explanatory speech: people truly made of clay, people tied for life into a bag which no one can undo. They are poorer than the gypsy, for their heart can speak no language under heaven. Such people we must learn slowly by the tenor of their acts, or through yea and nay communications; or we take them on trust on the strength of a general air, and now and again, when we see the spirit breaking through in a flash, correct or change our estimate. But these will be uphill intimacies, without charm or freedom, to the end; and freedom is the chief ingredient in confidence. Some minds, romantically dull, despise physical endowments. That is a doctrine for a misanthrope; to those who like their fellow-creatures it must always be meaningless; and, for my part, I can see few things more desirable, after the possession of such radical qualities as honour and humour and pathos, than to have a lively and not a stolid countenance; to have looks to correspond with every feeling; to be elegant and delightful in person, so that we shall please even in the intervals of active pleasing, and may never discredit speech with uncouth manners or become unconsciously our own burlesques. But of all unfortunates there is one creature (for I will not call him man) conspicuous in misfortune. This is he who has forfeited his birthright of expression, who has cultivated artful intonations, who has taught his face tricks,

45

like a pet monkey, and on every side perverted or cut off his means of communication with his fellow-men. The body is a house of many windows: there we all sit, showing ourselves and crying on the passers-by to come and love us. But this fellow has filled his windows with opaque glass, elegantly coloured. His house may be admired for its design, the crowd may pause before the stained windows, but meanwhile the poor proprietor must lie languishing within, uncomforted, unchangeably alone.

Truth of intercourse is something more difficult than to refrain from open lies. It is possible to avoid falsehood and yet not tell the truth. It is not enough to answer formal questions. To reach the truth by yea and nay communications implies a questioner with a share of inspiration, such as is often found in mutual love. *Yea* and *nay* mean nothing; the meaning must have been related in the question. Many words are often necessary to convey a very simple statement; for in this sort of exercise we never hit the gold; the most that we can hope is by many arrows, more or less far off on different sides, to indicate, in the course of time, for what target we are aiming, and after an hour's talk, back and forward, to convey the purport of a single principle or a single thought. And yet while the curt, pithy speaker misses the point entirely, a wordy, prolegomenous babbler will often add three new offences in the process of excusing one. It is really a most delicate affair. The world was made before the English language, and seemingly upon a different design. Suppose we held our converse not in words, but in music; those who have a bad ear would find themselves cut off from all near

CRABBED AGE AND YOUTH

"You know my mother now and then argues very notably; always very warmly at least. I happen often to differ from her; and we both think so well of our own arguments, that we very seldom are so happy as to convince one another. A pretty common case, I believe, in all *vehement* debatings. She says, I am *too witty;* Anglicè, *too pert;* I, that she is *too wise;* that is to say, being likewise put into English, *not so young as she has been.*"—Miss Howe to Miss Harlowe, *Clarissa,* vol. ii. Letter xiii.

THERE is a strong feeling in favour of cowardly and prudential proverbs. The sentiments of a man while he is full of ardour and hope are to be received, it is supposed, with some qualification. But when the same person has ignominiously failed and begins to eat up his words, he should be listened to like an oracle. Most of our pocket wisdom is conceived for the use of mediocre people, to discourage them from ambitious attempts, and generally console them in their mediocrity. And since mediocre people constitute the bulk of humanity, this is no doubt very properly so. But it does not follow that the one sort of proposition is any less true than the other, or that Icarus is not to be more praised, and perhaps more envied, than Mr. Samuel Budgett the Successful Merchant. The one is dead, to be sure, while the other is still in his counting-house counting out his money; and doubtless this is a consideration. But we have, on the other hand, some bold and magnanimous sayings common to high races and natures, which set forth the advantage of the losing side, and proclaim it better to be a dead lion than a living dog. It is difficult to fancy how the mediocrities reconcile such sayings with their proverbs. According to the latter, every lad who goes to sea is an egregious ass; never to forget your umbrella through a long life would seem a higher and wiser flight of achievement than to go smiling to the stake; and so long as you are a bit of a coward and inflexible in money matters, you fulfil the whole duty of man.

It is a still more difficult consideration for our average men, that while all their teachers, from Solomon down to Benjamin Franklin and the ungodly Binney, have inculcated the same ideal of manners, caution, and respectability, those characters in history who have most notoriously flown in the face of such precepts are spoken of in hyperbolical terms of praise, and honoured with public monuments in the streets of our commercial centres. This is very bewildering to the moral sense. You have Joan of Arc, who left a humble but honest and reputable livelihood under the eyes of her parents, to go a-colonelling, in the company of rowdy soldiers, against the enemies of France; surely a melancholy example for one's daughters! And then you have Columbus, who may have pioneered America, but, when all is said, was a most imprudent navigator. His life is not the kind of thing one would like to put into the hands of young people; rather, one would do one's utmost to keep it from their knowledge, as a red flag of adventure and

disintegrating influence in life. The time would fail me
if I were to recite all the big names in history whose exploits are perfectly irrational and even shocking to the
business mind. The incongruity is speaking; and I
imagine it must engender among the mediocrities a very
peculiar attitude towards the nobler and showier sides
of national life. They will read of the Charge of Balaclava in much the same spirit as they assist at a performance of the *Lyons Mail*. Persons of substance take in
the *Times* and sit composedly in pit or boxes according
to the degree of their prosperity in business. As for the
generals who go galloping up and down among bomb-
shells in absurd cocked hats — as for the actors who
raddle their faces and demean themselves for hire upon
the stage — they must belong, thank God! to a different order of beings, whom we watch as we watch the
clouds careering in the windy, bottomless inane, or read
about like characters in ancient and rather fabulous annals. Our offspring would no more think of copying
their behaviour, let us hope, than of doffing their clothes
and painting themselves blue in consequence of certain
admissions in the first chapter of their school history of
England.

Discredited as they are in practice, the cowardly proverbs hold their own in theory; and it is another instance
of the same spirit, that the opinions of old men about
life have been accepted as final. All sorts of allowances
are made for the illusions of youth; and none, or almost
none, for the disenchantments of age. It is held to be
a good taunt, and somehow or other to clinch the question logically, when an old gentleman waggles his head
and says: "Ah, so I thought when I was your age."

It is not thought an answer at all, if the young man retorts: "My venerable sir, so I shall most probably think
when I am yours." And yet the one is as good as the
other: pass for pass, tit for tat, a Roland for an Oliver.

"Opinion in good men," says Milton, "is but knowledge in the making." All opinions, properly so called,
are stages on the road to truth. It does not follow that
a man will travel any further; but if he has really considered the world and drawn a conclusion, he has travelled as far. This does not apply to formulæ got by
rote, which are stages on the road to nowhere but second childhood and the grave. To have a catchword in
your mouth is not the same thing as to hold an opinion; still less is it the same thing as to have made one
for yourself. There are too many of these catchwords in
the world for people to rap out upon you like an oath and
by way of an argument. They have a currency as intellectual counters; and many respectable persons pay
their way with nothing else. They seem to stand for
vague bodies of theory in the background. The im-
puted virtue of folios full of knockdown arguments is
supposed to reside in them, just as some of the majesty
of the British Empire dwells in the constable's truncheon.
They are used in pure superstition, as old clodhoppers
spoil Latin by way of an exorcism. And yet they are
vastly serviceable for checking unprofitable discussion
and stopping the mouths of babes and sucklings. And
when a young man comes to a certain stage of intellectual growth, the examination of these counters forms a
gymnastic at once amusing and fortifying to the mind.

Because I have reached Paris, I am not ashamed of
having passed through Newhaven and Dieppe. They

were very good places to pass through, and I am none the less at my destination. All my old opinions were only stages on the way to the one I now hold, as itself is only a stage on the way to something else. I am no more abashed at having been a red-hot Socialist with a panacea of my own than at having been a sucking infant. Doubtless the world is quite right in a million ways; but you have to be kicked about a little to convince you of the fact. And in the meanwhile you must do something, be something, believe something. It is not possible to keep the mind in a state of accurate balance and blank; and even if you could do so, instead of coming ultimately to the right conclusion, you would be very apt to remain in a state of balance and blank to perpetuity. Even in quite intermediate stages, a dash of enthusiasm is not a thing to be ashamed of in the retrospect: if St. Paul had not been a very zealous Pharisee, he would have been a colder Christian. For my part, I look back to the time when I was a Socialist with something like regret. I have convinced myself (for the moment) that we had better leave these great changes to what we call great blind forces; their blindness being so much more perspicacious than the little, peering, partial eyesight of men. I seem to see that my own scheme would not answer; and all the other schemes I ever heard propounded would depress some elements of goodness just as much as they encouraged others. Now I know that in thus turning Conservative with years, I am going through the normal cycle of change and travelling in the common orbit of men's opinions. I submit to this, as I would submit to gout or grey hair, as a concomitant of growing age or else of failing animal heat; but I do not acknowledge that it is necessarily a change for the better—I daresay it is deplorably for the worse. I have no choice in the business, and can no more resist this tendency of my mind than I could prevent my body from beginning to totter and decay. If I am spared (as the phrase runs) I shall doubtless outlive some troublesome desires; but I am in no hurry about that; nor, when the time comes, shall I plume myself on the immunity. Just in the same way, I do not greatly pride myself on having outlived my belief in the fairy tales of Socialism. Old people have faults of their own; they tend to become cowardly, niggardly, and suspicious. Whether from the growth of experience or the decline of animal heat, I see that age leads to these and certain other faults; and it follows, of course, that while in one sense I hope I am journeying towards the truth, in another I am indubitably posting towards these forms and sources of error.

As we go catching and catching at this or that corner of knowledge, now getting a foresight of generous possibilities, now chilled with a glimpse of prudence, we may compare the headlong course of our years to a swift torrent in which a man is carried away; now he is dashed against a boulder, now he grapples for a moment to a trailing spray; at the end, he is hurled out and overwhelmed in a dark and bottomless ocean. We have no more than glimpses and touches; we are torn away from our theories; we are spun round and round and shown this or the other view of life, until only fools or knaves can hold to their opinions. We take a sight at a condition in life, and say we have studied it; our most elaborate view is no more than an impression. If we had breathing space, we should take the occasion to modify and adjust; but at this breakneck hurry, we are no sooner boys than we are adult, no sooner in love than married or jilted, no sooner one age than we begin to be another, and no sooner in the fulness of our manhood than we begin to decline towards the grave. It is in vain to seek for consistency or expect clear and stable views in a medium so perturbed and fleeting. This is no cabinet science, in which things are tested to a scruple; we theorise with a pistol to our head; we are confronted with a new set of conditions on which we have not only to pass a judgment, but to take action, before the hour is at an end. And we cannot even regard ourselves as a constant; in this flux of things, our identity itself seems in a perpetual variation; and not infrequently we find our own disguise the strangest in the masquerade. In the course of time, we grow to love things we hated and hate things we loved. Milton is not so dull as he once was, nor perhaps Ainsworth so amusing. It is decidedly harder to climb trees, and not nearly so hard to sit still. There is no use pretending; even the thrice royal game of hide and seek has somehow lost in zest. All our attributes are modified or changed; and it will be a poor account of us if our views do not modify and change in a proportion. To hold the same views at forty as we held at twenty is to have been stupefied for a score of years, and take rank, not as a prophet, but as an unteachable brat, well birched and none the wiser. It is as if a ship captain should sail to India from the Port of London; and having brought a chart of the Thames on deck at his first setting out, should obstinately use no other for the whole voyage. And mark you, it would be no less foolish to begin at

Gravesend with a chart of the Red Sea. *Si Jeunesse savait, si Vieillesse pouvait,* is a very pretty sentiment, but not necessarily right. In five cases out of ten, it is not so much that the young people do not know, as that they do not choose. There is something irreverent in the speculation, but perhaps the want of power has more to do with the wise resolutions of age than we are always willing to admit. It would be an instructive experiment to make an old man young again and leave him all his *savoir.* I scarcely think he would put his money in the Savings Bank after all; I doubt if he would be such an admirable son as we are led to expect; and as for his conduct in love, I believe firmly he would out-Herod Herod, and put the whole of his new compeers to the blush. Prudence is a wooden Juggernaut, before whom Benjamin Franklin walks with the portly air of a high priest, and after whom dances many a successful merchant in the character of Atys. But it is not a deity to cultivate in youth. If a man lives to any considerable age, it cannot be denied that he laments his imprudences, but I notice he often laments his youth a deal more bitterly and with a more genuine intonation.

It is customary to say that age should be considered, because it comes last. It seems just as much to the point, that youth comes first. And the scale fairly kicks the beam, if you go on to add that age, in a majority of cases, never comes at all. Disease and accident make short work of even the most prosperous persons; death costs nothing, and the expense of a headstone is an inconsiderable trifle to the happy heir. To be suddenly snuffed out in the middle of ambitious schemes, is tragical enough at best; but when a man has been grudging himself his own life in the meanwhile, and saving up everything for the festival that was never to be, it becomes that hysterically moving sort of tragedy which lies on the confines of farce. The victim is dead — and he has cunningly overreached himself: a combination of calamities none the less absurd for being grim. To husband a favourite claret until the batch turns sour, is not at all an artful stroke of policy; and how much more with a whole cellar — a whole bodily existence! People may lay down their lives with cheerfulness in the sure expectation of a blessed immortality; but that is a different affair from giving up youth with all its admirable pleasures, in the hope of a better quality of gruel in a more than problematical, nay, more than improbable, old age. We should not compliment a hungry man, who should refuse a whole dinner and reserve all his appetite for the dessert, before he knew whether there was to be any dessert or not. If there be such a thing as imprudence in the world, we surely have it here. We sail in leaky bottoms and on great and perilous waters; and to take a cue from the dolorous old naval ballad, we have heard the mermaidens singing, and know that we shall never see dry land any more. Old and young, we are all on our last cruise. If there is a fill of tobacco among the crew, for God's sake pass it round, and let us have a pipe before we go!

Indeed, by the report of our elders, this nervous preparation for old age is only trouble thrown away. We fall on guard, and after all it is a friend who comes to meet us. After the sun is down and the west faded, the heavens begin to fill with shining stars. So, as we grow old, a sort of equable jog-trot of feeling is substituted for the violent ups and downs of passion and disgust; the same influence that restrains our hopes, quiets our apprehensions; if the pleasures are less intense, the troubles are milder and more tolerable; and in a word, this period for which we are asked to hoard up everything as for a time of famine, is, in its own right, the richest, easiest, and happiest of life. Nay, by managing its own work and following its own happy inspiration, youth is doing the best it can to endow the leisure of age. A full, busy youth is your only prelude to a self-contained and independent age; and the muff inevitably develops into the bore. There are not many Doctor Johnsons, to set forth upon their first romantic voyage at sixty-four. If we wish to scale Mont Blanc or visit a thieves' kitchen in the East End, to go down in a diving dress or up in a balloon, we must be about it while we are still young. It will not do to delay until we are clogged with prudence and limping with rheumatism, and people begin to ask us: "What does Gravity out of bed?" Youth is the time to go flashing from one end of the world to the other both in mind and body; to try the manners of different nations; to hear the chimes at midnight; to see sunrise in town and country; to be converted at a revival; to circumnavigate the metaphysics, write halting verses, run a mile to see a fire, and wait all day long in the theatre to applaud *Hernani*. There is some meaning in the old theory about wild oats; and a man who has not had his green-sickness and got done with it for good, is as little to be depended on as an unvaccinated infant. "It is extraordinary," says Lord Beaconsfield, one of the brightest and best preserved of youths up to the

date of his last novel,[1] "it is extraordinary how hourly
and how violently change the feelings of an inexperi-
enced young man." And this mobility is a special
talent entrusted to his care; a sort of indestructible vir-
ginity; a magic armour, with which he can pass un-
hurt through great dangers and come unbedaubed out
of the miriest passages. Let him voyage, speculate, see
all that he can, do all that he may; his soul has as many
lives as a cat, he will live in all weathers, and never be
a halfpenny the worse. Those who go to the devil in
youth, with anything like a fair chance, were probably
little worth saving from the first; they must have been
feeble fellows—creatures made of putty and pack-thread,
without steel or fire, anger or true joyfulness, in their
composition; we may sympathise with their parents,
but there is not much cause to go into mourning for
themselves; for to be quite honest, the weak brother is
the worst of mankind.

When the old man waggles his head and says, "Ah,
so I thought when I was your age," he has proved the
youth's case. Doubtless, whether from growth of experience or decline of animal heat, he thinks so no longer;
but he thought so while he was young; and all men have
thought so while they were young, since there was dew
in the morning or hawthorn in May; and here is another
young man adding his vote to those of previous generations and rivetting another link to the chain of testimony. It is as natural and as right for a young man to
be imprudent and exaggerated, to live in swoops and
circles, and beat about his cage like any other wild thing
newly captured, as it is for old men to turn grey, or

[1] *Lothair.*

mothers to love their offspring, or heroes to die for something worthier than their lives.

By way of an apologue for the aged, when they feel more than usually tempted to offer their advice, let me recommend the following little tale. A child who had been remarkably fond of toys (and in particular of lead soldiers) found himself growing to the level of acknowledged boyhood without any abatement of this childish taste. He was thirteen; already he had been taunted for dallying overlong about the playbox; he had to blush if he was found among his lead soldiers; the shades of the prison-house were closing about him with a vengeance. There is nothing more difficult than to put the thoughts of children into the language of their elders; but this is the effect of his meditations at this juncture: "Plainly," he said, "I must give up my playthings, in the meanwhile, since I am not in a position to secure myself against idle jeers. At the same time, I am sure that playthings are the very pick of life; all people give them up out of the same pusillanimous respect for those who are a little older; and if they do not return to them as soon as they can, it is only because they grow stupid and forget. I shall be wiser; I shall conform for a little to the ways of their foolish world; but so soon as I have made enough money, I shall retire and shut myself up among my playthings until the day I die." Nay, as he was passing in the train along the Esterel mountains between Cannes and Fréjus, he remarked a pretty house in an orange garden at the angle of a bay, and decided that this should be his Happy Valley. Astrea Redux; childhood was to come again! The idea has an air of simple nobility to me, not unworthy of Cincinnatus.

And yet, as the reader has probably anticipated, it is never likely to be carried into effect. There was a worm in the bud, a fatal error in the premises. Childhood must pass away, and then youth, as surely as age approaches. The true wisdom is to be always seasonable, and to change with a good grace in changing circumstances. To love playthings well as a child, to lead an adventurous and honourable youth, and to settle when the time arrives, into a green and smiling age, is to be a good artist in life and deserve well of yourself and your neighbour.

You need repent none of your youthful vagaries. They may have been over the score on one side, just as those of age are probably over the score on the other. But they had a point; they not only befitted your age and expressed its attitude and passions, but they had a relation to what was outside of you, and implied criticisms on the existing state of things, which you need not allow to have been undeserved, because you now see that they were partial. All error, not merely verbal, is a strong way of stating that the current truth is incomplete. The follies of youth have a basis in sound reason, just as much as the embarrassing questions put by babes and sucklings. Their most antisocial acts indicate the defects of our society. When the torrent sweeps the man against a boulder, you must expect him to scream, and you need not be surprised if the scream is sometimes a theory. Shelley, chafing at the Church of England, discovered the cure of all evils in universal atheism. Generous lads irritated at the injustices of society, see nothing for it but the abolishment of everything and Kingdom Come of anarchy. Shelley was a young fool; so are these cocksparrow revolutionaries. But it is better to be a fool than to be dead. It is better to emit a scream in the shape of a theory than to be entirely insensible to the jars and incongruities of life and take everything as it comes in a forlorn stupidity. Some people swallow the universe like a pill; they travel on through the world, like smiling images pushed from behind. For God's sake give me the young man who has brains enough to make a fool of himself! As for the others, the irony of facts shall take it out of their hands, and make fools of them in downright earnest, ere the farce be over. There shall be such a mopping and a mowing at the last day, and such blushing and confusion of countenance for all those who have been wise in their own esteem, and have not learnt the rough lessons that youth hands on to age. If we are indeed here to perfect and complete our own natures, and grow larger, stronger, and more sympathetic against some nobler career in the future, we had all best bestir ourselves to the utmost while we have the time. To equip a dull, respectable person with wings would be but to make a parody of an angel.

In short, if youth is not quite right in its opinions, there is a strong probability that age is not much more so. Undying hope is co-ruler of the human bosom with infallible credulity. A man finds he has been wrong at every preceding stage of his career, only to deduce the astonishing conclusion that he is at last entirely right. Mankind, after centuries of failure, are still upon the eve of a thoroughly constitutional millennium. Since we have explored the maze so long without result, it follows, for poor human reason, that we cannot have to explore much longer; close by must be the centre, with a champagne luncheon and a piece of ornamental water. How if there were no centre at all, but just one alley after another, and the whole world a labyrinth without end or issue?

I overheard the other day a scrap of conversation, which I take the liberty to reproduce. "What I advance is true," said one. "But not the whole truth," answered the other. "Sir," returned the first (and it seemed to me there was a smack of Dr. Johnson in the speech), "Sir, there is no such thing as the whole truth!" Indeed, there is nothing so evident in life as that there are two sides to a question. History is one long illustration. The forces of nature are engaged, day by day, in cudgelling it into our backward intelligences. We never pause for a moment's consideration, but we admit it as an axiom. An enthusiast sways humanity exactly by disregarding this great truth, and dinning it into our ears that this or that question has only one possible solution; and your enthusiast is a fine florid fellow, dominates things for a while and shakes the world out of a doze; but when once he is gone, an army of quiet and uninfluential people set to work to remind us of the other side and demolish the generous imposture. While Calvin is putting everybody exactly right in his *Institutes*, and hot-headed Knox is thundering in the pulpit, Montaigne is already looking at the other side in his library in Perigord, and predicting that they will find as much to quarrel about in the Bible as they had found already in the Church. Age may have one side, but assuredly Youth has the other. There is nothing more certain than that both are right, except perhaps that both are wrong. Let them agree to differ; for who knows but what agreeing to differ may not be a form of agreement rather than a form of difference?

I suppose it is written that any one who sets up for a bit of a philosopher, must contradict himself to his very face. For here have I fairly talked myself into thinking that we have the whole thing before us at last; that there is no answer to the mystery, except that there are as many as you please; that there is no centre to the maze because, like the famous sphere, its centre is everywhere; and that agreeing to differ with every ceremony of politeness, is the only "one undisturbed song of pure concent" to which we are ever likely to lend our musical voices.

AN APOLOGY FOR IDLERS

"BOSWELL: We grow weary when idle.

"JOHNSON: That is, sir, because others being busy, we want company; but if we were idle, there would be no growing weary; we should all entertain one another."

JUST now, when every one is bound, under pain of a decree in absence convicting them of *lèse*-respectability, to enter on some lucrative profession, and labour therein with something not far short of enthusiasm, a cry from the opposite party who are content when they have enough, and like to look on and enjoy in the meanwhile, savours a little of bravado and gasconade. And yet this should not be. Idleness so called, which does not consist in doing nothing, but in doing a great deal not recognized in the dogmatic formularies of the ruling class, has as good a right to state its position as industry itself. It is admitted that the presence of people who refuse to enter in the great handicap race for sixpenny pieces, is at once an insult and a disenchantment for those who do. A fine fellow (as we see so many) takes his determination, votes for the sixpences, and in the emphatic Americanism, "goes for" them. And while such an one is ploughing distressfully up the road, it is not hard to understand his resentment, when he perceives cool persons in the meadows by the wayside, lying with a handkerchief over their ears and a glass at their elbow. Alexander is touched in a very delicate place by the disregard of Diogenes. Where was the glory of having taken Rome for these tumultuous barbarians, who poured into the Senate house, and found the Fathers sitting silent and unmoved by their success? It is a sore thing to have laboured along and scaled the arduous hilltops, and when all is done, find humanity indifferent to your achievement. Hence physicists condemn the unphysical; financiers have only a superficial toleration for those who know little of stocks; literary persons despise the unlettered; and people of all pursuits combine to disparage those who have none.

But though this is one difficulty of the subject, it is not the greatest. You could not be put in prison for speaking against industry, but you can be sent to Coventry for speaking like a fool. The greatest difficulty with most subjects is to do them well; therefore, please to remember this is an apology. It is certain that much may be judiciously argued in favour of diligence; only there is something to be said against it, and that is what, on the present occasion, I have to say. To state one argument is not necessarily to be deaf to all others, and that a man has written a book of travels in Montenegro, is no reason why he should never have been to Richmond.

It is surely beyond a doubt that people should be a good deal idle in youth. For though here and there a Lord Macaulay may escape from school honours with all his wits about him, most boys pay so dear for their medals that they never afterwards have a shot in their locker, and begin the world bankrupt. And the same holds true during all the time a lad is educating himself, or suffer-

ing others to educate him. It must have been a very
foolish old gentleman who addressed Johnson at Oxford
in these words: "Young man, ply your book diligently
now, and acquire a stock of knowledge; for when years
come upon you, you will find that poring upon books
will be but an irksome task." The old gentleman
seems to have been unaware that many other things
besides reading grow irksome, and not a few become
impossible, by the time a man has to use spectacles and
cannot walk without a stick. Books are good enough
in their own way, but they are a mighty bloodless substitute for life. It seems a pity to sit, like the Lady of
Shalott, peering into a mirror, with your back turned on
all the bustle and glamour of reality. And if a man reads
very hard, as the old anecdote reminds us, he will have
little time for thoughts.

If you look back on your own education, I am sure it
will not be the full, vivid, instructive hours of truantry
that you regret; you would rather cancel some lack-
lustre periods between sleep and waking in the class.
For my own part, I have attended a good many lectures
in my time. I still remember that the spinning of a top
is a case of Kinetic Stability. I still remember that Em-
phyteusis is not a disease, nor Stillicide a crime. But
though I would not willingly part with such scraps of
science, I do not set the same store by them as by certain other odds and ends that I came by in the open
street while I was playing truant. This is not the moment to dilate on that mighty place of education, which
was the favourite school of Dickens and of Balzac, and
turns out yearly many inglorious masters in the Science
of the Aspects of Life. Suffice it to say this: if a lad

does not learn in the streets, it is because he has no faculty of learning. Nor is the truant always in the streets, for if he prefers, he may go out by the gardened suburbs into the country. He may pitch on some tuft of lilacs over a burn, and smoke innumerable pipes to the tune of the water on the stones. A bird will sing in the thicket. And there he may fall into a vein of kindly thought, and see things in a new perspective. Why, if this be not education, what is? We may conceive Mr. Worldly Wiseman accosting such an one, and the conversation that should thereupon ensue:—

"How now, young fellow, what dost thou here?"

"Truly, sir, I take mine ease."

"Is not this the hour of the class? and should'st thou not be plying thy Book with diligence, to the end thou mayest obtain knowledge?"

"Nay, but thus also I follow after Learning, by your leave."

"Learning, quotha! After what fashion, I pray thee? Is it mathematics?"

"No, to be sure."

"Is it metaphysics?"

"Nor that."

"Is it some language?"

"Nay, it is no language."

"Is it a trade?"

"Nor a trade neither."

"Why, then, what is't?"

"Indeed, sir, as a time may soon come for me to go upon Pilgrimage, I am desirous to note what is commonly done by persons in my case, and where are the ugliest Sloughs and Thickets on the Road; as also, what manner of Staff is of the best service. Moreover, I lie here, by this water, to learn by root-of-heart a lesson which my master teaches me to call Peace, or Contentment."

Hereupon Mr. Worldly Wiseman was much commoved with passion, and shaking his cane with a very threatful countenance, broke forth upon this wise: "Learning, quotha!" said he; "I would have all such rogues scourged by the Hangman!"

And so he would go his way, ruffling out his cravat with a crackle of starch, like a turkey when it spread its feathers.

Now this, of Mr. Wiseman's, is the common opinion. A fact is not called a fact, but a piece of gossip, if it does not fall into one of your scholastic categories. An inquiry must be in some acknowledged direction, with a name to go by; or else you are not inquiring at all, only lounging; and the work-house is too good for you. It is supposed that all knowledge is at the bottom of a well, or the far end of a telescope. Sainte-Beuve, as he grew older, came to regard all experience as a single great book, in which to study for a few years ere we go hence; and it seemed all one to him whether you should read in Chapter xx., which is the differential calculus, or in Chapter xxxix., which is hearing the band play in the gardens. As a matter of fact, an intelligent person, looking out of his eyes and hearkening in his ears, with a smile on his face all the time, will get more true education than many another in a life of heroic vigils. There is certainly some chill and arid knowledge to be found upon the summits of formal and laborious science; but it is all round about you, and for the trouble of looking,

71

that you will acquire the warm and palpitating facts
of life. While others are filling their memory with a
lumber of words, one-half of which they will forget before the week be out, your truant may learn some really
useful art: to play the fiddle, to know a good cigar, or
to speak with ease and opportunity to all varieties of
men. Many who have "plied their book diligently,"
and know all about some one branch or another of accepted lore, come out of the study with an ancient and
owl-like demeanour, and prove dry, stockish, and dys-
peptic in all the better and brighter parts of life. Many
make a large fortune, who remain underbred and pa-
thetically stupid to the last. And meantime there goes
the idler, who began life along with them — by your
leave, a different picture. He has had time to take care
of his health and his spirits; he has been a great deal in
the open air, which is the most salutary of all things for
both body and mind; and if he has never read the great
Book in very recondite places, he has dipped into it and
skimmed it over to excellent purpose. Might not the
student afford some Hebrew roots, and the business man
some of his half-crowns, for a share of the idler's knowledge of life at large, and Art of Living? Nay, and the
idler has another and more important quality than these.
I mean his wisdom. He who has much looked on at
the childish satisfaction of other people in their hobbies,
will regard his own with only a very ironical indulgence.
He will not be heard among the dogmatists. He will
have a great and cool allowance for all sorts of people
and opinions. If he finds no out-of-the-way truths, he
will identify himself with no very burning falsehood. His
way takes him along a by-road, not much frequented,

but very even and pleasant, which is called Common-place Lane, and leads to the Belvedere of Commonsense. Thence he shall command an agreeable, if no very noble prospect; and while others behold the East and West, the Devil and the Sunrise, he will be contentedly aware of a sort of morning hour upon all sublunary things, with an army of shadows running speedily and in many different directions into the great daylight of Eternity. The shadows and the generations, the shrill doctors and the plangent wars, go by into ultimate silence and emptiness; but underneath all this, a man may see, out of the Belvedere windows, much green and peaceful landscape; many firelit parlours; good people laughing, drinking, and making love as they did before the Flood or the French Revolution; and the old shepherd telling his tale under the hawthorn.

Extreme *busyness*, whether at school or college, kirk or market, is a symptom of deficient vitality; and a faculty for idleness implies a catholic appetite and a strong sense of personal identity. There is a sort of dead-alive, hackneyed people about, who are scarcely conscious of living except in the exercise of some conventional occupation. Bring these fellows into the country, or set them aboard ship, and you will see how they pine for their desk or their study. They have no curiosity; they cannot give themselves over to random provocations; they do not take pleasure in the exercise of their faculties for its own sake; and unless Necessity lays about them with a stick, they will even stand still. It is no good speaking to such folk: they *cannot* be idle, their nature is not generous enough; and they pass those hours in a sort of coma, which are not dedicated to furi-

ous moiling in the gold-mill. When they do not require to go to the office, when they are not hungry and
have no mind to drink, the whole breathing world is a
blank to them. If they have to wait an hour or so for a
train, they fall into a stupid trance with their eyes open.
To see them, you would suppose there was nothing to
look at and no one to speak with; you would imagine
they were paralysed or alienated; and yet very possibly
they are hard workers in their own way, and have good
eyesight for a flaw in a deed or a turn of the market.
They have been to school and college, but all the time
they had their eye on the medal; they have gone about
in the world and mixed with clever people, but all the
time they were thinking of their own affairs. As if a
man's soul were not too small to begin with, they have
dwarfed and narrowed theirs by a life of all work and
no play; until here they are at forty, with a listless attention, a mind vacant of all material of amusement, and not
one thought to rub against another, while they wait for
the train. Before he was breeched, he might have
clambered on the boxes ; when he was twenty, he
would have stared at the girls; but now the pipe is
smoked out, the snuffbox empty, and my gentleman
sits bolt upright upon a bench, with lamentable eyes.
This does not appeal to me as being Success in Life.

But it is not only the person himself who suffers from
his busy habits, but his wife and children, his friends
and relations, and down to the very people he sits with
in a railway carriage or an omnibus. Perpetual devotion to what a man calls his business, is only to be sus-
tained by perpetual neglect of many other things. And
it is not by any means certain that a man's business is

the most important thing he has to do. To an impartial estimate it will seem clear that many of the wisest, most virtuous, and most beneficent parts that are to be played upon the Theatre of Life are filled by gratuitous performers, and pass, among the world at large, as phases of idleness. For in that Theatre, not only the walking gentlemen, singing chambermaids, and diligent fiddlers in the orchestra, but those who look on and clap their hands from the benches, do really play a part and fulfil important offices towards the general result. You are no doubt very dependent on the care of your lawyer and stockbroker, of the guards and signalmen who convey you rapidly from place to place, and the policemen who walk the streets for your protection; but is there not a thought of gratitude in your heart for certain other benefactors who set you smiling when they fall in your way, or season your dinner with good company? Colonel Newcome helped to lose his friend's money; Fred Bayham had an ugly trick of borrowing shirts; and yet they were better people to fall among than Mr. Barnes. And though Falstaff was neither sober nor very honest, I think I could name one or two long-faced Barabbases whom the world could better have done without. Hazlitt mentions that he was more sensible of obligation to Northcote, who had never done him anything he could call a service, than to his whole circle of ostentatious friends; for he thought a good companion emphatically the greatest benefactor. I know there are people in the world who cannot feel grateful unless the favour has been done them at the cost of pain and difficulty. But this is a churlish disposition. A man may send you six sheets of letter-paper covered

75

with the most entertaining gossip, or you may pass half an hour pleasantly, perhaps profitably, over an article of his; do you think the service would be greater, if he had made the manuscript in his heart's blood, like a compact with the devil? Do you really fancy you should be more beholden to your correspondent, if he had been damning you all the while for your importunity? Pleasures are more beneficial than duties because, like the quality of mercy, they are not strained, and they are twice blest. There must always be two to a kiss, and there may be a score in a jest; but wherever there is an element of sacrifice, the favour is conferred with pain, and, among generous people, received with confusion. There is no duty we so much underrate as the duty of being happy. By being happy, we sow anonymous benefits upon the world, which remain unknown even to ourselves, or when they are disclosed, surprise nobody so much as the benefactor. The other day, a ragged, barefoot boy ran down the street after a marble, with so jolly an air that he set every one he passed into a good humour; one of these persons, who had been delivered from more than usually black thoughts, stopped the little fellow and gave him some money with this remark: "You see what sometimes comes of looking pleased." If he had looked pleased before, he had now to look both pleased and mystified. For my part, I justify this encouragement of smiling rather than tearful children; I do not wish to pay for tears anywhere but upon the stage; but I am prepared to deal largely in the opposite commodity. A happy man or woman is a better thing to find than a five-pound note. He or she is a radiating focus of goodwill; and their entrance into a room is as though another candle had been lighted. We need not care whether they could prove the forty-seventh proposition; they do a better thing than that, they practically demonstrate the great Theorem of the Liveableness of Life. Consequently, if a person cannot be happy without remaining idle, idle he should remain. It is a revolutionary precept; but thanks to hunger and the workhouse, one not easily to be abused; and within practical limits, it is one of the most incontestable truths in the whole Body of Morality. Look at one of your industrious fellows for a moment, I beseech you. He sows hurry and reaps indigestion; he puts a vast deal of activity out to interest, and receives a large measure of nervous derangement in return. Either he absents himself entirely from all fellowship, and lives a recluse in a garret, with carpet slippers and a leaden inkpot; or he comes among people swiftly and bitterly, in a contraction of his whole nervous system, to discharge some temper before he returns to work. I do not care how much or how well he works, this fellow is an evil feature in other people's lives. They would be happier if he were dead. They could easier do without his services in the Circumlocution Office, than they can tolerate his fractious spirits. He poisons life at the well-head. It is better to be beggared out of hand by a scapegrace nephew, than daily hag-ridden by a peevish uncle.

And what, in God's name, is all this pother about? For what cause do they embitter their own and other people's lives? That a man should publish three or thirty articles a year, that he should finish or not finish his great allegorical picture, are questions of little interest to

77

the world. The ranks of life are full; and although a thousand fall, there are always some to go into the breach. When they told Joan of Arc she should be at home minding women's work, she answered there were plenty to spin and wash. And so, even with your own rare gifts! When nature is " so careless of the single life," why should we coddle ourselves into the fancy that our own is of exceptional importance? Suppose Shakespeare had been knocked on the head some dark night in Sir Thomas Lucy's preserves, the world would have wagged on better or worse, the pitcher gone to the well, the scythe to the corn, and the student to his book; and no one been any the wiser of the loss. There are not many works extant, if you look the alternative all over, which are worth the price of a pound of tobacco to a man of limited means. This is a sobering reflection for the proudest of our earthly vanities. Even a tobacconist may, upon consideration, find no great cause for personal vainglory in the phrase; for although tobacco is an admirable sedative, the qualities necessary for retailing it are neither rare nor precious in themselves. Alas and alas! you may take it how you will, but the services of no single individual are indispensable. Atlas was just a gentleman with a protracted nightmare! And yet you see merchants who go and labour themselves into a great fortune and thence into the bankruptcy court; scribblers who keep scribbling at little articles until their temper is a cross to all who come about them, as though Pharaoh should set the Israelites to make a pin instead of a pyramid; and fine young men who work themselves into a decline, and are driven off in a hearse with white plumes upon it. Would you not suppose these

persons had been whispered, by the Master of the Cere-
monies, the promise of some momentous destiny ? and
that this lukewarm bullet on which they play their farces
was the bull's-eye and centrepoint of all the universe ?
And yet it is not so. The ends for which they give
away their priceless youth, for all they know, may be
chimerical or hurtful; the glory and riches they expect
may never come, or may find them indifferent; and they
and the world they inhabit are so inconsiderable that the
mind freezes at the thought.

BY a curious irony of fate, the places to which we are sent when health deserts us are often singularly beautiful. Often, too, they are places we have visited in former years, or seen briefly in passing by, and kept ever afterwards in pious memory; and we please ourselves with the fancy that we shall repeat many vivid and pleasurable sensations, and take up again the thread of our enjoyment in the same spirit as we let it fall. We shall now have an opportunity of finishing many pleasant excursions, interrupted of yore before our curiosity was fully satisfied. It may be that we have kept in mind, during all these years, the recollection of some valley into which we have just looked down for a moment before we lost sight of it in the disorder of the hills; it may be that we have lain awake at night, and agreeably tantalised ourselves with the thought of corners we had never turned, or summits we had all but climbed: we shall now be able, as we tell ourselves, to complete all these unfinished pleasures, and pass beyond the barriers that confined our recollections.

The promise is so great, and we are all so easily led away when hope and memory are both in one story, that I daresay the sick man is not very inconsolable when

he receives sentence of banishment, and is inclined to regard his ill-health as not the least fortunate accident of
his life.   Nor is he immediately undeceived.   The stir
and speed of the journey, and the restlessness that goes
to bed with him as he tries to sleep between two days
of noisy progress, fever him, and stimulate his dull
nerves into something of their old quickness and sensibility.   And so he can enjoy the faint autumnal splendour
of the landscape, as he sees hill and plain, vineyard and
forest, clad in one wonderful glory of fairy gold, which
the first great winds of winter will transmute, as in the
fable, into withered leaves.   And so too he can enjoy the
admirable brevity and simplicity of such litfle glimpses
of country and country ways as flash upon him through
the windows of the train; little glimpses that have a character all their own; sights seen as a travelling swallow
might see them from the wing, or Iris as she went
abroad over the land on some Olympian errand.   Here
and there, indeed, a few children huzzah and wave their
hands to the express; but for the most part, it is an in-
terruption too brief and isolated to attract much notice;
the sheep do not cease from browsing; a girl sits bal-
anced on the projecting tiller of a canal boat, so precari-
ously that it seems as if a fly or the splash of a leaping
fish would be enough to overthrow the dainty equi-
librium, and yet all these hundreds of tons of coal and
wood and iron have been precipitated roaring past her
very ear, and there is not a start, not a tremor, not a turn
of the averted head, to indicate that she has been even
conscious of its passage.   Herein, I think, lies the chief
attraction of railway travel.   The speed is so easy, and
the train disturbs so little the scenes through which it

takes us, that our heart becomes full of the placidity and
stillness of the country; and while the body is borne forward in the flying chain of carriages, the thoughts alight,
as the humour moves them, at unfrequented stations;
they make haste up the poplar alley that leads towards the
town; they are left behind with the signalman as, shad-
ing his eyes with his hand, he watches the long train
sweep away into the golden distance.

Moreover, there is still before the invalid the shock
of wonder and delight with which he will learn that he
has passed the indefinable line that separates South from
North. And this is an uncertain moment; for sometimes the consciousness is forced upon him early, on
the occasion of some slight association, a colour, a
flower, or a scent; and sometimes not until, one fine
morning, he wakes up with the southern sunshine
peeping through the *persiennes,* and the southern patois
confusedly audible below the windows. Whether it
come early or late, however, this pleasure will not end
with the anticipation, as do so many others of the same
family. It will leave him wider awake than it found
him, and give a new significance to all he may see for
many days to come. There is something in the mere
name of the South that carries enthusiasm along with it.
At the sound of the word, he pricks up his ears; he becomes as anxious to seek out beauties and to get by
heart the permanent lines and character of the landscape,
as if he had been told that it was all his own — an estate out of which he had been kept unjustly, and which
he was now to receive in free and full possession. Even
those who have never been there before feel as if they
had been; and everybody goes comparing, and seeking

for the familiar, and finding it with such ecstasies of recognition, that one would think they were coming home after a weary absence, instead of travelling hourly farther abroad.

It is only after he is fairly arrived and settled down in his chosen corner, that the invalid begins to understand the change that has befallen him. Everything about him is as he had remembered, or as he had anticipated. Here, at his feet, under his eyes, are the olive gardens and the blue sea. Nothing can change the eternal magnificence of form of the naked Alps behind Mentone; nothing, not even the crude curves of the railway, can utterly deform the suavity of contour of one bay after another along the whole reach of the Riviera. And of all this, he has only a cold head knowledge that is divorced from enjoyment. He recognises with his intelligence that this thing and that thing is beautiful, while in his heart of hearts he has to confess that it is not beautiful for him. It is in vain that he spurs his discouraged spirit; in vain that he chooses out points of view, and stands there, looking with all his eyes, and waiting for some return of the pleasure that he remembers in other days, as the sick folk may have awaited the coming of the angel at the pool of Bethesda. He is like an enthusiast leading about with him a stolid, indifferent tourist. There is some one by who is out of sympathy with the scene, and is not moved up to the measure of the occasion; and that some one is himself. The world is disenchanted for him. He seems to himself to touch things with muffled hands, and to see them through a veil. His life becomes a palsied fumbling after notes that are silent when he has found and struck them. He cannot

recognise that this phlegmatic and unimpressionable body with which he now goes burthened, is the same that he knew heretofore so quick and delicate and alive.

He is tempted to lay the blame on the very softness and amenity of the climate, and to fancy that in the rigours of the winter at home, these dead emotions would revive and flourish. A longing for the brightness and silence of fallen snow seizes him at such times. He is homesick for the hale rough weather; for the tracery of the frost upon his window-panes at morning, the reluctant descent of the first flakes, and the white roofs relieved against the sombre sky. And yet the stuff of which these yearnings are made, is of the flimsiest: if but the thermometer fall a little below its ordinary Mediterranean level, or a wind come down from the snow-clad Alps behind, the spirit of his fancies changes upon the instant, and many a doleful vignette of the grim wintry streets at home returns to him, and begins to haunt his memory. The hopeless, huddled attitude of tramps in doorways; the flinching gait of barefoot children on the icy pavement; the sheen of the rainy streets towards afternoon; the meagre anatomy of the poor defined by the clinging of wet garments; the high canorous note of the North-easter on days when the very houses seem to stiffen with cold: these, and such as these, crowd back upon him, and mockingly substitute themselves for the fanciful winter scenes with which he had pleased himself a while before. He cannot be glad enough that he is where he is. If only the others could be there also; if only those tramps could lie down for a little in the sunshine, and those children warm their feet, this once, upon a kindlier earth; if only there were

no cold anywhere, and no nakedness, and no hunger; if only it were as well with all men as it is with him!

For it is not altogether ill with the invalid, after all. If it is only rarely that anything penetrates vividly into his numbed spirit, yet, when anything does, it brings with it a joy that is all the more poignant for its very rarity. There is something pathetic in these occasional returns of a glad activity of heart. In his lowest hours he will be stirred and awakened by many such; and they will spring perhaps from very trivial sources; as a friend once said to me, the "spirit of delight" comes often on small wings. For the pleasure that we take in beautiful nature is essentially capricious. It comes sometimes when we least look for it; and sometimes, when we expect it most certainly, it leaves us to gape joylessly for days together, in the very home-land of the beautiful. We may have passed a place a thousand times and one; and on the thousand and second it will be transfigured, and stand forth in a certain splendour of reality from the dull circle of surroundings; so that we see it "with a child's first pleasure," as Wordsworth saw the daffodils by the lake side. And if this falls out capriciously with the healthy, how much more so with the invalid. Some day he will find his first violet, and be lost in pleasant wonder, by what alchemy the cold earth of the clods, and the vapid air and rain, can be transmuted into colour so rich and odour so touchingly sweet. Or perhaps he may see a group of washerwomen relieved, on a spit of shingle, against the blue sea, or a meeting of flower-gatherers in the tempered daylight of an olive-garden; and something significant or monumental in the grouping, something in the har-

mony of faint colour that is always characteristic of the
dress of these southern women, will come home to him
unexpectedly, and awake in him that satisfaction with
which we tell ourselves that we are the richer by one
more beautiful experience.   Or it may be something
even slighter: as when the opulence of the sunshine,
which somehow gets lost and fails to produce its effect
on the large scale, is suddenly revealed to him by the
chance isolation — as he changes the position of his sun-
shade — of a yard or two of roadway with its stones
and weeds.   And then, there is no end to the infinite
variety of the olive-yards themselves.   Even the colour
is indeterminate and continually shifting: now you
would say it was green, now grey, now blue; now tree
stands above tree, like "cloud on cloud," massed into
filmy indistinctness; and now, at the wind's will, the
whole sea of foliage is shaken and broken up with little
momentary silverings and shadows.   But every one
sees the world in his own way.   To some the glad moment may have arrived on other provocations; and their
recollection may be most vivid of the stately gait of
women carrying burthens on their heads; of tropical effects with canes and naked rock and sunlight; of the
relief of cypresses; of the troubled, busy-looking groups
of sea-pines, that seem always as if they were being
wielded and swept together by a whirlwind; of the air
coming, laden with virginal perfumes, over the myrtles
and the scented underwood; of the empurpled hills
standing up, solemn and sharp, out of the green-gold
air of the east at evening.

There go many elements, without doubt, to the making of one such moment of intense perception; and it is

on the happy agreement of these many elements, on the harmonious vibration of many nerves, that the whole delight of the moment must depend. Who can forget how, when he has chanced upon some attitude of complete restfulness, after long uneasy rolling to and fro on grass or heather, the whole fashion of the landscape has been changed for him, as though the sun had just broken forth, or a great artist had only then completed, by some cunning touch, the composition of the picture? And not only a change of posture — a snatch of perfume, the sudden singing of a bird, the freshness of some pulse of air from an invisible sea, the light shadow of a travelling cloud, the merest nothing that sends a little shiver along the most infinitesimal nerve of a man's body — not one of the least of these but has a hand somehow in the general effect, and brings some refinement of its own into the character of the pleasure we feel.

And if the external conditions are thus varied and subtle, even more so are those within our own bodies. No man can find out the world, says Solomon, from beginning to end, because the world is in his heart; and so it is impossible for any of us to understand, from beginning to end, that agreement of harmonious circumstances that creates in us the highest pleasure of admiration, precisely because some of these circumstances are hidden from us for ever in the constitution of our own bodies. After we have reckoned up all that we can see or hear or feel, there still remains to be taken into account some sensibility more delicate than usual in the nerves affected, or some exquisite refinement in the architecture of the brain, which is indeed to the sense of the beautiful as the eye or the ear to the sense of hearing or sight. We admire splendid views and great pictures; and yet what is truly admirable is rather the mind within us, that gathers together these scattered details for its delight, and makes out of certain colours, certain distributions of graduated light and darkness, that intelligible whole which alone we call a picture or a view. Hazlitt, relating in one of his essays how he went on foot from one great man's house to another's in search of works of art, begins suddenly to triumph over these noble and wealthy owners, because he was more capable of enjoying their costly possessions than they were; because they had paid the money and he had received the pleasure. And the occasion is a fair one for self-complacency. While the one man was working to be able to buy the picture, the other was working to be able to enjoy the picture. An inherited aptitude will have been diligently improved in either case; only the one man has made for himself a fortune, and the other has made for himself a living spirit. It is a fair occasion for self-complacency, I repeat, when the event shows a man to have chosen the better part, and laid out his life more wisely, in the long run, than those who have credit for most wisdom. And yet even this is not a good unmixed; and like all other possessions, although in a less degree, the possession of a brain that has been thus improved and cultivated, and made into the prime organ of a man's enjoyment, brings with it certain inevitable cares and disappointments. The happiness of such an one comes to depend greatly upon those fine shades of sensation that heighten and harmonise the coarser elements of beauty. And thus a degree of nervous prostration, that to other men would be hardly disagreeable, is enough to overthrow for him the whole fabric of his life, to take, except at rare moments, the edge off his pleasures, and to meet him wherever he goes with failure, and the sense of want, and disenchantment of the world and life.

It is not in such numbness of spirit only that the life of the invalid resembles a premature old age. Those excursions that he had promised himself to finish, prove too long or too arduous for his feeble body; and the barrier-hills are as impassable as ever. Many a white town that sits far out on the promontory, many a comely fold of wood on the mountain side, beckons and allures his imagination day after day, and is yet as inaccessible to his feet as the clefts and gorges of the clouds. The sense of distance grows upon him wonderfully; and after some feverish efforts and the fretful uneasiness of the first few days, he falls contentedly in with the restrictions of his weakness. His narrow round becomes pleasant and familiar to him as the cell to a contented prisoner. Just as he has fallen already out of the mid race of active life, he now falls out of the little eddy that circulates in the shallow waters of the sanatorium. He sees the country people come and go about their everyday affairs, the foreigners stream out in goodly pleasure parties; the stir of man's activity is all about him, as he suns himself inertly in some sheltered corner; and he looks on with a patriarchal impersonality of interest, such as a man may feel when he pictures to himself the fortunes of his remote descendants, or the robust old age of the oak he has planted over-night.

In this falling aside, in this quietude and desertion of other men, there is no inharmonious prelude to the last

quietude and desertion of the grave; in this dulness of
the senses there is a gentle preparation for the final insensibility of death. And to him the idea of mortality
comes in a shape less violent and harsh than is its wont,
less as an abrupt catastrophe than as a thing of infinitesimal gradation, and the last step on a long decline of way.
As we turn to and fro in bed, and every moment the move-
ments grow feebler and smaller and the attitude more
restful and easy, until sleep overtakes us at a stride and
we move no more, so desire after desire leaves him;
day by day his strength decreases, and the circle of his
activity grows ever narrower; and he feels, if he is to
be thus tenderly weaned from the passion of life, thus
gradually inducted into the slumber of death, that when
at last the end comes, it will come quietly and fitly. If
anything is to reconcile poor spirits to the coming of
the last enemy, surely it should be such a mild approach
as this; not to hale us forth with violence, but to per-
suade us from a place we have no further pleasure in.
It is not so much, indeed, death that approaches as life
that withdraws and withers up from round about him.
He has outlived his own usefulness, and almost his own
enjoyment; and if there is to be no recovery; if never
again will he be young and strong and passionate, if the
actual present shall be to him always like a thing read
in a book or remembered out of the far-away past; if,
in fact, this be veritably nightfall, he will not wish
greatly for the continuance of a twilight that only strains
and disappoints the eyes, but steadfastly await the perfect darkness. He will pray for Medea: when she
comes, let her either rejuvenate or slay.

And yet the ties that still attach him to the world are

many and kindly. The sight of children has a significance for him such as it may have for the aged also, but not for others. If he has been used to feel humanely, and to look upon life somewhat more widely than from the narrow loophole of personal pleasure and advancement, it is strange how small a portion of his thoughts will be changed or embittered by this proximity of death. He knows that already, in English counties, the sower follows the ploughman up the face of the field, and the rooks follow the sower; and he knows also that he may not live to go home again and see the corn spring and ripen, and be cut down at last, and brought home with gladness. And yet the future of this harvest, the continuance of drought or the coming of rain unseasonably, touch him as sensibly as ever. For he has long been used to wait with interest the issue of events in which his own concern was nothing; and to be joyful in a plenty, and sorrowful for a famine, that did not increase or diminish, by one half loaf, the equable sufficiency of his own supply. Thus there remain unaltered all the disinterested hopes for mankind and a better future which have been the solace and inspiration of his life. These he has set beyond the reach of any fate that only menaces himself; and it makes small difference whether he die five thousand years, or five thousand and fifty years, before the good epoch for which he faithfully labours. He has not deceived himself; he has known from the beginning that he followed the pillar of fire and cloud, only to perish himself in the wilderness, and that it was reserved for others to enter joyfully into possession of the land. And so, as everything grows greyer and quieter about him, and slopes towards

extinction, these unfaded visions accompany his sad
decline, and follow him, with friendly voices and hopeful words, into the very vestibule of death. The desire
of love or of fame scarcely moved him, in his days of
health, more strongly than these generous aspirations
move him now; and so life is carried forward beyond
life, and a vista kept open for the eyes of hope, even when
his hands grope already on the face of the impassable.

Lastly, he is bound tenderly to life by the thought of
his friends; or shall we not say rather, that by their
thought for him, by their unchangeable solicitude and
love, he remains woven into the very stuff of life, beyond
the power of bodily dissolution to undo? In a thousand
ways will he survive and be perpetuated. Much of
Etienne de la Boetie survived during all the years in
which Montaigne continued to converse with him on
the pages of the ever-delightful essays. Much of what
was truly Goethe was dead already when he revisited
places that knew him no more, and found no better consolation than the promise of his own verses, that soon
he too would be at rest. Indeed, when we think of
what it is that we most seek and cherish, and find most
pride and pleasure in calling ours, it will sometimes
seem to us as if our friends, at our decease, would suffer
loss more truly than ourselves. As a monarch who should
care more for the outlying colonies he knows on the map
or through the report of his vicegerents, than for the
trunk of his empire under his eyes at home, are we not
more concerned about the shadowy life that we have in
the hearts of others, and that portion in their thoughts
and fancies which, in a certain far-away sense, belongs
to us, than about the real knot of our identity — that

central metropolis of self, of which alone we are immediately aware — or the diligent service of arteries and veins and infinitesimal activity of ganglia, which we know (as we know a proposition in Euclid) to be the source and substance of the whole? At the death of every one whom we love, some fair and honourable portion of our existence falls away, and we are dislodged from one of these dear provinces; and they are not, perhaps, the most fortunate who survive a long series of such impoverishments, till their life and influence narrow gradually into the meagre limit of their own spirits, and death, when he comes at last, can destroy them at one blow.

NOTE. — To this essay I must in honesty append a word or two of qualification; for this is one of the points on which a slightly greater age teaches us a slightly different wisdom:

A youth delights in generalities, and keeps loose from particular obligations; he jogs on the footpath way, himself pursuing butterflies, but courteously lending his applause to the advance of the human species and the coming of the kingdom of justice and love. As he grows older, he begins to think more narrowly of man's action in the general, and perhaps more arrogantly of his own in the particular. He has not that same unspeakable trust in what he would have done had he been spared, seeing finally that that would have been little; but he has a far higher notion of the blank that he will make by dying. A young man feels himself one too many in the world; his is a painful situation: he has no calling; no obvious utility; no ties, but to his parents, and these he is sure to disregard. I do not think that a proper allowance has been made for this true cause of suffering in youth; but by the mere fact of a prolonged existence, we outgrow either the fact or else the feeling. Either we become so callously accustomed to our own useless figure in the world, or else — and this, thank God, in the majority of cases — we so collect about us the interest or the love of our fellows, so multiply our effective part in the affairs of life, that we need to entertain no longer the question of our right to be.

And so in the majority of cases, a man who fancies himself dying, will get cold comfort from the very youthful view expressed in this essay. He, as a living man, has some to help, some to love, some to correct; it may be, some to punish. These duties cling, not upon humanity, but upon the man himself. It is he, not another, who is one woman's son and a second woman's husband and a third woman's father. That life which began so small, has now grown, with a myriad filaments, into the lives of others. It is not indispensable; another will take the place and shoulder the discharged responsibility; but the better the man and the nobler his purposes, the more will he be tempted to regret the extinction of his powers and the deletion of his personality. To have lived a generation, is not only to have grown at home in that perplexing medium, but to have assumed innumerable duties. To die at such an age, has, for all but the entirely base, something of the air of a betrayal. A man does not only reflect upon what he might have done in a future that is never to be his; but beholding himself so early a deserter from the fight, he eats his heart for the good he might have done already. To have been so useless and now to lose all hope of being useful any more — there it is that death and memory assail him. And even if mankind shall go on, founding heroic cities, practising heroic virtues, rising steadily from strength to strength; even if his work shall be fulfilled, his friends consoled, his wife remarried by a better than he; how shall this alter, in one jot, his estimation of a career which was his only business in this world, which was so fitfully pursued, and which is now so ineffectively to end?

ÆS TRIPLEX

THE changes wrought by death are in themselves so sharp and final, and so terrible and melancholy in their consequences, that the thing stands alone in man's experience, and has no parallel upon earth. It outdoes all other accidents because it is the last of them. Sometimes it leaps suddenly upon its victims, like a Thug; sometimes it lays a regular siege and creeps upon their citadel during a score of years. And when the business is done, there is sore havoc made in other people's lives, and a pin knocked out by which many subsidiary friendships hung together. There are empty chairs, solitary walks, and single beds at night. Again, in taking away our friends, death does not take them away utterly, but leaves behind a mocking, tragical, and soon intolerable residue, which must be hurriedly concealed. Hence a whole chapter of sights and customs striking to the mind, from the pyramids of Egypt to the gibbets and dule trees of mediæval Europe. The poorest persons have a bit of pageant going towards the tomb; memorial stones are set up over the least memorable; and, in order to preserve some show of respect for what remains of our old loves and friendships, we must accompany it with much grimly ludicrous cere-

monial, and the hired undertaker parades before the
door. All this, and much more of the same sort, accompanied by the eloquence of poets, has gone a great
way to put humanity in error; nay, in many philosophies the error has been embodied and laid down with
every circumstance of logic; although in real life the
bustle and swiftness, in leaving people little time to
think, have not left them time enough to go danger-
ously wrong in practice.

As a matter of fact, although few things are spoken of
with more fearful whisperings than this prospect of
death, few have less influence on conduct under healthy
circumstances. We have all heard of cities in South
America built upon the side of fiery mountains, and
how, even in this tremendous neighbourhood, the inhabitants are not a jot more impressed by the solemnity
of mortal conditions than if they were delving gardens
in the greenest corner of England. There are serenades
and suppers and much gallantry among the myrtles
overhead; and meanwhile the foundation shudders un-
derfoot, the bowels of the mountain growl, and at any
moment living ruin may leap sky-high into the moonlight, and tumble man and his merry-making in the
dust. In the eyes of very young people, and very dull
old ones, there is something indescribably reckless and
desperate in such a picture. It seems not credible that
respectable married people, with umbrellas, should find
appetite for a bit of supper within quite a long distance
of a fiery mountain; ordinary life begins to smell of
high-handed debauch when it is carried on so close to a
catastrophe; and even cheese and salad, it seems, could
hardly be relished in such circumstances without some-

thing like a defiance of the Creator. It should be a place
for nobody but hermits dwelling in prayer and macera-
tion, or mere born-devils drowning care in a perpetual
carouse.

And yet, when one comes to think upon it calmly,
the situation of these South American citizens forms only
a very pale figure for the state of ordinary mankind.
This world itself, travelling blindly and swiftly in over-
crowded space, among a million other worlds travelling
blindly and swiftly in contrary directions, may very well
come by a knock that would set it into explosion like a
penny squib. And what, pathologically looked at, is
the human body with all its organs, but a mere bagful
of petards? The least of these is as dangerous to the
whole economy as the ship's powder-magazine to the
ship; and with every breath we breathe, and every meal
we eat, we are putting one or more of them in peril. If
we clung as devotedly as some philosophers pretend we
do to the abstract idea of life, or were half as frightened
as they make out we are, for the subversive accident
that ends it all, the trumpets might sound by the hour
and no one would follow them into battle — the blue-
peter might fly at the truck, but who would climb into
a sea-going ship? Think (if these philosophers were
right) with what a preparation of spirit we should af-
front the daily peril of the dinner-table: a deadlier spot
than any battle-field in history, where the far greater
proportion of our ancestors have miserably left their
bones! What woman would ever be lured into marriage, so much more dangerous than the wildest sea?
And what would it be to grow old? For, after a certain
distance, every step we take in life we find the ice grow-

ing thinner below our feet, and all around us and behind us we see our contemporaries going through. By the time a man gets well into the seventies, his continued existence is a mere miracle; and when he lays his old bones in bed for the night, there is an overwhelming probability that he will never see the day. Do the old men mind it, as a matter of fact? Why, no. They were never merrier; they have their grog at night, and tell the raciest stories; they hear of the death of people about their own age, or even younger, not as if it was a grisly warning, but with a simple childlike pleasure at having outlived some one else; and when a draught might puff them out like a guttering candle, or a bit of a stumble shatter them like so much glass, their old hearts keep sound and unaffrighted, and they go on, bubbling with laughter, through years of man's age compared to which the valley at Balaclava was as safe and peaceful as a village cricket-green on Sunday. It may fairly be questioned (if we look to the peril only) whether it was a much more daring feat for Curtius to plunge into the gulf, than for any old gentleman of ninety to doff his clothes and clamber into bed.

Indeed, it is a memorable subject for consideration, with what unconcern and gaiety mankind pricks on along the Valley of the Shadow of Death. The whole way is one wilderness of snares, and the end of it, for those who fear the last pinch, is irrevocable ruin. And yet we go spinning through it all, like a party for the Derby. Perhaps the reader remembers one of the humorous devices of the deified Caligula: how he encouraged a vast concourse of holiday-makers on to his bridge over Baiæ bay; and when they were in the height

of their enjoyment, turned loose the Prætorian guards
among the company, and had them tossed into the sea.
This is no bad miniature of the dealings of nature with
the transitory race of man. Only, what a chequered
picnic we have of it, even while it lasts! and into what
great waters, not to be crossed by any swimmer, God's
pale Prætorian throws us over in the end!

We live the time that a match flickers; we pop the
cork of a ginger-beer bottle, and the earthquake swallows us on the instant. Is it not odd, is it not incongruous, is it not, in the highest sense of human speech,
incredible, that we should think so highly of the ginger-
beer, and regard so little the devouring earthquake?
The love of Life and the fear of Death are two famous
phrases that grow harder to understand the more we
think about them. It is a well-known fact that an immense proportion of boat accidents would never happen if people held the sheet in their hands instead of
making it fast; and yet, unless it be some martinet of a
professional mariner or some landsman with shattered
nerves, every one of God's creatures makes it fast. A
strange instance of man's unconcern and brazen bold-
ness in the face of death !

We confound ourselves with metaphysical phrases,
which we import into daily talk with noble inappro-
priateness. We have no idea of what death is, apart
from its circumstances and some of its consequences to
others; and although we have some experience of living,
there is not a man on earth who has flown so high into
abstraction as to have any practical guess at the meaning of the word *life*. All literature, from Job and Omar
Khayyam to Thomas Carlyle or Walt Whitman, is but an

attempt to look upon the human state with such large-
ness of view as shall enable us to rise from the consideration of living to the Definition of Life. And our sages
give us about the best satisfaction in their power when
they say that it is a vapour, or a show, or made out
of the same stuff with dreams. Philosophy, in its
more rigid sense, has been at the same work for ages;
and after a myriad bald heads have wagged over the
problem, and piles of words have been heaped one upon
another into dry and cloudy volumes without end, philosophy has the honour of laying before us, with modest
pride, her contribution towards the subject : that life is
a Permanent Possibility of Sensation. Truly a fine result ! A man may very well love beef, or hunting, or
a woman; but surely, surely, not a Permanent Possibility of Sensation ! He may be afraid of a precipice, or a
dentist, or a large enemy with a club, or even an undertaker's man; but not certainly of abstract death. We
may trick with the word life in its dozen senses until
we are weary of tricking; we may argue in terms of all
the philosophies on earth, but one fact remains true
throughout — that we do not love life, in the sense that
we are greatly preoccupied about its conservation; that
we do not, properly speaking, love life at all, but living.
Into the views of the least careful there will enter some
degree of providence; no man's eyes are fixed entirely
on the passing hour; but although we have some anticipation of good health, good weather, wine, active employment, love, and self-approval, the sum of these an-
ticipations does not amount to anything like a general
view of life's possibilities and issues; nor are those who
cherish them most vividly, at all the most scrupulous of

their personal safety. To be deeply interested in the accidents of our existence, to enjoy keenly the mixed texture of human experience, rather leads a man to disregard precautions, and risk his neck against a straw. For surely the love of living is stronger in an Alpine climber roping over a peril, or a hunter riding merrily at a stiff fence, than in a creature who lives upon a diet and walks a measured distance in the interest of his constitution.

There is a great deal of very vile nonsense talked upon both sides of the matter: tearing divines reducing life to the dimensions of a mere funeral procession, so short as to be hardly decent; and melancholy unbelievers yearning for the tomb as if it were a world too far away. Both sides must feel a little ashamed of their performances now and again when they draw in their chairs to dinner. Indeed, a good meal and a bottle of wine is an answer to most standard works upon the question. When a man's heart warms to his viands, he forgets a great deal of sophistry, and soars into a rosy zone of contemplation. Death may be knocking at the door, like the Commander's statue; we have something else in hand, thank God, and let him knock. Passing bells are ringing all the world over. All the world over, and every hour, some one is parting company with all his aches and ecstasies. For us also the trap is laid. But we are so fond of life that we have no leisure to entertain the terror of death. It is a honeymoon with us all through, and none of the longest. Small blame to us if we give our whole hearts to this glowing bride of ours, to the appetites, to honour, to the hungry curiosity of the mind, to the pleasure of the eyes in nature, and the pride of our own nimble bodies.

We all of us appreciate the sensations; but as for car-
ing about the Permanence of the Possibility, a man's
head is generally very bald, and his senses very dull,
before he comes to that. Whether we regard life as a
lane leading to a dead wall—a mere bag's end, as the
French say—or whether we think of it as a vestibule or
gymnasium, where we wait our turn and prepare our
faculties for some more noble destiny; whether we
thunder in a pulpit, or pule in little atheistic poetry-
books, about its vanity and brevity; whether we look
justly for years of health and vigour, or are about to
mount into a Bath-chair, as a step towards the hearse;
in each and all of these views and situations there is but
one conclusion possible: that a man should stop his ears
against paralysing terror, and run the race that is set before him with a single mind. No one surely could have
recoiled with more heartache and terror from the thought
of death than our respected lexicographer; and yet we
know how little it affected his conduct, how wisely and
boldly he walked, and in what a fresh and lively vein
he spoke of life. Already an old man, he ventured on
his Highland tour; and his heart, bound with triple
brass, did not recoil before twenty-seven individual cups
of tea. As courage and intelligence are the two qualities best worth a good man's cultivation, so it is the first
part of intelligence to recognise our precarious estate in
life, and the first part of courage to be not at all abashed
before the fact. A frank and somewhat headlong carriage, not looking too anxiously before, not dallying in
maudlin regret over the past, stamps the man who is
well armoured for this world.

And not only well armoured for himself, but a good

friend and a good citizen to boot. We do not go to cowards for tender dealing; there is nothing so cruel as panic; the man who has least fear for his own carcass, has most time to consider others. That eminent chemist who took his walks abroad in tin shoes, and subsisted wholly upon tepid milk, had all his work cut out for him in considerate dealings with his own digestion. So soon as prudence has begun to grow up in the brain, like a dismal fungus, it finds its first expression in a paralysis of generous acts. The victim begins to shrink spiritually; he develops a fancy for parlours with a regulated temperature, and takes his morality on the principle of tin shoes and tepid milk. The care of one important body or soul becomes so engrossing, that all the noises of the outer world begin to come thin and faint into the parlour with the regulated temperature; and the tin shoes go equably forward over blood and rain. To be overwise is to ossify; and the scruple-monger ends by standing stockstill. Now the man who has his heart on his sleeve, and a good whirling weathercock of a brain, who reckons his life as a thing to be dashingly used and cheerfully hazarded, makes a very different acquaintance of the world, keeps all his pulses going true and fast, and gathers impetus as he runs, until, if he be running towards anything better than wildfire, he may shoot up and become a constellation in the end. Lord look after his health, Lord have a care of his soul, says he; and he has at the key of the position, and swashes through incongruity and peril towards his aim. Death is on all sides of him with pointed batteries, as he is on all sides of all of us; unfortunate surprises gird him round; mim-mouthed friends and relations hold up their hands in

quite a little elegiacal synod about his path: and what
cares he for all this? Being a true lover of living, a
fellow with something pushing and spontaneous in his
inside, he must, like any other soldier, in any other stirring, deadly warfare, push on at his best pace until he
touch the goal. "A peerage or Westminster Abbey!"
cried Nelson in his bright, boyish, heroic manner. These
are great incentives; not for any of these, but for the
plain satisfaction of living, of being about their business
in some sort or other, do the brave, serviceable men of
every nation tread down the nettle danger, and pass fly-
ingly over all the stumbling-blocks of prudence. Think
of the heroism of Johnson, think of that superb indifference to mortal limitation that set him upon his dictionary, and carried him through triumphantly until the end!
Who, if he were wisely considerate of things at large,
would ever embark upon any work much more considerable than a halfpenny post card? Who would project a
serial novel, after Thackeray and Dickens had each fallen
in mid-course? Who would find heart enough to begin
to live, if he dallied with the consideration of death?

And, after all, what sorry and pitiful quibbling all this
is! To forego all the issues of living in a parlour with a
regulated temperature — as if that were not to die a
hundred times over, and for ten years at a stretch! As
if it were not to die in one's own lifetime, and without
even the sad immunities of death! As if it were not to
die, and yet be the patient spectators of our own piti-
able change! The Permanent Possibility is preserved,
but the sensations carefully held at arm's length, as if
one kept a photographic plate in a dark chamber. It is
better to lose health like a spendthrift than to waste it

like a miser. It is better to live and be done with it, than to die daily in the sickroom. By all means begin your folio; even if the doctor does not give you a year, even if he hesitates about a month, make one brave push and see what can be accomplished in a week. It is not only in finished undertakings that we ought to honour useful labour. A spirit goes out of the man who means execution, which outlives the most untimely ending. All who have meant good work with their whole hearts, have done good work, although they may die before they have the time to sign it. Every heart that has beat strong and cheerfully has left a hopeful impulse behind it in the world, and bettered the tradition of mankind. And even if death catch people, like an open pitfall, and in mid-career, laying out vast projects, and planning monstrous foundations, flushed with hope, and their mouths full of boastful language, they should be at once tripped up and silenced: is there not something brave and spirited in such a termination? and does not life go down with a better grace, foaming in full body over a preci-pice, than miserably straggling to an end in sandy del-tas? When the Greeks made their fine saying that those whom the gods love die young, I cannot help be-lieving they had this sort of death also in their eye. For surely, at whatever age it overtake the man, this is to die young. Death has not been suffered to take so much as an illusion from his heart. In the hot-fit of life, a-tip-toe on the highest point of being, he passes at a bound on to the other side. The noise of the mallet and chisel is scarcely quenched, the trumpets are hardly done blow-ing, when, trailing with him clouds of glory, this happy-starred, full-blooded spirit shoots into the spiritual land.

EL DORADO

IT seems as if a great deal were attainable in a world where there are so many marriages and decisive battles, and where we all, at certain hours of the day, and with great gusto and despatch, stow a portion of victuals finally and irretrievably into the bag which contains us. And it would seem also, on a hasty view, that the attainment of as much as possible was the one goal of man's contentious life. And yet, as regards the spirit, this is but a semblance. We live in an ascending scale when we live happily, one thing leading to another in an endless series. There is always a new horizon for onward-looking men, and although we dwell on a small planet, immersed in petty business and not enduring beyond a brief period of years, we are so constituted that our hopes are inaccessible, like stars, and the term of hoping is prolonged until the term of life. To be truly happy is a question of how we begin and not of how we end, of what we want and not of what we have. An aspiration is a joy for ever, a possession as solid as a landed estate, a fortune which we can never exhaust and which gives us year by year a revenue of pleasurable activity. To have many of these is to be spiritually rich. Life is only a very dull and ill-

directed theatre unless we have some interests in the
piece; and to those who have neither art nor science,
the world is a mere arrangement of colours, or a rough
footway where they may very well break their shins.
It is in virtue of his own desires and curiosities that any
man continues to exist with even patience, that he is
charmed by the look of things and people, and that he
wakens every morning with a renewed appetite for
work and pleasure. Desire and curiosity are the two
eyes through which he sees the world in the most enchanted colours: it is they that make women beautiful
or fossils interesting: and the man may squander his
estate and come to beggary, but if he keeps these two
amulets he is still rich in the possibilities of pleasure.
Suppose he could take one meal so compact and com-
prehensive that he should never hunger any more; suppose him, at a glance, to take in all the features of the
world and allay the desire for knowledge; suppose him
to do the like in any province of experience— would not
that man be in a poor way for amusement ever after?

One who goes touring on foot with a single volume
in his knapsack reads with circumspection, pausing often
to reflect, and often laying the book down to contemplate the landscape or the prints in the inn parlour; for
he fears to come to an end of his entertainment, and be
left companionless on the last stages of his journey. A
young fellow recently finished the works of Thomas
Carlyle, winding up, if we remember aright, with the
ten note-books upon Frederick the Great. "What!"
cried the young fellow, in consternation, "is there no
more Carlyle? Am I left to the daily papers?" A more
celebrated instance is that of Alexander, who wept bit-

terly because he had no more worlds to subdue. And when Gibbon had finished the *Decline and Fall*, he had only a few moments of joy; and it was with a "sober melancholy" that he parted from his labours.

Happily we all shoot at the moon with ineffectual arrows; our hopes are set on inaccessible El Dorado; we come to an end of nothing here below. Interests are only plucked up to sow themselves again, like mustard. You would think, when the child was born, there would be an end to trouble; and yet it is only the beginning of fresh anxieties; and when you have seen it through its teething and its education, and at last its marriage, alas! it is only to have new fears, new quivering sensibilities, with every day; and the health of your children's children grows as touching a concern as that of your own. Again, when you have married your wife, you would think you were got upon a hilltop, and might begin to go downward by an easy slope. But you have only ended courting to begin marriage. Falling in love and winning love are often difficult tasks to overbearing and rebellious spirits; but to keep in love is also a business of some importance, to which both man and wife must bring kindness and goodwill. The true love story commences at the altar, when there lies before the married pair a most beautiful contest of wisdom and generosity, and a life-long struggle towards an unattainable ideal. Unattainable? Ay, surely unattainable, from the very fact that they are two instead of one.

"Of making books there is no end," complained the Preacher; and did not perceive how highly he was praising letters as an occupation. There is no end, indeed, to making books or experiments, or to travel, or to gathering wealth. Problem gives rise to problem. We may study for ever, and we are never as learned as we would. We have never made a statue worthy of our dreams. And when we have discovered a continent, or crossed a chain of mountains, it is only to find another ocean or another plain upon the further side. In the infinite universe there is room for our swiftest diligence and to spare. It is not like the works of Carlyle, which can be read to an end. Even in a corner of it, in a private park, or in the neighbourhood of a single hamlet, the weather and the seasons keep so deftly changing that although we walk there for a lifetime there will be always something new to startle and delight us.

There is only one wish realisable on the earth; only one thing that can be perfectly attained: Death. And from a variety of circumstances we have no one to tell us whether it be worth attaining.

A strange picture we make on our way to our chimæras, ceaselessly marching, grudging ourselves the time for rest; indefatigable, adventurous pioneers. It is true that we shall never reach the goal; it is even more than probable that there is no such place; and if we lived for centuries and were endowed with the powers of a god, we should find ourselves not much nearer what we wanted at the end. O toiling hands of mortals! O unwearied feet, travelling ye know not whither! Soon, soon, it seems to you, you must come forth on some conspicuous hilltop, and but a little way further, against the setting sun, descry the spires of El Dorado. Little do ye know your own blessedness; for to travel hopefully is a better thing than to arrive, and the true success is to labour.

THE ENGLISH ADMIRALS

"Whether it be wise in men to do such actions or no, I am sure it is so in States to honour them." — SIR WILLIAM TEMPLE.

THERE is one story of the wars of Rome which I have always very much envied for England. Germanicus was going down at the head of the legions into a dangerous river — on the opposite bank the woods were full of Germans — when there flew out seven great eagles which seemed to marshal the Romans on their way; they did not pause or waver, but disappeared into the forest where the enemy lay concealed. "Forward!" cried Germanicus, with a fine rhetorical inspiration, "Forward! and follow the Roman birds." It would be a very heavy spirit that did not give a leap at such a signal, and a very timorous one that continued to have any doubt of success. To appropriate the eagles as fellow-countrymen was to make imaginary allies of the forces of nature; the Roman Empire and its military fortunes, and along with these the prospects of those individual Roman legionaries now fording a river in Germany, looked altogether greater and more hopeful. It is a kind of illusion easy to produce. A particular shape of cloud, the appearance of a particular star, the holiday of some particular saint, anything in short to remind the combatants of patriotic legends or old successes, may be enough to change the issue of a pitched battle; for it gives to the one party a feeling that Right and the larger interests are with them.

If an Englishman wishes to have such a feeling, it must be about the sea. The lion is nothing to us; he has not been taken to the hearts of the people, and naturalised as an English emblem. We know right well that a lion would fall foul of us as grimly as he would of a Frenchman or a Moldavian Jew, and we do not carry him before us in the smoke of battle. But the sea is our approach and bulwark; it has been the scene of our greatest triumphs and dangers; and we are accustomed in lyrical strains to claim it as our own. The prostrating experiences of foreigners between Calais and Dover have always an agreeable side to English prepossessions. A man from Bedfordshire, who does not know one end of the ship from the other until she begins to move, swaggers among such persons with a sense of hereditary nautical experience. To suppose yourself endowed with natural parts for the sea because you are the countryman of Blake and mighty Nelson, is perhaps just as unwarrantable as to imagine Scotch extraction a sufficient guarantee that you will look well in a kilt. But the feeling is there, and seated beyond the reach of argument. We should consider ourselves unworthy of our descent if we did not share the arrogance of our progenitors, and please ourselves with the pretension that the sea is English. Even where it is looked upon by the guns and battlements of another nation we regard it as a kind of English cemetery, where the bones of our seafaring fathers take their rest until the last trumpet; for I suppose no other nation has lost as many ships, or sent as many brave fellows to the bottom.

There is nowhere such a background for heroism as the noble, terrifying, and picturesque conditions of some of our sea fights. Hawke's battle in the tempest, and Aboukir at the moment when the French Admiral blew up, reach the limit of what is imposing to the imagination. And our naval annals owe some of their interest to the fantastic and beautiful appearance of old warships and the romance that invests the sea and everything sea-going in the eyes of English lads on a half-holiday at the coast. Nay, and what we know of the misery between decks enhances the bravery of what was done by giving it something for contrast. We like to know that these bold and honest fellows contrived to live, and to keep bold and honest, among absurd and vile surroundings. No reader can forget the description of the *Thunder* in *Roderick Random:* the disorderly tyranny; the cruelty and dirt of officers and men; deck after deck, each with some new object of offence; the hospital, where the hammocks were huddled together with but fourteen inches space for each; the cockpit, far under water, where, "in an intolerable stench," the spectacled steward kept the accounts of the different messes; and the canvas enclosure, six feet square, in which Morgan made flip and salmagundi, smoked his pipe, sang his Welsh songs, and swore his queer Welsh imprecations. There are portions of this business on board the *Thunder* over which the reader passes lightly and hurriedly, like a traveller in a malarious country. It is easy enough to understand the opinion of Dr. Johnson: "Why, sir," he said, "no man will be a sailor who has contrivance enough to get himself into a jail." You would fancy any one's spirit would die out under such an accumulation of darkness, noisomeness, and injustice, above all when he had not come there of his own free will, but under the cutlasses and bludgeons of the press-gang. But perhaps a watch on deck in the sharp sea air put a man on his mettle again; a battle must have been a capital relief; and prize-money, bloodily earned and grossly squandered, opened the doors of the prison for a twinkling. Somehow or other, at least, this worst of possible lives could not overlie the spirit and gaiety of our sailors; they did their duty as though they had some interest in the fortune of that country which so cruelly oppressed them, they served their guns merrily when it came to fighting, and they had the readiest ear for a bold, honourable sentiment, of any class of men the world ever produced.

Most men of high destinies have high-sounding names. Pym and Habakkuk may do pretty well, but they must not think to cope with the Cromwells and Isaiahs. And you could not find a better case in point than that of the English Admirals. Drake and Rooke and Hawke are picked names for men of execution. Frobisher, Rodney, Boscawen, Foul-Weather Jack Byron, are all good to catch the eye in a page of a naval history. Cloudesley Shovel is a mouthful of quaint and sounding syllables. Benbow has a bulldog quality that suits the man's character, and it takes us back to those English archers who were his true comrades for plainness, tenacity, and pluck. Raleigh is spirited and martial, and signifies an act of bold conduct in the field. It is impossible to judge of Blake or Nelson, no names current among men being worthy of such heroes. But still it is odd enough, and very appropriate in this connection, that the latter was greatly taken with his Sicilian title. "The signification, perhaps, pleased him," says Southey; "Duke of Thunder was what in Dahomey would have been called a *strong name;* it was to a sailor's taste, and certainly to no man could it be more applicable." Admiral in itself is one of the most satisfactory of distinctions; it has a noble sound and a very proud history; and Columbus thought so highly of it, that he enjoined his heirs to sign themselves by that title as long as the house should last.

But it is the spirit of the men, and not their names, that I wish to speak about in this paper. That spirit is truly English; they, and not Tennyson's cotton-spinners or Mr. D'Arcy Thompson's Abstract Bagman, are the true and typical Englishmen. There may be more *head* of bagmen in the country, but human beings are reckoned by number only in political constitutions. And the Admirals are typical in the full force of the word. They are splendid examples of virtue, indeed, but of a virtue in which most Englishmen can claim a moderate share; and what we admire in their lives is a sort of apotheosis of ourselves. Almost everybody in our land, except humanitarians and a few persons whose youth has been depressed by exceptionally æsthetic surroundings, can understand and sympathise with an Admiral or a prize-fighter. I do not wish to bracket Benbow and Tom Cribb; but, depend upon it, they are practically bracketed for admiration in the minds of many frequenters of ale-houses. If you told them about Germanicus and the eagles, or Regulus going back to Carthage, they would very likely fall asleep; but tell them about Harry Pearce and Jem Belcher, or about Nelson and the Nile, and they put down their pipes to listen. I have by me a copy of

Boxiana, on the fly-leaves of which a youthful member of the fancy kept a chronicle of remarkable events and an obituary of great men. Here we find piously chronicled the demise of jockeys, watermen, and pugilists — Johnny Moore, of the Liverpool Prize Ring; Tom Spring, aged fifty-six; "Pierce Egan, senior, writer of *Boxiana* and other sporting works"—and among all these, the Duke of Wellington! If Benbow had lived in the time of this annalist, do you suppose his name would not have been added to the glorious roll? In short, we do not all feel warmly towards Wesley or Laud, we cannot all take pleasure in *Paradise Lost;* but there are certain common sentiments and touches of nature by which the whole nation is made to feel kinship. A little while ago everybody, from Hazlitt and John Wilson down to the imbecile creature who scribbled his register on the fly-leaves of *Boxiana*, felt a more or less shamefaced satisfaction in the exploits of prize-fighters. And the exploits of the Admirals are popular to the same degree, and tell in all ranks of society. Their sayings and doings stir English blood like the sound of a trumpet; and if the Indian Empire, the trade of London, and all the outward and visible ensigns of our greatness should pass away, we should still leave behind us a durable monument of what we were in these sayings and doings of the English Admirals.

Duncan, lying off the Texel with his own flagship, the *Venerable*, and only one other vessel, heard that the whole Dutch fleet was putting to sea. He told Captain Hotham to anchor alongside of him in the narrowest part of the channel, and fight his vessel till she sank. "I have taken the depth of the water," added he, "and

when the *Venerable* goes down, my flag will still fly."
And you observe this is no naked Viking in a prehistoric
period; but a Scotch member of Parliament, with a
smattering of the classics, a telescope, a cocked hat of
great size, and flannel underclothing. In the same spirit,
Nelson went into Aboukir with six colours flying; so
that even if five were shot away, it should not be imagined he had struck. He too must needs wear his four
stars outside his Admiral's frock, to be a butt for sharp-
shooters. "In honour I gained them," he said to ob-
jectors, adding with sublime illogicality, "in honour I
will die with them." Captain Douglas of the *Royal Oak,*
when the Dutch fired his vessel in the Thames, sent his
men ashore, but was burned along with her himself
rather than desert his post without orders. Just then,
perhaps the Merry Monarch was chasing a moth round
the supper-table with the ladies of his court. When
Raleigh sailed into Cadiz, and all the forts and ships
opened fire on him at once, he scorned to shoot a gun,
and made answer with a flourish of insulting trumpets.
I like this bravado better than the wisest dispositions to
insure victory; it comes from the heart and goes to it.
God has made nobler heroes, but he never made a finer
gentleman than Walter Raleigh. And as our Admirals
were full of heroic superstitions, and had a strutting and
vainglorious style of fight, so they discovered a startling
eagerness for battle, and courted war like a mistress.
When the news came to Essex before Cadiz that the attack had been decided, he threw his hat into the sea.
It is in this way that a schoolboy hears of a half-holiday;
but this was a bearded man of great possessions who
had just been allowed to risk his life. Benbow could

not lie still in his bunk after he had lost his leg; he must be on deck in a basket to direct and animate the fight. I said they loved war like a mistress; yet I think there are not many mistresses we should continue to woo under similar circumstances. Trowbridge went ashore with the *Culloden,* and was able to take no part in the battle of the Nile. "The merits of that ship and her gallant captain," wrote Nelson to the Admiralty, "are too well known to benefit by anything I could say. Her misfortune was great in getting aground, *while her more fortunate companions were in the full tide of happiness.*" This is a notable expression, and depicts the whole great-hearted, big-spoken stock of the English Admirals to a hair. It was to be "in the full tide of happiness" for Nelson to destroy five thousand five hundred and twenty-five of his fellow-creatures, and have his own scalp torn open by a piece of langridge shot. Hear him again at Copenhagen: "A shot through the mainmast knocked the splinters about; and he observed to one of his officers with a smile, 'It is warm work, and this may be the last to any of us at any moment;' and then, stopping short at the gangway, added, with emotion, *'But, mark you — I would not be elsewhere for thousands.'*"

I must tell one more story, which has lately been made familiar to us all, and that in one of the noblest ballads in the English language. I had written my tame prose abstract, I shall beg the reader to believe, when I had no notion that the sacred bard designed an immortality for Greenville. Sir Richard Greenville was Vice-Admiral to Lord Thomas Howard, and lay off the Azores with the English squadron in 1591. He was a noted tyrant to his crew: a dark, bullying fellow apparently; and it is related of him that he would chew and swallow wineglasses, by way of convivial levity, till the blood ran out of his mouth. When the Spanish fleet of fifty sail came within sight of the English, his ship, the *Revenge,* was the last to weigh anchor, and was so far circumvented by the Spaniards, that there were but two courses open—either to turn her back upon the enemy or sail through one of his squadrons. The first alternative Greenville dismissed as dishonourable to himself, his country, and her Majesty's ship. Accordingly, he chose the latter, and steered into the Spanish armament. Several vessels he forced to luff and fall under his lee; until, about three o'clock of the afternoon, a great ship of three decks of ordnance took the wind out of his sails, and immediately boarded. Thenceforward, and all night long, the *Revenge* held her own single-handed against the Spaniards. As one ship was beaten off, another took its place. She endured, according to Raleigh's computation, "eight hundred shot of great artillery, besides many assaults and entries." By morning the powder was spent, the pikes all broken, not a stick was standing, "nothing left overhead either for flight or defence;" six feet of water in the hold; almost all the men hurt; and Greenville himself in a dying condition. To bring them to this pass, a fleet of fifty sail had been mauling them for fifteen hours, the *Admiral of the Hulks* and the *Ascension* of Seville had both gone down alongside, and two other vessels had taken refuge on shore in a sinking state. In Hawke's words, they had "taken a great deal of drubbing." The captain and crew thought they had done about

118

enough; but Greenville was not of this opinion; he gave orders to the master gunner, whom he knew to be a fellow after his own stamp, to scuttle the *Revenge* where she lay. The others, who were not mortally wounded like the Admiral, interfered with some decision, locked the master gunner in his cabin, after having deprived him of his sword, for he manifested an intention to kill himself if he were not to sink the ship; and sent to the Spaniards to demand terms. These were granted. The second or third day after, Greenville died of his wounds aboard the Spanish flagship, leaving his contempt upon the "traitors and dogs" who had not chosen to do as he did, and engage fifty vessels, well found and fully manned, with six inferior craft ravaged by sickness and short of stores. He at least, he said, had done his duty as he was bound to do, and looked for everlasting fame.

Some one said to me the other day that they considered this story to be of a pestilent example. I am not inclined to imagine we shall ever be put into any practical difficulty from a superfluity of Greenvilles. And besides, I demur to the opinion. The worth of such actions is not a thing to be decided in a quaver of sensibility or a flush of righteous commonsense. The man who wished to make the ballads of his country, coveted a small matter compared to what Richard Greenville accomplished. I wonder how many people have been inspired by this mad story, and how many battles have been actually won for England in the spirit thus engendered. It is only with a measure of habitual foolhardiness that you can be sure, in the common run of men, of courage on a reasonable occasion. An army or a fleet, if it is not led by quixotic fancies, will not be led far by terror of the Provost Marshal. Even German warfare, in addition to maps and telegraphs, is not above employing the *Wacht am Rhein*. Nor is it only in the profession of arms that such stories may do good to a man. In this desperate and gleeful fighting, whether it is Greenville or Benbow, Hawke or Nelson, who flies his colours in the ship, we see men brought to the test and giving proof of what we call heroic feeling. Prosperous humanitarians tell me, in my club smoking-room, that they are a prey to prodigious heroic feelings, and that it costs them more nobility of soul to do nothing in particular, than would carry on all the wars, by sea or land, of bellicose humanity. It may very well be so, and yet not touch the point in question. For what I desire is to see some of this nobility brought face to face with me in an inspiriting achievement. A man may talk smoothly over a cigar in my club smoking-room from now to the Day of Judgment, without adding anything to mankind's treasury of illustrious and encouraging examples. It is not over the virtues of a curate-and-tea-party novel, that people are abashed into high resolutions. It may be because their hearts are crass, but to stir them properly they must have men entering into glory with some pomp and circumstance. And that is why these stories of our sea-captains, printed, so to speak, in capitals, and full of bracing moral influence, are more valuable to England than any material benefit in all the books of political economy between Westminster and Birmingham. Greenville chewing wineglasses at table makes no very pleasant figure, any more than a thousand other artists when they are viewed in the body, or met in private life; but his work of art, his finished tragedy, is an eloquent performance; and I contend it ought not only to enliven men of the sword as they go into battle, but send back merchant clerks with more heart and spirit to their book-keeping by double entry.

There is another question which seems bound up in this; and that is Temple's problem: whether it was wise of Douglas to burn with the *Royal Oak?* and by implication, what it was that made him do so? Many will tell you it was the desire of fame.

"To what do Cæsar and Alexander owe the infinite grandeur of their renown, but to fortune? How many men has she extinguished in the beginning of their progress, of whom we have no knowledge; who brought as much courage to the work as they, if their adverse hap had not cut them off in the first sally of their arms? Amongst so many and so great dangers, I do not remember to have anywhere read that Cæsar was ever wounded; a thousand have fallen in less dangers than the least of these he went through. A great many brave actions must be expected to be performed without witness, for one that comes to some notice. A man is not always at the top of a breach, or at the head of an army in the sight of his general, as upon a platform. He is often surprised between the hedge and the ditch; he must run the hazard of his life against a henroost; he must dislodge four rascally musketeers out of a barn; he must prick out single from his party, as necessity arises, and meet adventures alone."

Thus far Montaigne, in a characteristic essay on *Glory*. Where death is certain, as in the cases of Douglas or Greenville, it seems all one from a personal point of

view. The man who lost his life against a henroost, is
in the same pickle with him who lost his life against a
fortified place of the first order. Whether he has missed
a peerage or only the corporal's stripes, it is all one if he
has missed them and is quietly in the grave. It was by
a hazard that we learned the conduct of the four marines
of the *Wager*. There was no room for these brave fellows in the boat, and they were left behind upon the
island to a certain death. They were soldiers, they said,
and knew well enough it was their business to die; and
as their comrades pulled away, they stood upon the
beach, gave three cheers, and cried "God bless the
king!" Now, one or two of those who were in the boat
escaped, against all likelihood, to tell the story. That
was a great thing for us; but surely it cannot, by any
possible twisting of human speech, be construed into
anything great for the marines. You may suppose, if
you like, that they died hoping their behaviour would
not be forgotten; or you may suppose they thought nothing on the subject, which is much more likely. What
can be the signification of the word "fame" to a private of marines, who cannot read and knows nothing of
past history beyond the reminiscences of his grand-
mother? But whichever supposition you make, the fact
is unchanged. They died while the question still hung
in the balance; and I suppose their bones were already
white, before the winds and the waves and the humour
of Indian chiefs and Spanish governors had decided
whether they were to be unknown and useless martyrs
or honoured heroes. Indeed, I believe this is the lesson:
if it is for fame that men do brave actions, they are only
silly fellows after all.

It is at best but a pettifogging, pickthank business to decompose actions into little personal motives, and explain heroism away. The Abstract Bagman will grow like an Admiral at heart, not by ungrateful carping, but in a heat of admiration. But there is another theory of the personal motive in these fine sayings and doings, which I believe to be true and wholesome. People usually do things, and suffer martyrdoms, because they have an inclination that way. The best artist is not the man who fixes his eye on posterity, but the one who loves the practice of his art. And instead of having a taste for being successful merchants and retiring at thirty, some people have a taste for high and what we call heroic forms of excitement. If the Admirals courted war like a mistress; if, as the drum beat to quarters, the sailors came gaily out of the forecastle,—it is because a fight is a period of multiplied and intense experiences, and, by Nelson's computation, worth "thousands" to any one who has a heart under his jacket. If the marines of the *Wager* gave three cheers and cried "God bless the king," it was because they liked to do things nobly for their own satisfaction. They were giving their lives, there was no help for that; and they made it a point of self-respect to give them handsomely. And there were never four happier marines in God's world than these four at that moment. If it was worth thousands to be at the Baltic, I wish a Benthamite arithmetician would calculate how much it was worth to be one of these four marines; or how much their story is worth to each of us who read it. And mark you, undemonstrative men would have spoiled the situation. The finest action is the better for a piece of purple. If the soldiers of the *Birkenhead* had not gone down in line, or these marines of the *Wager* had walked away simply into the island, like plenty of other brave fellows in the like circumstances, my Benthamite arithmetician would assign a far lower value to the two stories. We have to desire a grand air in our heroes; and such a knowledge of the human stage as shall make them put the dots on their own i's, and leave us in no suspense as to when they mean to be heroic. And hence, we should congratulate ourselves upon the fact that our Admirals were not only great-hearted but big-spoken.

The heroes themselves say, as often as not, that fame is their object; but I do not think that is much to the purpose. People generally say what they have been taught to say; that was the catchword they were given in youth to express the aims of their way of life; and men who are gaining great battles are not likely to take much trouble in reviewing their sentiments and the words in which they were told to express them. Almost every person, if you will believe himself, holds a quite different theory of life from the one on which he is patently acting. And the fact is, fame may be a forethought and an afterthought, but it is too abstract an idea to move people greatly in moments of swift and momentous decision. It is from something more immediate, some determination of blood to the head, some trick of the fancy, that the breach is stormed or the bold word spoken. I am sure a fellow shooting an ugly weir in a canoe has exactly as much thought about fame as most commanders going into battle; and yet the action, fall out how it will, is not one of those the muse delights to celebrate. Indeed it is difficult to see why the fellow does a thing so nameless and yet so formidable to look at, unless on the theory that he likes it. I suspect that is why; and I suspect it is at least ten per cent of why Lord Beaconsfield and Mr. Gladstone have debated so much in the House of Commons, and why Burnaby rode to Khiva the other day, and why the Admirals courted war like a mistress.

SOME PORTRAITS BY RAEBURN

THROUGH the initiative of a prominent citizen, Edinburgh has been in possession, for some autumn weeks, of a gallery of paintings of singular merit and interest. They were exposed in the apartments of the Scotch Academy; and filled those who are accustomed to visit the annual spring exhibition, with astonishment and a sense of incongruity. Instead of the too common purple sunsets, and pea-green fields, and distances executed in putty and hog's lard, he beheld, looking down upon him from the walls of room after room, a whole army of wise, grave, humorous, capable, or beautiful countenances, painted simply and strongly by a man of genuine instinct. It was a complete act of the Human Drawing-Room Comedy. Lords and ladies, soldiers and doctors, hanging judges, and heretical divines, a whole generation of good society was resuscitated; and the Scotchman of to-day walked about among the Scotchmen of two generations ago. The moment was well chosen, neither too late nor too early. The people who sat for these pictures are not yet ancestors, they are still relations. They are not yet altogether a part of the dusty past, but occupy a middle distance within cry of our affections. The little

child who looks wonderingly on his grandfather's watch
in the picture, is now the veteran Sheriff *emeritus* of
Perth. And I hear a story of a lady who returned the
other day to Edinburgh, after an absence of sixty years:
"I could see none of my old friends," she said, "until
I went into the Raeburn Gallery, and found them all
there."

It would be difficult to say whether the collection was
more interesting on the score of unity or diversity.
Where the portraits were all of the same period, almost
all of the same race, and all from the same brush, there
could not fail to be many points of similarity. And yet
the similarity of the handling seems to throw into more
vigorous relief those personal distinctions which Raeburn was so quick to seize. He was a born painter of
portraits. He looked people shrewdly between the
eyes, surprised their manners in their face, and had possessed himself of what was essential in their character
before they had been many minutes in his studio.
What he was so swift to perceive, he conveyed to the
canvas almost in the moment of conception. He had
never any difficulty, he said, about either hands or faces.
About draperies or light or composition, he might see
room for hesitation or afterthought. But a face or a
hand was something plain and legible. There were no
two ways about it, any more than about the person's
name. And so each of his portraits is not only (in
Doctor Johnson's phrase, aptly quoted on the catalogue)
"a piece of history," but a piece of biography into the
bargain. It is devoutly to be wished that all biography
were equally amusing, and carried its own credentials
equally upon its face. These portraits are racier than

many anecdotes, and more complete than many a volume of sententious memoirs. You can see whether you get a stronger and clearer idea of Robertson the historian from Raeburn's palette or Dugald Stewart's woolly and evasive periods. And then the portraits are both signed and countersigned. For you have, first, the authority of the artist, whom you recognise as no mean critic of the looks and manners of men; and next you have the tacit acquiescence of the subject, who sits looking out upon you with inimitable innocence, and apparently under the impression that he is in a room by himself. For Raeburn could plunge at once through all the constraint and embarrassment of the sitter, and present the face, clear, open, and intelligent as at the most disengaged moments. This is best seen in portraits where the sitter is represented in some appropriate action: Neil Gow with his fiddle, Doctor Spens shooting an arrow, or Lord Bannatyne hearing a cause. Above all, from this point of view, the portrait of Lieutenant-Colonel Lyon is notable. A strange enough young man, pink, fat about the lower part of the face, with a lean forehead, a narrow nose and a fine nostril, sits with a drawing-board upon his knees. He has just paused to render himself account of some difficulty, to disentangle some complication of line or compare neighbouring values. And there, without any perceptible wrinkling, you have rendered for you exactly the fixed look in the eyes, and the unconscious compression of the mouth, that befit and signify an effort of the kind. The whole pose, the whole expression, is absolutely direct and simple. You are ready to take your oath to it that Colonel Lyon had no idea he was sitting for his picture, and thought of nothing in the world besides his own occupation of the moment.

Although the collection did not embrace, I understand, nearly the whole of Raeburn's works, it was too large not to contain some that were indifferent, whether as works of art or as portraits. Certainly the standard was remarkably high, and was wonderfully maintained, but there were one or two pictures that might have been almost as well away — one or two that seemed wanting in salt, and some that you can only hope were not successful likenesses. Neither of the portraits of Sir Walter Scott, for instance, were very agreeable to look upon. You do not care to think that Scott looked quite so rustic and puffy. And where is that peaked forehead which, according to all written accounts and many portraits, was the distinguishing characteristic of his face? Again, in spite of his own satisfaction and in spite of Dr. John Brown, I cannot consider that Raeburn was very happy in hands. Without doubt, he could paint one if he had taken the trouble to study it; but it was by no means always that he gave himself the trouble. Looking round one of these rooms hung about with his portraits, you were struck with the array of expressive faces, as compared with what you may have seen in looking round a room full of living people. But it was not so with the hands. The portraits differed from each other in face perhaps ten times as much as they differed by the hand; whereas with living people the two go pretty much together; and where one is remarkable, the other will almost certainly not be commonplace.

One interesting portrait was that of Duncan of Camperdown. He stands in uniform beside a table, his feet slightly straddled with the balance of an old sailor, his hand poised upon a chart by the finger tips. The mouth is pursed, the nostril spread and drawn up, the eyebrows very highly arched. The cheeks lie along the jaw in folds of iron, and have the redness that comes from much exposure to salt sea winds. From the whole figure, attitude and countenance, there breathes something precise and decisive, something alert, wiry, and strong. You can understand, from the look of him, that sense, not so much of humour, as of what is grimmest and driest in pleasantry, which inspired his address before the fight at Camperdown. He had just overtaken the Dutch fleet under Admiral de Winter. "Gentlemen," says he, "you see a severe winter approaching; I have only to advise you to keep up a good fire." Somewhat of this same spirit of adamantine drollery must have supported him in the days of the mutiny at the Nore, when he lay off the Texel with his own flagship, the *Venerable*, and only one other vessel, and kept up active signals, as though he had a powerful fleet in the offing, to intimidate the Dutch.

Another portrait which irresistibly attracted the eye, was the half-length of Robert M'Queen, of Braxfield, Lord Justice-Clerk. If I know gusto in painting when I see it, this canvas was painted with rare enjoyment. The tart, rosy, humorous look of the man, his nose like a cudgel, his face resting squarely on the jowl, has been caught and perpetuated with something that looks like brotherly love. A peculiarly subtle expression haunts the lower part, sensual and incredulous, like that of a man tasting good Bordeaux with half a fancy it has been somewhat too long uncorked. From under the pen-

dulous eyelids of old age, the eyes look out with a half-
youthful, half-frosty twinkle. Hands, with no pretence
to distinction, are folded on the judge's stomach. So
sympathetically is the character conceived by the portrait painter, that it is hardly possible to avoid some
movement of sympathy on the part of the spectator.
And sympathy is a thing to be encouraged, apart from
humane considerations, because it supplies us with the
materials for wisdom. It is probably more instructive
to entertain a sneaking kindness for any unpopular person, and, among the rest, for Lord Braxfield, than to
give way to perfect raptures of moral indignation against
his abstract vices. He was the last judge on the Scotch
bench to employ the pure Scotch idiom. His opinions,
thus given in Doric, and conceived in a lively, rugged,
conversational style, were full of point and authority.
Out of the bar, or off the bench, he was a convivial man,
a lover of wine, and one who "shone peculiarly" at
tavern meetings. He has left behind him an unrivalled
reputation for rough and cruel speech; and to this day
his name smacks of the gallows. It was he who presided at the trials of Muir and Skirving in 1793 and 1794;
and his appearance on these occasions was scarcely cut
to the pattern of to-day. His summing up on Muir began
thus — the reader must supply for himself "the growl-
ing, blacksmith's voice" and the broad Scotch accent :
"Now this is the question for consideration — Is the
panel guilty of sedition, or is he not? Now, before this
can be answered, two things must be attended to that
require no proof : *First*, that the British constitution is
the best that ever was since the creation of the world,
and it is not possible to make it better." It's a pretty fair

start, is it not, for a political trial? A little later, he has occasion to refer to the relations of Muir with "those wretches," the French. "I never liked the French all my days," said his lordship, "but now I hate them." And yet a little further on: "A government in any country should be like a corporation; and in this country it is made up of the landed interest, which alone has a right to be represented. As for the rabble who have nothing but personal property, what hold has the nation of them? They may pack up their property on their backs, and leave the country in the twinkling of an eye." After having made profession of sentiments so cynically antipopular as these, when the trials were at an end, which was generally about midnight, Braxfield would walk home to his house in George Square with no better escort than an easy conscience. I think I see him getting his cloak about his shoulders, and, with perhaps a lantern in one hand, steering his way along the streets in the mirk January night. It might have been that very day that Skirving had defied him in these words : "It is altogether unavailing for your lordship to menace me; for I have long learned to fear not the face of man;" and I can fancy, as Braxfield reflected on the number of what he called *Grumbletonians* in Edinburgh, and of how many of them must bear special malice against so upright and inflexible a judge, nay, and might at that very moment be lurking in the mouth of a dark close with hostile intent—I can fancy that he indulged in a sour smile, as he reflected that he also was not especially afraid of men's faces or men's fists, and had hitherto found no occasion to embody this insensibility in heroic words. For if he was an inhumane old gentleman (and

I am afraid it is a fact that he was inhumane), he was also perfectly intrepid. You may look into the queer face of that portrait for as long as you will, but you will not see any hole or corner for timidity to enter in.

Indeed, there would be no end to this paper if I were even to name half of the portraits that were remarkable for their execution, or interesting by association. There was one picture of Mr. Wardrop, of Torbane Hill, which you might palm off upon most laymen as a Rembrandt; and close by, you saw the white head of John Clerk, of Eldin, that country gentleman who, playing with pieces of cork on his own dining-table, invented modern naval warfare. There was that portrait of Neil Gow, to sit for which the old fiddler walked daily through the streets of Edinburgh arm in arm with the Duke of Athole. There was good Harry Erskine, with his satirical nose and upper lip, and his mouth just open for a witticism to pop out; Hutton the geologist, in quakerish raiment, and looking altogether trim and narrow, and as if he cared more about fossils than young ladies; full-blown John Robieson, in hyperbolical red dressing-gown, and, every inch of him, a fine old man of the world; Constable the publisher, upright beside a table, and bearing a corporation with commercial dignity; Lord Bannatyne hearing a cause, if ever anybody heard a cause since the world began; Lord Newton just awakened from clandestine slumber on the bench; and the second President Dundas, with every feature so fat that he reminds you, in his wig, of some droll old court officer in an illustrated nursery story-book, and yet all these fat features instinct with meaning, the fat lips curved and compressed, the nose combining somehow the dignity of a beak with the

good nature of a bottle, and the very double chin with
an air of intelligence and insight. And all these portraits
are so pat and telling, and look at you so spiritedly from
the walls, that, compared with the sort of living people
one sees about the streets, they are as bright new sovereigns to fishy and obliterated sixpences. Some dis-
paraging thoughts upon our own generation could
hardly fail to present themselves; but it is perhaps only
the *sacer vates* who is wanting; and we also, painted
by such a man as Carolus Duran, may look in holiday
immortality upon our children and grandchildren.

Raeburn's young women, to be frank, are by no means
of the same order of merit. No one, of course, could be
insensible to the presence of Miss Janet Suttie or Mrs.
Campbell of Possil. When things are as pretty as that,
criticism is out of season. But, on the whole, it is only
with women of a certain age that he can be said to have
succeeded, in at all the same sense as we say he succeeded with men. The younger women do not seem to
be made of good flesh and blood. They are not painted
in rich and unctuous touches. They are dry and di-
aphanous. And although young ladies in Great Britain
are all that can be desired of them, I would fain hope
they are not quite so much of that as Raeburn would
have us believe. In all these pretty faces, you miss
character, you miss fire, you miss that spice of the devil
which is worth all the prettiness in the world; and what
is worst of all, you miss sex. His young ladies are not
womanly to nearly the same degree as his men are masculine; they are so in a negative sense; in short, they
are the typical young ladies of the male novelist.

To say truth, either Raeburn was timid with young

and pretty sitters; or he had stupefied himself with sentimentalities; or else (and here is about the truth of it) Raeburn and the rest of us labour under an obstinate blindness in one direction, and know very little more about women after all these centuries than Adam when he first saw Eve. This is all the more likely, because we are by no means so unintelligent in the matter of old women. There are some capital old women, it seems to me, in books written by men. And Raeburn has some, such as Mrs. Colin Campbell, of Park, or the anonymous "Old lady with a large cap," which are done in the same frank, perspicacious spirit as the very best of his men. He could look into their eyes without trouble; and he was not withheld, by any bashful sentimentalism, from recognising what he saw there and unsparingly putting it down upon the canvas. But where people cannot meet without some confusion and a good deal of involuntary humbug, and are occupied, for as long as they are together, with a very different vein of thought, there cannot be much room for intelligent study nor much result in the shape of genuine comprehension. Even women, who understand men so well for practical purposes, do not know them well enough for the purposes of art. Take even the very best of their male creations, take Tito Melema, for instance, and you will find he has an equivocal air, and every now and again remembers he has a comb at the back of his head. Of course, no woman will believe this, and many men will be so very polite as to humour their incredulity.

CHILD'S PLAY

THE regret we have for our childhood is not wholly
justifiable: so much a man may lay down without
fear of public ribaldry; for although we shake our heads
over the change, we are not unconscious of the manifold advantages of our new state. What we lose in
generous impulse, we more than gain in the habit of
generously watching others; and the capacity to enjoy
Shakespeare may balance a lost aptitude for playing at
soldiers. Terror is gone out of our lives, moreover;
we no longer see the devil in the bed-curtains nor lie
awake to listen to the wind. We go to school no
more; and if we have only exchanged one drudgery for
another (which is by no means sure), we are set free
for ever from the daily fear of chastisement. And yet a
great change has overtaken us; and although we do
not enjoy ourselves less, at least we take our pleasure
differently. We need pickles nowadays to make
Wednesday's cold mutton please our Friday's appetite;
and I can remember the time when to call it red veni-
son, and tell myself a hunter's story, would have made
it more palatable than the best of sauces. To the grown
person, cold mutton is cold mutton all the world over;
not all the mythology ever invented by man will make

it better or worse to him; the broad fact, the clamant
reality, of the mutton carries away before it such seduc-
tive figments. But for the child it is still possible to
weave an enchantment over eatables; and if he has but
read of a dish in a story-book, it will be heavenly manna
to him for a week.

If a grown man does not like eating and drinking and
exercise, if he is not something positive in his tastes, it
means he has a feeble body and should have some medicine; but children may be pure spirits, if they will, and
take their enjoyment in a world of moonshine. Sensation does not count for so much in our first years as afterwards; something of the swaddling numbness of infancy clings about us; we see and touch and hear through
a sort of golden mist. Children, for instance, are able
enough to see, but they have no great faculty for looking; they do not use their eyes for the pleasure of using
them, but for by-ends of their own; and the things I call
to mind seeing most vividly, were not beautiful in themselves, but merely interesting or enviable to me as I
thought they might be turned to practical account in play.
Nor is the sense of touch so clean and poignant in children
as it is in a man. If you will turn over your old memories, I think the sensations of this sort you remember
will be somewhat vague, and come to not much more
than a blunt, general sense of heat on summer days, or
a blunt, general sense of wellbeing in bed. And here,
of course, you will understand pleasurable sensations;
for overmastering pain — the most deadly and tragical
element in life, and the true commander of man's soul
and body — alas! pain has its own way with all of us;
it breaks in, a rude visitant, upon the fairy garden where

137

the child wanders in a dream, no less surely than it rules
upon the field of battle, or sends the immortal war-god
whimpering to his father; and innocence, no more than
philosophy, can protect us from this sting.   As for taste,
when we bear in mind the excesses of unmitigated sugar
which delight a youthful palate, "it is surely no very
cynical asperity" to think taste a character of the maturer growth.   Smell and hearing are perhaps more de-
veloped; I remember many scents, many voices, and a
great deal of spring singing in the woods.   But hearing
is capable of vast improvement as a means of pleasure;
and there is all the world between gaping wonderment
at the jargon of birds, and the emotion with which a
man listens to articulate music.

At the same time, and step by step with this increase
in the definition and intensity of what we feel which accompanies our growing age, another change takes place
in the sphere of intellect, by which all things are trans-
formed and seen through theories and associations as
through coloured windows.   We make to ourselves
day by day, out of history, and gossip, and econom-
ical speculations, and God knows what, a medium in
which we walk and through which we look abroad.
We study shop windows with other eyes than in our
childhood, never to wonder, not always to admire,
but to make and modify our little incongruous theories about life.   It is no longer the uniform of a soldier that arrests our attention; but perhaps the flowing
carriage of a woman, or perhaps a countenance that has
been vividly stamped with passion and carries an adventurous story written in its lines.   The pleasure of
surprise is passed away; sugar-loaves and water-carts

seem mighty tame to encounter; and we walk the streets to make romances and to sociologise. Nor must we deny that a good many of us walk them solely for the purposes of transit or in the interest of a livelier digestion. These, indeed, may look back with mingled thoughts upon their childhood, but the rest are in a better case; they know more than when they were children, they understand better, their desires and sympathies answer more nimbly to the provocation of the senses, and their minds are brimming with interest as they go about the world.

According to my contention, this is a flight to which children cannot rise. They are wheeled in perambulators or dragged about by nurses in a pleasing stupor. A vague, faint, abiding wonderment possesses them. Here and there some specially remarkable circumstance, such as a water-cart or a guardsman, fairly penetrates into the seat of thought and calls them, for half a moment, out of themselves; and you may see them, still towed forward sideways by the inexorable nurse as by a sort of destiny, but still staring at the bright object in their wake. It may be some minutes before another such moving spectacle reawakens them to the world in which they dwell. For other children, they almost invariably show some intelligent sympathy. "There is a fine fellow making mud pies," they seem to say; "that I can understand, there is some sense in mud pies." But the doings of their elders, unless where they are speakingly picturesque or recommend themselves by the quality of being easily imitable, they let them go over their heads (as we say) without the least regard. If it were not for this perpetual imitation, we should be tempted to fancy they despised us outright, or only considered us in the light of creatures brutally strong and brutally silly; among whom they condescended to dwell in obedience like a philosopher at a barbarous court. At times, indeed, they display an arrogance of disregard that is truly staggering. Once, when I was groaning aloud with physical pain, a young gentleman came into the room and nonchalantly inquired if I had seen his bow and arrow. He made no account of my groans, which he accepted, as he had to accept so much else, as a piece of the inexplicable conduct of his elders; and like a wise young gentleman, he would waste no wonder on the subject. Those elders, who care so little for rational enjoyment, and are even the enemies of rational enjoyment for others, he had accepted without understanding and without complaint, as the rest of us accept the scheme of the universe.

We grown people can tell ourselves a story, give and take strokes until the bucklers ring, ride far and fast, marry, fall, and die; all the while sitting quietly by the fire or lying prone in bed. This is exactly what a child cannot do, or does not do, at least, when he can find anything else. He works all with lay figures and stage properties. When his story comes to the fighting, he must rise, get something by way of a sword and have a set-to with a piece of furniture, until he is out of breath. When he comes to ride with the king's pardon, he must bestride a chair, which he will so hurry and belabour and on which he will so furiously demean himself, that the messenger will arrive, if not bloody with spurring, at least fiery red with haste. If his romance involves an accident upon a cliff, he must clamber in person about the chest of drawers and fall bodily upon the carpet, before his imagination is satisfied. Lead soldiers, dolls, all toys, in short, are in the same category and answer the same end. Nothing can stagger a child's faith; he accepts the clumsiest substitutes and can swallow the most staring incongruities. The chair he has just been besieging as a castle, or valiantly cutting to the ground as a dragon, is taken away for the accommodation of a morning visitor, and he is nothing abashed; he can skirmish by the hour with a stationary coal-scuttle; in the midst of the enchanted pleasance, he can see, without sensible shock, the gardener soberly digging potatoes for the day's dinner. He can make abstraction of whatever does not fit into his fable; and he puts his eyes into his pocket, just as we hold our noses in an unsavoury lane. And so it is, that although the ways of children cross with those of their elders in a hundred places daily, they never go in the same direction nor so much as lie in the same element. So may the telegraph wires intersect the line of the high-road, or so might a landscape painter and a bagman visit the same country, and yet move in different worlds.

People struck with these spectacles, cry aloud about the power of imagination in the young. Indeed there may be two words to that. It is, in some ways, but a pedestrian fancy that the child exhibits. It is the grown people who make the nursery stories; all the children do, is jealously to preserve the text. One out of a dozen reasons why *Robinson Crusoe* should be so popular with youth, is that it hits their level in this matter to a nicety; Crusoe was always at makeshifts and had, in so many words, to *play* at a great variety of professions; and then the book is all about tools, and there is nothing that de-

lights a child so much. Hammers and saws belong to
a province of life that positively calls for imitation. The
juvenile lyrical drama, surely of the most ancient Thes-
pian model, wherein the trades of mankind are successively simulated to the running burthen "On a cold and
frosty morning," gives a good instance of the artistic
taste in children. And this need for overt action and
lay figures testifies to a defect in the child's imagination
which prevents him from carrying out his novels in
the privacy of his own heart. He does not yet know
enough of the world and men. His experience is incomplete. That stage-wardrobe and scene-room that we
call the memory is so ill provided, that he can overtake
few combinations and body out few stories, to his own
content, without some external aid. He is at the experi-
mental stage; he is not sure how one would feel in certain circumstances; to make sure, he must come as near
trying it as his means permit. And so here is young
heroism with a wooden sword, and mothers practise
their kind vocation over a bit of jointed stick. It may be
laughable enough just now; but it is these same people
and these same thoughts, that not long hence, when they
are on the theatre of life, will make you weep and tremble. For children think very much the same thoughts
and dream the same dreams, as bearded men and mar-
riageable women. No one is more romantic. Fame
and honour, the love of young men and the love of
mothers, the business man's pleasure in method, all
these and others they anticipate and rehearse in their
play hours. Upon us, who are further advanced and
fairly dealing with the threads of destiny, they only
glance from time to time to glean a hint for their own

mimetic reproduction. Two children playing at soldiers are far more interesting to each other than one of the scarlet beings whom both are busy imitating. This is perhaps the greatest oddity of all. "Art for art" is their motto; and the doings of grown folk are only interesting as the raw material for play. Not Théophile Gautier, not Flaubert, can look more callously upon life, or rate the reproduction more highly over the reality; and they will parody an execution, a deathbed, or the funeral of the young man of Nain, with all the cheerfulness in the world.

The true parallel for play is not to be found, of course, in conscious art, which, though it be derived from play, is itself an abstract, impersonal thing, and depends largely upon philosophical interests beyond the scope of childhood. It is when we make castles in the air and personate the leading character in our own romances, that we return to the spirit of our first years. Only, there are several reasons why the spirit is no longer so agreeable to indulge. Nowadays, when we admit this personal element into our divagations we are apt to stir up uncomfortable and sorrowful memories, and remind ourselves sharply of old wounds. Our day-dreams can no longer lie all in the air like a story in the *Arabian Nights;* they read to us rather like the history of a period in which we ourselves had taken part, where we come across many unfortunate passages and find our own conduct smartly reprimanded. And then the child, mind you, acts his parts. He does not merely repeat them to himself; he leaps, he runs, and sets the blood agog over all his body. And so his play breathes him; and he no sooner assumes a passion than he gives it

vent. Alas! when we betake ourselves to our intellectual form of play, sitting quietly by the fire or lying prone
in bed, we rouse many hot feelings for which we can
find no outlet. Substitutes are not acceptable to the
mature mind, which desires the thing itself; and even
to rehearse a triumphant dialogue with one's enemy,
although it is perhaps the most satisfactory piece of play
still left within our reach, is not entirely satisfying, and
is even apt to lead to a visit and an interview which
may be the reverse of triumphant after all.

In the child's world of dim sensation, play is all in
all. "Making believe" is the gist of his whole life,
and he cannot so much as take a walk except in character. I could not learn my alphabet without some
suitable *mise-en-scène*, and had to act a business man
in an office before I could sit down to my book. Will
you kindly question your memory, and find out how
much you did, work or pleasure, in good faith and
soberness, and for how much you had to cheat yourself
with some invention? I remember, as though it were
yesterday, the expansion of spirit, the dignity and self-
reliance, that came with a pair of mustachios in burnt
cork, even when there was none to see. Children are
even content to forego what we call the realities, and
prefer the shadow to the substance. When they might
be speaking intelligibly together, they chatter senseless
gibberish by the hour, and are quite happy because
they are making believe to speak French. I have said
already how even the imperious appetite of hunger suffers itself to be gulled and led by the nose with the fag
end of an old song. And it goes deeper than this:
when children are together even a meal is felt as an in-

terruption in the business of life; and they must find
some imaginative sanction, and tell themselves some
sort of story, to account for, to colour, to render entertaining, the simple processes of eating and drinking.
What wonderful fancies I have heard evolved out of the
pattern upon tea - cups! — from which there followed a
code of rules and a whole world of excitement, until
tea - drinking began to take rank as a game. When my
cousin and I took our porridge of a morning, we had a
device to enliven the course of the meal. He ate his
with sugar, and explained it to be a country continually
buried under snow. I took mine with milk, and explained it to be a country suffering gradual inundation.
You can imagine us exchanging bulletins; how here
was an island still unsubmerged, here a valley not yet
covered with snow; what inventions were made; how
his population lived in cabins on perches and travelled
on stilts, and how mine was always in boats; how the
interest grew furious, as the last corner of safe ground
was cut off on all sides and grew smaller every moment; and how, in fine, the food was of altogether
secondary importance, and might even have been nau-
seous, so long as we seasoned it with these dreams.
But perhaps the most exciting moments I ever had over
a meal, were in the case of calves' feet jelly. It was
hardly possible not to believe — and you may be sure,
so far from trying, I did all I could to favour the illusion
— that some part of it was hollow, and that sooner or
later my spoon would lay open the secret tabernacle of
the golden rock. There, might some miniature *Red
Beard* await his hour; there, might one find the treasures of the *Forty Thieves,* and bewildered Cassim beating

about the walls. And so I quarried on slowly, with bated breath, savouring the interest. Believe me, I had little palate left for the jelly; and though I preferred the taste when I took cream with it, I used often to go without, because the cream dimmed the transparent fractures.

Even with games, this spirit is authoritative with right-minded children. It is thus that hide-and-seek has so pre-eminent a sovereignty, for it is the well-spring of romance, and the actions and the excitement to which it gives rise lend themselves to almost any sort of fable. And thus cricket, which is a mere matter of dexterity, palpably about nothing and for no end, often fails to satisfy infantile craving. It is a game, if you like, but not a game of play. You cannot tell yourself a story about cricket; and the activity it calls forth can be justified on no rational theory. Even football, although it admirably simulates the tug and the ebb and flow of battle, has presented difficulties to the mind of young sticklers after verisimilitude; and I knew at least one little boy who was mightily exercised about the presence of the ball, and had to spirit himself up, whenever he came to play, with an elaborate story of enchantment, and take the missile as a sort of talisman bandied about in conflict between two Arabian nations.

To think of such a frame of mind, is to become disquieted about the bringing up of children. Surely they dwell in a mythological epoch, and are not the contemporaries of their parents. What can they think of them? what can they make of these bearded or petticoated giants who look down upon their games? who move upon a cloudy Olympus, following unknown designs

apart from rational enjoyment? who profess the tender-
est solicitude for children, and yet every now and again
reach down out of their altitude and terribly vindicate
the prerogatives of age? Off goes the child, corporally
smarting, but morally rebellious. Were there ever such
unthinkable deities as parents? I would give a great
deal to know what, in nine cases out of ten, is the child's
unvarnished feeling. A sense of past cajolery; a sense
of personal attraction, at best very feeble; above all, I
should imagine, a sense of terror for the untried residue
of mankind: go to make up the attraction that he feels.
No wonder, poor little heart, with such a weltering
world in front of him, if he clings to the hand he knows!
The dread irrationality of the whole affair, as it seems to
children, is a thing we are all too ready to forget. "O,
why," I remember passionately wondering, "why can
we not all be happy and devote ourselves to play?"
And when children do philosophise, I believe it is usually to very much the same purpose.

One thing, at least, comes very clearly out of these
considerations; that whatever we are to expect at the
hands of children, it should not be any peddling exacti-
tude about matters of fact. They walk in a vain show,
and among mists and rainbows; they are passionate
after dreams and unconcerned about realities; speech is
a difficult art not wholly learned; and there is nothing
in their own tastes or purposes to teach them what we
mean by abstract truthfulness. When a bad writer is
inexact, even if he can look back on half a century of
years, we charge him with incompetence and not with
dishonesty. And why not extend the same allowance
to imperfect speakers? Let a stockbroker be dead stupid

about poetry, or a poet inexact in the details of business, and we excuse them heartily from blame. But show us a miserable, unbreeched, human entity, whose whole profession it is to take a tub for a fortified town and a shaving-brush for the deadly stiletto, and who passes three-fourths of his time in a dream and the rest in open self-deception, and we expect him to be as nice upon a matter of fact as a scientific expert bearing evidence. Upon my heart, I think it less than decent.   You do not consider how little the child sees, or how swift he is to weave what he has seen into bewildering fiction; and that he cares no more for what you call truth, than you for a gingerbread dragoon.

I am reminded, as I write, that the child is very in-quiring as to the precise truth of stories.   But indeed this is a very different matter, and one bound up with the subject of play, and the precise amount of play-fulness, or playability, to be looked for in the world. Many such burning questions must arise in the course of nursery education.   Among the fauna of this planet, which already embraces the pretty soldier and the ter-rifying Irish beggarman, is, or is not, the child to expect a Bluebeard or a Cormoran ? Is he, or is he not, to look out for magicians, kindly and potent ? May he, or may he not, reasonably hope to be cast away upon a desert island, or turned to such diminutive proportions that he can live on equal terms with his lead soldiery, and go a cruise in his own toy schooner ?   Surely all these are practical questions to a neophyte entering upon life with a view to play.   Precision upon such a point, the child can understand.   But if you merely ask him of his past behaviour, as to who threw such a stone, for instance, or struck such and such a match; or whether he had looked into a parcel or gone by a forbidden path,—why, he can see no moment in the inquiry, and it is ten to one, he has already half forgotten and half bemused himself with subsequent imaginings.

It would be easy to leave them in their native cloud-land, where they figure so prettily — pretty like flowers and innocent like dogs. They will come out of their gardens soon enough, and have to go into offices and the witness-box. Spare them yet a while, O conscientious parent! Let them doze among their playthings yet a little! for who knows what a rough, warfaring existence lies before them in the future?

WALKING TOURS

I T must not be imagined that a walking tour, as some would have us fancy, is merely a better or worse way of seeing the country. There are many ways of seeing landscape quite as good; and none more vivid, in spite of canting dilettantes, than from a railway train. But landscape on a walking tour is quite accessory. He who is indeed of the brotherhood does not voyage in quest of the picturesque, but of certain jolly humours — of the hope and spirit with which the march begins at morning, and the peace and spiritual repletion of the evening's rest. He cannot tell whether he puts his knapsack on, or takes it off, with more delight. The excitement of the departure puts him in key for that of the arrival. Whatever he does is not only a reward in itself, but will be further rewarded in the sequel; and so pleasure leads on to pleasure in an endless chain. It is this that so few can understand; they will either be always lounging or always at five miles an hour; they do not play off the one against the other, prepare all day for the evening, and all evening for the next day. And, above all, it is here that your overwalker fails of comprehension. His heart rises against those who drink their curaçoa in liqueur glasses, when he himself can swill it in

a brown john. He will not believe that the flavour is
more delicate in the smaller dose. He will not believe
that to walk this unconscionable distance is merely to
stupefy and brutalise himself, and come to his inn, at
night, with a sort of frost on his five wits, and a starless
night of darkness in his spirit. Not for him the mild
luminous evening of the temperate walker! He has nothing left of man but a physical need for bedtime and a
double nightcap; and even his pipe, if he be a smoker,
will be savourless and disenchanted. It is the fate of
such an one to take twice as much trouble as is needed
to obtain happiness, and miss the happiness in the end;
he is the man of the proverb, in short, who goes further
and fares worse.

Now, to be properly enjoyed, a walking tour should
be gone upon alone. If you go in a company, or even
in pairs, it is no longer a walking tour in anything but
name; it is something else and more in the nature of a
picnic. A walking tour should be gone upon alone,
because freedom is of the essence; because you should
be able to stop and go on, and follow this way or that,
as the freak takes you; and because you must have your
own pace, and neither trot alongside a champion walker,
nor mince in time with a girl. And then you must be
open to all impressions and let your thoughts take colour
from what you see. You should be as a pipe for any
wind to play upon. "I cannot see the wit," says Hazlitt, "of walking and talking at the same time. When
I am in the country I wish to vegetate like the country,"
— which is the gist of all that can be said upon the matter. There should be no cackle of voices at your elbow,
to jar on the meditative silence of the morning. And so

long as a man is reasoning he cannot surrender himself to that fine intoxication that comes of much motion in the open air, that begins in a sort of dazzle and sluggishness of the brain, and ends in a peace that passes comprehension.

During the first day or so of any tour there are moments of bitterness, when the traveller feels more than coldly towards his knapsack, when he is half in a mind to throw it bodily over the hedge and, like Christian on a similar occasion, "give three leaps and go on singing." And yet it soon acquires a property of easiness. It becomes magnetic; the spirit of the journey enters into it. And no sooner have you passed the straps over your shoulder than the lees of sleep are cleared from you, you pull yourself together with a shake, and fall at once into your stride. And surely, of all possible moods, this, in which a man takes the road, is the best. Of course, if he *will* keep thinking of his anxieties, if he *will* open the merchant Abudah's chest and walk arm-in-arm with the hag — why, wherever he is, and whether he walk fast or slow, the chances are that he will not be happy. And so much the more shame to himself! There are perhaps thirty men setting forth at that same hour, and I would lay a large wager there is not another dull face among the thirty. It would be a fine thing to follow, in a coat of darkness, one after another of these wayfarers, some summer morning, for the first few miles upon the road. This one, who walks fast, with a keen look in his eyes, is all concentrated in his own mind; he is up at his loom, weaving and weaving, to set the landscape to words. This one peers about, as he goes, among the grasses; he waits by the canal to watch the dragon-flies; he leans on the gate of the pasture, and cannot look enough upon the complacent kine. And here comes another, talking, laughing, and gesticulating to himself. His face changes from time to time, as indignation flashes from his eyes or anger clouds his forehead. He is composing articles, delivering orations, and conducting the most impassioned interviews, by the way. A little farther on, and it is as like as not he will begin to sing. And well for him, supposing him to be no great master in that art, if he stumble across no stolid peasant at a corner; for on such an occasion, I scarcely know which is the more troubled, or whether it is worse to suffer the confusion of your troubadour, or the unfeigned alarm of your clown. A sedentary population, accustomed, besides, to the strange mechanical bearing of the common tramp, can in no wise explain to itself the gaiety of these passers-by. I knew one man who was arrested as a runaway lunatic, because, although a full-grown person with a red beard, he skipped as he went like a child. And you would be astonished if I were to tell you all the grave and learned heads who have confessed to me that, when on walking tours, they sang—and sang very ill—and had a pair of red ears when, as described above, the inauspicious peasant plumped into their arms from round a corner. And here, lest you should think I am exaggerating, is Hazlitt's own confession, from his essay *On Going a Journey*, which is so good that there should be a tax levied on all who have not read it:—

"Give me the clear blue sky over my head," says he, "and the green turf beneath my feet, a winding road before me, and a three hours' march to dinner—and then to thinking! It is hard if I cannot start some game on these lone heaths. I laugh, I run, I leap, I sing for joy."

Bravo! After that adventure of my friend with the policeman, you would not have cared, would you, to publish that in the first person ? But we have no bravery nowadays, and, even in books, must all pretend to be as dull and foolish as our neighbours. It was not so with Hazlitt. And notice how learned he is (as, indeed, throughout the essay) in the theory of walking tours. He is none of your athletic men in purple stockings, who walk their fifty miles a day : three hours' march is his ideal. And then he must have a winding road, the epicure!

Yet there is one thing I object to in these words of his, one thing in the great master's practice that seems to me not wholly wise. I do not approve of that leaping and running. Both of these hurry the respiration; they both shake up the brain out of its glorious open-air confusion; and they both break the pace. Uneven walking is not so agreeable to the body, and it distracts and irritates the mind. Whereas, when once you have fallen into an equable stride, it requires no conscious thought from you to keep it up, and yet it prevents you from thinking earnestly of anything else. Like knitting, like the work of a copying clerk, it gradually neutralises and sets to sleep the serious activity of the mind. We can think of this or that, lightly and laughingly, as a child thinks, or as we think in a morning doze; we can make puns or puzzle out acrostics, and trifle in a thousand ways with words and rhymes; but when it comes to honest work, when we come to gather ourselves together for an effort, we may sound the trumpet as loud and long as we please; the great barons of the mind will not rally to the standard, but sit, each one, at home, warming his hands over his own fire and brooding on his own private thought!

In the course of a day's walk, you see, there is much variance in the mood. From the exhilaration of the start, to the happy phlegm of the arrival, the change is certainly great. As the day goes on, the traveller moves from the one extreme towards the other. He becomes more and more incorporated with the material landscape, and the open-air drunkenness grows upon him with great strides, until he posts along the road, and sees everything about him, as in a cheerful dream. The first is certainly brighter, but the second stage is the more peaceful. A man does not make so many articles towards the end, nor does he laugh aloud; but the purely animal pleasures, the sense of physical wellbeing, the delight of every inhalation, of every time the muscles tighten down the thigh, console him for the absence of the others, and bring him to his destination still content.

Nor must I forget to say a word on bivouacs. You come to a milestone on a hill, or some place where deep ways meet under trees; and off goes the knapsack, and down you sit to smoke a pipe in the shade. You sink into yourself, and the birds come round and look at you; and your smoke dissipates upon the afternoon under the blue dome of heaven; and the sun lies warm upon your feet, and the cool air visits your neck and turns aside your open shirt. If you are not happy, you must have an evil conscience. You may dally as long as you like by the roadside. It is almost as if the millennium were arrived, when we shall throw our clocks and watches over the housetop, and remember time and seasons no more.   Not to keep hours for a lifetime is, I was going to say, to live for ever.   You have no idea, unless you have tried it, how endlessly long is a summer's day, that you measure out only by hunger, and bring to an end only when you are drowsy.   I know a village where there are hardly any clocks, where no one knows more of the days of the week than by a sort of instinct for the fête on Sundays, and where only one person can tell you the day of the month, and she is generally wrong; and if people were aware how slow Time journeyed in that village, and what armfuls of spare hours he gives, over and above the bargain, to its wise inhabitants, I believe there would be a stampede out of London, Liverpool, Paris, and a variety of large towns, where the clocks lose their heads, and shake the hours out each one faster than the other, as though they were all in a wager.   And all these foolish pilgrims would each bring his own misery along with him, in a watch-pocket!   It is to be noticed, there were no clocks and watches in the much-vaunted days before the flood.   It follows, of course, there were no appointments, and punctuality was not yet thought upon.   "Though ye take from a covetous man all his treasure," says Milton, "he has yet one jewel left; ye cannot deprive him of his covetousness."   And so I would say of a modern man of business, you may do what you will for him, put him in Eden, give him the elixir of life — he has still a flaw at heart, he still has his business habits.   Now, there is no time when business habits are more mitigated than on a walking tour.   And so during these halts, as I say, you will feel almost free.

But it is at night, and after dinner, that the best hour

156

comes.   There are no such pipes to be smoked as those that follow a good day's march; the flavour of the tobacco is a thing to be remembered, it is so dry and aromatic, so full and so fine.   If you wind up the evening with grog, you will own there was never such grog; at every sip a jocund tranquillity spreads about your limbs, and sits easily in your heart.   If you read a book — and you will never do so save by fits and starts — you find the language strangely racy and harmonious; words take a new meaning; single sentences possess the ear for half an hour together; and the writer endears himself to you, at every page, by the nicest coincidence of sentiment.   It seems as if it were a book you had written yourself in a dream.   To all we have read on such occasions we look back with special favour.   "It was on the 10th of April, 1798," says Hazlitt, with amorous precision, "that I sat down to a volume of the new *Héloïse,* at the Inn at Llangollen, over a bottle of sherry and a cold chicken."   I should wish to quote more, for though we are mighty fine fellows nowadays, we cannot write like Hazlitt.   And, talking of that, a volume of Hazlitt's essays would be a capital pocket-book on such a journey; so would a volume of Heine's songs; and for *Tristram Shandy* I can pledge a fair experience.

If the evening be fine and warm, there is nothing better in life than to lounge before the inn door in the sunset, or lean over the parapet of the bridge, to watch the weeds and the quick fishes.   It is then, if ever, that you taste Joviality to the full significance of that audacious word.   Your muscles are so agreeably slack, you feel so clean and so strong and so idle, that whether you move or sit still, whatever you do is done with pride and a kingly sort of pleasure. You fall in talk with any one, wise or foolish, drunk or sober. And it seems as if a hot walk purged you, more than of anything else, of all narrowness and pride, and left curiosity to play its part freely, as in a child or a man of science. You lay aside all your own hobbies, to watch provincial humours develop themselves before you, now as a laughable farce, and now grave and beautiful like an old tale.

Or perhaps you are left to your own company for the night, and surly weather imprisons you by the fire. You may remember how Burns, numbering past pleasures, dwells upon the hours when he has been "happy thinking." It is a phrase that may well perplex a poor modern, girt about on every side by clocks and chimes, and haunted, even at night, by flaming dial-plates. For we are all so busy, and have so many far-off projects to realise, and castles in the fire to turn into solid habitable mansions on a gravel soil, that we can find no time for pleasure trips into the Land of Thought and among the Hills of Vanity. Changed times, indeed, when we must sit all night, beside the fire, with folded hands; and a changed world for most of us, when we find we can pass the hours without discontent, and be happy thinking. We are in such haste to be doing, to be writing, to be gathering gear, to make our voice audible a moment in the derisive silence of eternity, that we forget that one thing, of which these are but the parts — namely, to live. We fall in love, we drink hard, we run to and fro upon the earth like frightened sheep. And now you are to ask yourself if, when all is done, you would not have been better to sit by the fire at home, and be happy thinking. To sit still and contemplate,— to remember the faces of women without desire, to be pleased by the great deeds of men without envy, to be everything and everywhere in sympathy, and yet content to remain where and what you are — is not this to know both wisdom and virtue, and to dwell with happiness? After all, it is not they who carry flags, but they who look upon it from a private chamber, who have the fun of the procession. And once you are at that, you are in the very humour of all social heresy. It is no time for shuffling, or for big, empty words. If you ask yourself what you mean by fame, riches, or learning, the answer is far to seek; and you go back into that kingdom of light imaginations, which seem so vain in the eyes of Philistines perspiring after wealth, and so momentous to those who are stricken with the disproportions of the world, and, in the face of the gigantic stars, cannot stop to split differences between two degrees of the infinitesimally small, such as a tobacco pipe or the Roman Empire, a million of money or a fiddlestick's end.

You lean from the window, your last pipe reeking whitely into the darkness, your body full of delicious pains, your mind enthroned in the seventh circle of content; when suddenly the mood changes, the weathercock goes about, and you ask yourself one question more: whether, for the interval, you have been the wisest philosopher or the most egregious of donkeys? Human experience is not yet able to reply; but at least you have had a fine moment, and looked down upon all the kingdoms of the earth. And whether it was wise or foolish, to-morrow's travel will carry you, body and mind, into some different parish of the infinite.

PAN'S PIPES

THE world in which we live has been variously said and sung by the most ingenious poets and philosophers: these reducing it to formulæ and chemical ingredients, those striking the lyre in high-sounding measures for the handiwork of God. What experience supplies is of a mingled tissue, and the choosing mind has much to reject before it can get together the materials of a theory. Dew and thunder, destroying Attila and the Spring lambkins, belong to an order of contrasts which no repetition can assimilate. There is an uncouth, outlandish strain throughout the web of the world, as from a vexatious planet in the house of life. Things are not congruous and wear strange disguises: the consummate flower is fostered out of dung, and after nourishing itself awhile with heaven's delicate distillations, decays again into indistinguishable soil; and with Cæsar's ashes, Hamlet tells us, the urchins make dirt pies and filthily besmear their countenance. Nay, the kindly shine of summer, when tracked home with the scientific spyglass, is found to issue from the most portentous nightmare of the universe—the great, conflagrant sun: a world of hell's squibs, tumultuary, roaring aloud, inimical to life. The sun itself is enough

to disgust a human being of the scene which he inhabits; and you would not fancy there was a green or
habitable spot in the universe thus awfully lighted up.
And yet it is by the blaze of such a conflagration, to
which the fire of Rome was but a spark, that we do
all our fiddling, and hold domestic tea-parties at the
arbour door.

The Greeks figured Pan, the god of Nature, now terribly stamping his foot, so that armies were dispersed;
now by the woodside on a summer noon trolling on his
pipe until he charmed the hearts of upland ploughmen.
And the Greeks, in so figuring, uttered the last word of
human experience. To certain smoke-dried spirits matter and motion and elastic ethers, and the hypothesis of
this or that other spectacled professor, tell a speaking
story; but for youth and all ductile and congenial minds,
Pan is not dead, but of all the classic hierarchy alone
survives in triumph; goat-footed, with a gleeful and an
angry look, the type of the shaggy world: and in every
wood, if you go with a spirit properly prepared, you
shall hear the note of his pipe.

For it is a shaggy world, and yet studded with gardens; where the salt and tumbling sea receives clear
rivers running from among reeds and lilies; fruitful and
austere; a rustic world; sunshiny, lewd, and cruel.
What is it the birds sing among the trees in pairing-
time ? What means the sound of the rain falling far and
wide upon the leafy forest ? To what tune does the fish-
erman whistle, as he hauls in his net at morning, and
the bright fish are heaped inside the boat ? These are
all airs upon Pan's pipe; he it was who gave them
breath in the exultation of his heart, and gleefully modu-

lated their outflow with his lips and fingers. The coarse
mirth of herdsmen, shaking the dells with laughter and
striking out high echoes from the rock; the tune of
moving feet in the lamplit city, or on the smooth ball-
room floor; the hooves of many horses, beating the
wide pastures in alarm; the song of hurrying rivers; the
colour of clear skies; and smiles and the live touch of
hands; and the voice of things, and their significant look,
and the renovating influence they breathe forth — these
are his joyful measures, to which the whole earth treads
in choral harmony. To this music the young lambs
bound as to a tabor, and the London shop-girl skips
rudely in the dance. For it puts a spirit of gladness in
all hearts; and to look on the happy side of nature is
common, in their hours, to all created things. Some
are vocal under a good influence, are pleasing whenever they are pleased, and hand on their happiness to
others, as a child who, looking upon lovely things,
looks lovely. Some leap to the strains with unapt foot,
and make a halting figure in the universal dance. And
some, like sour spectators at the play, receive the music
into their hearts with an unmoved countenance, and
walk like strangers through the general rejoicing. But
let him feign never so carefully, there is not a man but
has his pulses shaken when Pan trolls out a stave of
ecstasy and sets the world a-singing.

Alas if that were all! But oftentimes the air is changed;
and in the screech of the night wind, chasing navies,
subverting the tall ships and the rooted cedar of the
hills; in the random deadly levin or the fury of headlong floods, we recognise the "dread foundation" of
life and the anger in Pan's heart. Earth wages open

war against her children, and under her softest touch
hides treacherous claws. The cool waters invite us in
to drown; the domestic hearth burns up in the hour of
sleep, and makes an end of all. Everything is good or
bad, helpful or deadly, not in itself, but by its circumstances. For a few bright days in England the hurri-
cane must break forth and the North Sea pay a toll of
populous ships. And when the universal music has
led lovers into the paths of dalliance, confident of Nature's sympathy, suddenly the air shifts into a minor, and
death makes a clutch from his ambuscade below the
bed of marriage. For death is given in a kiss; the dearest kindnesses are fatal; and into this life, where one
thing preys upon another, the child too often makes its
entrance from the mother's corpse. It is no wonder,
with so traitorous a scheme of things, if the wise people who created for us the idea of Pan thought that of
all fears the fear of him was the most terrible, since it
embraces all. And still we preserve the phrase: a panic
terror. To reckon dangers too curiously, to hearken too
intently for the threat that runs through all the winning
music of the world, to hold back the hand from the
rose because of the thorn, and from life because of death:
this it is to be afraid of Pan. Highly respectable citizens who flee life's pleasures and responsibilities and
keep, with upright hat, upon the midway of custom,
avoiding the right hand and the left, the ecstasies and
the agonies, how surprised they would be if they could
hear their attitude mythologically expressed, and knew
themselves as tooth-chattering ones, who flee from Nature because they fear the hand of Nature's God! Shrilly
sound Pan's pipes; and behold the banker instantly con-

cealed in the bank parlour! For to distrust one's impulses is to be recreant to Pan.

There are moments when the mind refuses to be satisfied with evolution, and demands a ruddier presentation of the sum of man's experience. Sometimes the mood is brought about by laughter at the humorous side of life, as when, abstracting ourselves from earth, we imagine people plodding on foot, or seated in ships and speedy trains, with the planet all the while whirling in the opposite direction, so that, for all their hurry, they travel back-foremost through the universe of space. Sometimes it comes by the spirit of delight, and sometimes by the spirit of terror. At least, there will always be hours when we refuse to be put off by the feint of explanation, nicknamed science; and demand instead some palpitating image of our estate, that shall represent the troubled and uncertain element in which we dwell, and satisfy reason by the means of art. Science writes of the world as if with the cold finger of a starfish; it is all true; but what is it when compared to the reality of which it discourses? where hearts beat high in April, and death strikes, and hills totter in the earthquake, and there is a glamour over all the objects of sight, and a thrill in all noises for the ear, and Romance herself has made her dwelling among men? So we come back to the old myth, and hear the goat-footed piper making the music which is itself the charm and terror of things; and when a glen invites our visiting footsteps, fancy that Pan leads us thither with a gracious tremolo; or when our hearts quail at the thunder of the cataract, tell ourselves that he has stamped his hoof in the nigh thicket.

A PLEA FOR GAS LAMPS

CITIES given, the problem was to light them. How to conduct individual citizens about the burgess-warren, when once heaven had withdrawn its leading luminary? or — since we live in a scientific age — when once our spinning planet has turned its back upon the sun? The moon, from time to time, was doubtless very helpful; the stars had a cheery look among the chimney-pots; and a cresset here and there, on church or citadel, produced a fine pictorial effect, and, in places where the ground lay unevenly, held out the right hand of conduct to the benighted. But sun, moon, and stars abstracted or concealed, the night-faring inhabitant had to fall back — we speak on the authority of old prints — upon stable lanthorns, two stories in height. Many holes, drilled in the conical turret-roof of this vagabond Pharos, let up spouts of dazzlement into the bearer's eyes; and as he paced forth in the ghostly darkness, carrying his own sun by a ring about his finger, day and night swung to and fro and up and down about his footsteps. Black-ness haunted his path; he was beleaguered by goblins as he went; and, curfew being struck, he found no light but that he travelled in throughout the township.

Closely following on this epoch of migratory lanthorns

in a world of extinction, came the era of oil-lights, hard to kindle, easy to extinguish, pale and wavering in the hour of their endurance. Rudely puffed the winds of heaven; roguishly clomb up the all-destructive urchin; and, lo! in a moment night re-established her void empire, and the cit groped along the wall, suppered but bedless, occult from guidance, and sorrily wading in the kennels. As if gamesome winds and gamesome youths were not sufficient, it was the habit to sling these feeble luminaries from house to house above the fairway. There, on invisible cordage, let them swing! And suppose some crane-necked general to go speeding by on a tall charger, spurring the destiny of nations, red-hot in expedition, there would indubitably be some effusion of military blood, and oaths, and a certain crash of glass; and while the chieftain rode forward with a purple coxcomb, the street would be left to original darkness, unpiloted, unvoyageable, a province of the desert night.

The conservative, looking before and after, draws from each contemplation the matter for content. Out of the age of gas lamps he glances back slightingly at the mirk and glimmer in which his ancestors wandered; his heart waxes jocund at the contrast; nor do his lips refrain from a stave, in the highest style of poetry, lauding progress and the golden mean. When gas first spread along a city, mapping it forth about evenfall for the eye of observant birds, a new age had begun for sociality and corporate pleasure-seeking, and begun with proper circumstance, becoming its own birthright. The work of Prometheus had advanced by another stride. Mankind and its supper parties were no longer at the mercy of a few miles of sea-fog; sundown no longer emptied the promenade; and the day was lengthened out to every man's fancy. The city-folk had stars of their own; biddable, domesticated stars.

It is true that these were not so steady, nor yet so clear, as their originals; nor indeed was their lustre so elegant as that of the best wax candles. But then the gas stars, being nearer at hand, were more practically efficacious than Jupiter himself. It is true, again, that they did not unfold their rays with the appropriate spontaneity of the planets, coming out along the firmament one after another, as the need arises. But the lamplighters took to their heels every evening, and ran with a good heart. It was pretty to see man thus emulating the punctuality of heaven's orbs; and though perfection was not absolutely reached, and now and then an individual may have been knocked on the head by the ladder of the flying functionary, yet people commended his zeal in a proverb, and taught their children to say, "God bless the lamplighter!" And since his passage was a piece of the day's programme, the children were well pleased to repeat the benediction, not, of course, in so many words, which would have been improper, but in some chaste circumlocution, suitable for infant lips.

God bless him, indeed! For the term of his twilight diligence is near at hand; and for not much longer shall we watch him speeding up the street and, at measured intervals, knocking another luminous hole into the dusk. The Greeks would have made a noble myth of such an one; how he distributed starlight, and, as soon as the need was over, re-collected it; and the little bull's-eye, which was his instrument, and held enough fire to kindle a whole parish, would have been fitly commemorated in the legend. Now, like all heroic tasks, his labours draw towards apotheosis, and in the light of victory himself shall disappear. For another advance has been effected. Our tame stars are to come out in future, not one by one, but all in a body and at once. A sedate electrician somewhere in a back office touches a spring — and behold! from one end to another of the city, from east to west, from the Alexandra to the Crystal Palace, there is light! *Fiat Lux,* says the sedate electrician. What a spectacle, on some clear, dark nightfall, from the edge of Hampstead Hill, when in a moment, in the twinkling of an eye, the design of the monstrous city flashes into vision — a glittering hieroglyph many square miles in extent; and when, to borrow and debase an image, all the evening street-lamps burst together into song! Such is the spectacle of the future, preluded the other day by the experiment in Pall Mall. Star-rise by electricity, the most romantic flight of civilisation; the compensatory benefit for an innumerable array of factories and bankers' clerks. To the artistic spirit exercised about Thirlmere, here is a crumb of consolation; consolatory, at least, to such of them as look out upon the world through seeing eyes, and contentedly accept beauty where it comes.

But the conservative, while lauding progress, is ever timid of innovation; his is the hand upheld to counsel pause; his is the signal advising slow advance. The word *electricity* now sounds the note of danger. In Paris, at the mouth of the Passage des Princes, in the place before the Opera portico, and in the Rue Drouot at the *Figaro* office, a new sort of urban star now shines out nightly, horrible, unearthly, obnoxious to the human eye; a lamp for a nightmare! Such a light as this should shine only on murders and public crime, or along the corridors of lunatic asylums, a horror to heighten horror. To look at it only once is to fall in love with gas, which gives a warm domestic radiance fit to eat by. Mankind, you would have thought, might have remained content with what Prometheus stole for them and not gone fishing the profound heaven with kites to catch and domesticate the wildfire of the storm. Yet here we have the levin brand at our doors, and it is proposed that we should henceforward take our walks abroad in the glare of permanent lightning. A man need not be very superstitious if he scruple to follow his pleasures by the light of the Terror that Flieth, nor very epicurean if he prefer to see the face of beauty more becomingly displayed. That ugly blinding glare may not improperly advertise the home of slanderous *Figaro,* which is a back-shop to the infernal regions; but where soft joys prevail, where people are convoked to pleasure and the philosopher looks on smiling and silent, where love and laughter and deifying wine abound, there, at least, let the old mild lustre shine upon the ways of man.

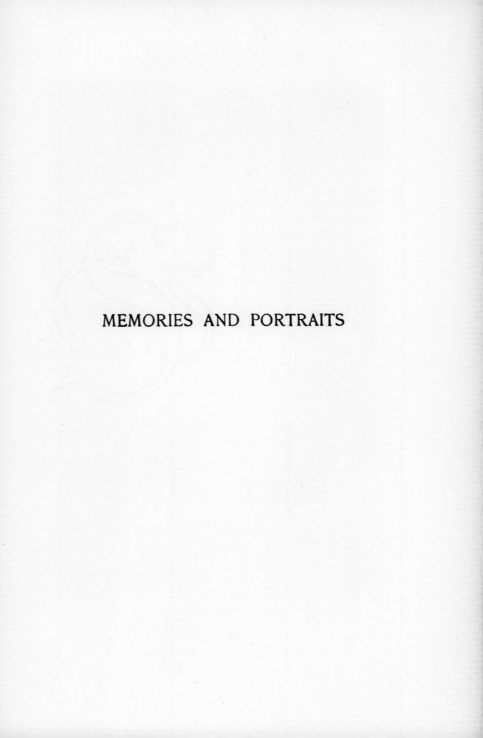

MEMORIES AND PORTRAITS

TO

MY MOTHER

IN THE NAME OF PAST JOY AND PRESENT SORROW

𝕴 𝕯𝖊𝖉𝖎𝖈𝖆𝖙𝖊

THESE MEMORIES AND PORTRAITS

S. S. "Ludgate Hill"
within sight of Cape Race

NOTE

THIS volume of papers, unconnected as they are, it will be better to read through from the beginning, rather than dip into at random. A certain thread of meaning binds them. Memories of childhood and youth, portraits of those who have gone before us in the battle, — taken together, they build up a face that "I have loved long since and lost awhile," the face of what was once myself. This has come by accident; I had no design at first to be autobiographical; I was but led away by the charm of beloved memories and by regret for the irrevocable dead; and when my own young face (which is a face of the dead also) began to appear in the well as by a kind of magic, I was the first to be surprised at the occurrence.

My grandfather the pious child, my father the idle eager sentimental youth, I have thus unconsciously exposed. Of their descendant, the person of to-day, I wish to keep the secret : not because I love him better, but because, with him, I am still in a business partnership, and cannot divide interests.

Of the papers which make up the volume, some have appeared already in *The Cornhill, Longman's, Scribner, The English Illustrated, The Magazine of Art, The Contemporary Review;* three are here in print for the first time; and two others have enjoyed only what may be regarded as a private circulation.

R. L. S.

I. THE FOREIGNER AT HOME

" This is no my ain house;
I ken by the biggin' o't."

TWO recent books,[1] one by Mr. Grant White on England, one on France by the diabolically clever Mr. Hillebrand, may well have set people thinking on the divisions of races and nations. Such thoughts should arise with particular congruity and force to inhabitants of that United Kingdom, peopled from so many different stocks, babbling so many different dialects, and offering in its extent such singular contrasts, from the busiest over-population to the unkindliest desert, from the Black Country to the Moor of Rannoch. It is not only when we cross the seas that we go abroad; there are foreign parts of England; and the race that has conquered so wide an empire has not yet managed to assimilate the islands whence she sprang. Ireland, Wales, and the Scottish mountains still cling, in part, to their old Gaelic speech. It was but the other day that English triumphed in Cornwall, and they still show in Mousehole, on St. Michael's Bay, the house of the last Cornish-speaking woman. English itself, which will now frank the traveller through the most of North America, through the greater South Sea Islands, in India, along much of the

[1] 1881.

coast of Africa, and in the ports of China and Japan, is still to be heard, in its home country, in half a hundred varying stages of transition. You may go all over the States, and — setting aside the actual intrusion and influence of foreigners, negro, French, or Chinese — you shall scarce meet with so marked a difference of accent as in the forty miles between Edinburgh and Glasgow, or of dialect as in the hundred miles between Edinburgh and Aberdeen. Book English has gone round the world, but at home we still preserve the racy idioms of our fathers, and every county, in some parts every dale, has its own quality of speech, vocal or verbal. In like manner, local custom and prejudice, even local religion and local law, linger on into the latter end of the nineteenth century — *imperia in imperio*, foreign things at home.

In spite of these promptings to reflection, ignorance of his neighbours is the character of the typical John Bull. His is a domineering nature, steady in fight, imperious to command, but neither curious nor quick about the life of others. In French colonies, and still more in the Dutch, I have read that there is an immediate and lively contact between the dominant and the dominated race, that a certain sympathy is begotten, or at the least a transfusion of prejudices, making life easier for both. But the Englishman sits apart, bursting with pride and ignorance. He figures among his vassals in the hour of peace with the same disdainful air that led him on to victory. A passing enthusiasm for some foreign art or fashion may deceive the world, it cannot impose upon his intimates. He may be amused by a foreigner as by a monkey, but he will never condescend to study him with any patience. Miss Bird, an authoress with whom

I profess myself in love, declares all the viands of Japan
to be uneatable — a staggering pretension. So, when
the Prince of Wales's marriage was celebrated at Mentone by a dinner to the Mentonese, it was proposed to
give them solid English fare — roast beef and plum pud-
ding, and no tomfoolery. Here we have either pole of
the Britannic folly. We will not eat the food of any foreigner; nor, when we have the chance, will we suffer
him to eat of it himself. The same spirit inspired Miss
Bird's American missionaries, who had come thousands
of miles to change the faith of Japan, and openly pro-
fessed their ignorance of the religions they were trying
to supplant.

I quote an American in this connection without scruple.
Uncle Sam is better than John Bull, but he is tarred with
the English stick. For Mr. Grant White the States are
the New England States and nothing more. He wonders at the amount of drinking in London; let him try
San Francisco. He wittily reproves English ignorance
as to the status of women in America; but has he not
himself forgotten Wyoming? The name Yankee, of
which he is so tenacious, is used over the most of
the great Union as a term of reproach. The Yankee
States, of which he is so staunch a subject, are but
a drop in the bucket. And we find in his book a
vast virgin ignorance of the life and prospects of America; every view partial, parochial, not raised to the horizon; the moral feeling proper, at the largest, to a clique
of States; and the whole scope and atmosphere not
American, but merely Yankee. I will go far beyond
him in reprobating the assumption and the incivility of
my countryfolk to their cousins from beyond the sea; I

grill in my blood over the silly rudeness of our news-
paper articles; and I do not know where to look when
I find myself in company with an American and see my
countrymen unbending to him as to a performing dog.
But in the case of Mr. Grant White example were better
than precept. Wyoming is, after all, more readily accessible to Mr. White than Boston to the English, and
the New England self-sufficiency no better justified than
the Britannic.

It is so, perhaps, in all countries; perhaps in all, men
are most ignorant of the foreigners at home. John Bull
is ignorant of the States; he is probably ignorant of India; but considering his opportunities, he is far more
ignorant of countries nearer his own door. There is one
country, for instance — its frontier not so far from London, its people closely akin, its language the same in all
essentials with the English — of which I will go bail he
knows nothing. His ignorance of the sister kingdom
cannot be described; it can only be illustrated by anecdote. I once travelled with a man of plausible manners
and good intelligence, — a University man, as the phrase
goes, — a man, besides, who had taken his degree in life
and knew a thing or two about the age we live in. We
were deep in talk, whirling between Peterborough and
London; among other things, he began to describe some
piece of legal injustice he had recently encountered, and
I observed in my innocence that things were not so in
Scotland. "I beg your pardon," said he, "this is a
matter of law." He had never heard of the Scots law;
nor did he choose to be informed. The law was the
same for the whole country, he told me roundly; every
child knew that. At last, to settle matters, I explained

to him that I was a member of a Scottish legal body, and
had stood the brunt of an examination in the very law in
question. Thereupon he looked me for a moment full
in the face and dropped the conversation. This is a
monstrous instance, if you like, but it does not stand
alone in the experience of Scots.

England and Scotland differ, indeed, in law, in history, in religion, in education, and in the very look of
nature and men's faces, not always widely, but always
trenchantly. Many particulars that struck Mr. Grant
White, a Yankee, struck me, a Scot, no less forcibly;
he and I felt ourselves foreigners on many common provocations. A Scotchman may tramp the better part of
Europe and the United States, and never again receive
so vivid an impression of foreign travel and strange
lands and manners as on his first excursion into England. The change from a hilly to a level country strikes
him with delighted wonder. Along the flat horizon
there arise the frequent venerable towers of churches.
He sees at the end of airy vistas the revolution of the
windmill sails. He may go where he pleases in the
future; he may see Alps, and Pyramids, and lions; but
it will be hard to beat the pleasure of that moment.
There are, indeed, few merrier spectacles than that of
many windmills bickering together in a fresh breeze
over a woody country; their halting alacrity of movement, their pleasant business, making bread all day
with uncouth gesticulations, their air, gigantically human, as of a creature half alive, put a spirit of romance
into the tamest landscape. When the Scotch child sees
them first he falls immediately in love; and from that
time forward windmills keep turning in his dreams.

And so, in their degree, with every feature of the life and landscape. The warm, habitable age of towns and hamlets, the green, settled, ancient look of the country; the lush hedgerows, stiles and privy pathways in the fields; the sluggish, brimming rivers; chalk and smock-frocks; chimes of bells and the rapid, pertly-sounding English speech — they are all new to the curiosity; they are all set to English airs in the child's story that he tells himself at night. The sharp edge of novelty wears off; the feeling is scotched, but I doubt whether it is ever killed. Rather it keeps returning, ever the more rarely and strangely, and even in scenes to which you have been long accustomed suddenly awakes and gives a relish to enjoyment or heightens the sense of isolation.

One thing especially continues unfamiliar to the Scotchman's eye — the domestic architecture, the look of streets and buildings; the quaint, venerable age of many, and the thin walls and warm colouring of all. We have, in Scotland, far fewer ancient buildings, above all in country places; and those that we have are all of hewn or harled masonry. Wood has been sparingly used in their construction; the window-frames are sunken in the wall, not flat to the front, as in England; the roofs are steeper-pitched; even a hill farm will have a massy, square, cold and permanent appearance. English houses, in comparison, have the look of cardboard toys, such as a puff might shatter. And to this the Scotchman never becomes used. His eye can never rest consciously on one of these brick houses — rickles of brick, as he might call them — or on one of these flat-chested streets, but he is instantly reminded where he is, and instantly travels back in fancy to his home. "This is no my ain house;

I ken by the biggin' o't." And yet perhaps it is his
own, bought with his own money, the key of it long
polished in his pocket; but it has not yet, and never
will be, thoroughly adopted by his imagination; nor
does he cease to remember that, in the whole length
and breadth of his native country, there was no building
even distantly resembling it.

But it is not alone in scenery and architecture that we
count England foreign. The constitution of society, the
very pillars of the empire, surprise and even pain us.
The dull, neglected peasant, sunk in matter, insolent,
gross and servile, makes a startling contrast with our
own long-legged, long-headed, thoughtful, Bible-quot-
ing ploughman. A week or two in such a place as Suffolk leaves the Scotchman gasping. It seems incredible
that within the boundaries of his own island a class
should have been thus forgotten. Even the educated
and intelligent, who hold our own opinions and speak
in our own words, yet seem to hold them with a difference or from another reason, and to speak on all things
with less interest and conviction. The first shock of
English society is like a cold plunge. It is possible that
the Scot comes looking for too much, and to be sure his
first experiment will be in the wrong direction. Yet
surely his complaint is grounded; surely the speech of
Englishmen is too often lacking in generous ardour, the
better part of the man too often withheld from the social
commerce, and the contact of mind with mind evaded
as with terror. A Scotch peasant will talk more liber-
ally out of his own experience. He will not put you by
with conversational counters and small jests; he will
give you the best of himself, like one interested in life

and man's chief end. A Scotchman is vain, interested in himself and others, eager for sympathy, setting forth his thoughts and experience in the best light. The egoism of the Englishman is self-contained. He does not seek to proselytise. He takes no interest in Scotland or the Scotch, and, what is the unkindest cut of all, he does not care to justify his indifference. Give him the wages of going on and being an Englishman, that is all he asks; and in the meantime, while you continue to associate, he would rather not be reminded of your baser origin. Compared with the grand, tree-like self-sufficiency of his demeanour, the vanity and curiosity of the Scot seem uneasy, vulgar and immodest. That you should continually try to establish human and serious relations, that you should actually feel an interest in John Bull, and desire and invite a return of interest from him, may argue something more awake and lively in your mind, but it still puts you in the attitude of a suitor and a poor relation. Thus even the lowest class of the educated English towers over a Scotchman by the head and shoulders.

Different indeed is the atmosphere in which Scotch and English youth begin to look about them, come to themselves in life, and gather up those first apprehensions which are the material of future thought and, to a great extent, the rule of future conduct. I have been to school in both countries, and I found, in the boys of the North, something at once rougher and more tender, at once more reserve and more expansion, a greater habitual distance chequered by glimpses of a nearer intimacy, and on the whole wider extremes of temperament and sensibility. The boy of the South seems more wholesome, but less thoughtful; he gives himself to games as

to a business, striving to excel, but is not readily trans-
ported by imagination; the type remains with me as
cleaner in mind and body, more active, fonder of eating,
endowed with a lesser and a less romantic sense of life
and of the future, and more immersed in present circumstances. And certainly, for one thing, English boys are
younger for their age. Sabbath observance makes a
series of grim, and perhaps serviceable, pauses in the
tenor of Scotch boyhood — days of great stillness and
solitude for the rebellious mind, when in the dearth of
books and play, and in the intervals of studying the
Shorter Catechism, the intellect and senses prey upon
and test each other. The typical English Sunday, with
the huge midday dinner and the plethoric afternoon,
leads perhaps to different results. About the very cradle
of the Scot there goes a hum of metaphysical divinity;
and the whole of two divergent systems is summed up,
not merely speciously, in the two first questions of the
rival catechisms, the English tritely inquiring, "What
is your name?" the Scottish striking at the very roots of
life with, "What is the chief end of man?" and answer-
ing nobly, if obscurely, "To glorify God and to enjoy
Him for ever." I do not wish to make an idol of the
Shorter Catechism; but the fact of such a question being
asked opens to us Scotch a great field of speculation;
and the fact that it is asked of all of us, from the peer to
the ploughboy, binds us more nearly together. No Englishman of Byron's age, character and history, would
have had patience for long theological discussions on
the way to fight for Greece; but the daft Gordon blood
and the Aberdonian schooldays kept their influence to
the end. We have spoken of the material conditions;

nor need much more be said of these: of the land lying everywhere more exposed, of the wind always louder and bleaker, of the black, roaring winters, of the gloom of high-lying, old stone cities, imminent on the windy seaboard; compared with the level streets, the warm colouring of the brick, the domestic quaintness of the architecture, among which English children begin to grow up and come to themselves in life. As the stage of the University approaches, the contrast becomes more express. The English lad goes to Oxford or Cambridge; there, in an ideal world of gardens, to lead a semi-scenic life, costumed, disciplined and drilled by proctors. Nor is this to be regarded merely as a stage of education; it is a piece of privilege besides, and a step that separates him further from the bulk of his compatriots. At an earlier age the Scottish lad begins his greatly different experience of crowded class-rooms, of a gaunt quadrangle, of a bell hourly booming over the traffic of the city to recall him from the public-house where he has been lunching, or the streets where he has been wandering fancy-free. His college life has little of restraint, and nothing of necessary gentility. He will find no quiet clique of the exclusive, studious and cultured; no rotten borough of the arts. All classes rub shoulders on the greasy benches. The raffish young gentleman in gloves must measure his scholarship with the plain, clownish laddie from the parish school. They separate, at the session's end, one to smoke cigars about a watering-place, the other to resume the labours of the field beside his peasant family. The first muster of a college class in Scotland is a scene of curious and painful interest; so many lads, fresh from the heather, hang round the stove in cloddish embarrassment, ruffled by the presence of their smarter comrades, and afraid of the sound of their own rustic voices. It was in these early days, I think, that Professor Blackie won the affection of his pupils, putting these uncouth, umbrageous students at their ease with ready human geniality. Thus, at least, we have a healthy democratic atmosphere to breathe in while at work; even when there is no cordiality there is always a juxtaposition of the different classes, and in the competition of study the intellectual power of each is plainly demonstrated to the other. Our tasks ended, we of the North go forth as freemen into the humming, lamplit city. At five o'clock you may see the last of us hiving from the college gates, in the glare of the shop windows, under the green glimmer of the winter sunset. The frost tingles in our blood; no proctor lies in wait to intercept us; till the bell sounds again, we are the masters of the world; and some portion of our lives is always Saturday, *la trêve de Dieu*.

Nor must we omit the sense of the nature of his country and his country's history gradually growing in the child's mind from story and from observation. A Scottish child hears much of shipwreck, outlying iron skerries, pitiless breakers, and great sea-lights; much of heathery mountains, wild clans, and hunted Covenanters. Breaths come to him in song of the distant Cheviots and the ring of foraying hoofs. He glories in his hard-fisted forefathers, of the iron girdle and the handful of oatmeal, who rode so swiftly and lived so sparely on their raids. Poverty, ill-luck, enterprise, and constant resolution are the fibres of the legend of his country's history. The heroes and kings of Scot-

187

land have been tragically fated; the most marking incidents in Scottish history—Flodden, Darien, or the
Forty-five—were still either failures or defeats; and the
fall of Wallace and the repeated reverses of the Bruce
combine with the very smallness of the country to teach
rather a moral than a material criterion for life. Britain
is altogether small, the mere taproot of her extended
empire; Scotland, again, which alone the Scottish boy
adopts in his imagination, is but a little part of that,
and avowedly cold, sterile and unpopulous. It is not
so for nothing. I once seemed to have perceived in an
American boy a greater readiness of sympathy for lands
that are great, and rich, and growing, like his own. It
proved to be quite otherwise: a mere dumb piece of
boyish romance, that I had lacked penetration to divine.
But the error serves the purpose of my argument; for
I am sure, at least, that the heart of young Scotland will
be always touched more nearly by paucity of number
and Spartan poverty of life.

So we may argue, and yet the difference is not explained. That Shorter Catechism which I took as being
so typical of Scotland, was yet composed in the city of
Westminster. The division of races is more sharply
marked within the borders of Scotland itself than between the countries. Galloway and Buchan, Lothian
and Lochaber, are like foreign parts; yet you may
choose a man from any of them, and, ten to one, he
shall prove to have the headmark of a Scot. A century
and a half ago the Highlander wore a different costume,
spoke a different language, worshipped in another
church, held different morals, and obeyed a different
social constitution from his fellow-countrymen either

of the south or north. Even the English, it is recorded, did not loathe the Highlander and the Highland costume as they were loathed by the remainder of the Scotch. Yet the Highlander felt himself a Scot. He would willingly raid into the Scotch lowlands; but his courage failed him at the border, and he regarded England as a perilous, unhomely land. When the Black Watch, after years of foreign service, returned to Scotland, veterans leaped out and kissed the earth at Port Patrick. They had been in Ireland, stationed among men of their own race and language, where they were well liked and treated with affection; but it was the soil of Galloway that they kissed at the extreme end of the hostile lowlands, among a people who did not understand their speech, and who had hated, harried, and hanged them since the dawn of history. Last, and perhaps most curious, the sons of chieftains were often educated on the continent of Europe. They went abroad speaking Gaelic; they returned speaking, not English, but the broad dialect of Scotland. Now, what idea had they in their minds when they thus, in thought, identified themselves with their ancestral enemies? What was the sense in which they were Scotch and not English, or Scotch and not Irish? Can a bare name be thus influential on the minds and affections of men, and a political aggregation blind them to the nature of facts? The story of the Austrian Empire would seem to answer, No; the far more galling business of Ireland clenches the negative from nearer home. Is it common education, common morals, a common language or a common faith, that join men into nations? There were practically none of these in the case we are considering.

The fact remains: in spite of the difference of blood and language, the Lowlander feels himself the sentimental countryman of the Highlander. When they meet abroad, they fall upon each other's necks in spirit; even at home there is a kind of clannish intimacy in their talk. But from his compatriot in the south the Lowlander stands consciously apart. He has had a different training; he obeys different laws; he makes his will in other terms, is otherwise divorced and married; his eyes are not at home in an English landscape or with English houses; his ear continues to remark the English speech; and even though his tongue acquire the Southern knack, he will still have a strong Scotch accent of the mind.

II. SOME COLLEGE MEMORIES[1]

I AM asked to write something (it is not specifically
stated what) to the profit and glory of my *Alma
Mater;* and the fact is I seem to be in very nearly the
same case with those who addressed me, for while I am
willing enough to write something, I know not what to
write.   Only one point I see, that if I am to write at all,
it should be of the University itself and my own days
under its shadow; of the things that are still the same
and of those that are already changed : such talk, in
short, as would pass naturally between a student of to-
day and one of yesterday, supposing them to meet and
grow confidential.

The generations pass away swiftly enough on the high
seas of life; more swiftly still in the little bubbling back-
water of the quadrangle; so that we see there, on a scale
startlingly diminished, the flight of time and the succes-
sion of men.   I looked for my name the other day in last
year's case book of the Speculative.   Naturally enough
I looked for it near the end; it was not there, nor yet in
the next column, so that I began to think it had been
dropped at press; and when at last I found it, mounted
on the shoulders of so many successors, and looking in

[1] Written for the " Book " of the Edinburgh University Union Fancy
Fair.

that posture like the name of a man of ninety, I was conscious of some of the dignity of years. This kind of dignity of temporal precession is likely, with prolonged life, to become more familiar, possibly less welcome; but I felt it strongly then, it is strongly on me now, and I am the more emboldened to speak with my successors in the tone of a parent and a praiser of things past.

For, indeed, that which they attend is but a fallen University; it has doubtless some remains of good, for human institutions decline by gradual stages; but decline, in spite of all seeming embellishments, it does; and what is perhaps more singular, began to do so when I ceased to be a student. Thus, by an odd chance, I had the very last of the very best of *Alma Mater;* the same thing, I hear (which makes it the more strange), had previously happened to my father; and if they are good and do not die, something not at all unsimilar will be found in time to have befallen my successors of to-day. Of the specific points of change, of advantage in the past, of shortcoming in the present, I must own that, on a near examination, they look wondrous cloudy. The chief and far the most lamentable change is the absence of a certain lean, ugly, idle, unpopular student, whose presence was for me the gist and heart of the whole matter; whose changing humours, fine occasional purposes of good, flinching acceptance of evil, shiverings on wet, east-windy, morning journeys up to class, infinite yawnings during lecture and unquenchable gusto in the delights of truantry, made up the sunshine and shadow of my college life. You cannot fancy what you missed in missing him; his virtues, I make sure, are inconceivable to his successors, just as they were apparently concealed from his contemporaries, for I was practically alone in the pleasure I had in his society.   Poor soul, I remember how much he was cast down at times, and how life (which had not yet begun) seemed to be already at an end, and hope quite dead, and misfortune and dishonour, like physical presences, dogging him as he went.   And it may be worth while to add that these clouds rolled away in their season, and that all clouds roll away at last, and the troubles of youth in particular are things but of a moment.   So this student, whom I have in my eye, took his full share of these concerns, and that very largely by his own fault; but he still clung to his fortune, and in the midst of much misconduct, kept on in his own way learning how to work; and at last, to his wonder, escaped out of the stage of studentship not openly shamed; leaving behind him the University of Edinburgh shorn of a good deal of its interest for myself.

But while he is (in more senses than one) the first person, he is by no means the only one whom I regret, or whom the students of to-day, if they knew what they had lost, would regret also.   They have still Tait, to be sure — long may they have him! — and they have still Tait's class-room, cupola and all; but think of what a different place it was when this youth of mine (at least on roll days) would be present on the benches, and, at the near end of the platform, Lindsay senior[1] was airing his robust old age.   It is possible my successors may have never even heard of Old Lindsay; but when he went, a link snapped with the last century.   He had something of a rustic air, sturdy and fresh and plain; he

[1] Professor Tait's laboratory assistant.

193

spoke with a ripe east-country accent, which I used to admire; his reminiscences were all of journeys on foot or highways busy with post-chaises — a Scotland before steam; he had seen the coal fire on the Isle of May, and he regaled me with tales of my own grandfather. Thus he was for me a mirror of things perished; it was only in his memory that I could see the huge shock of flames of the May beacon stream to leeward, and the watchers, as they fed the fire, lay hold unscorched of the windward bars of the furnace; it was only thus that I could see my grandfather driving swiftly in a gig along the seaboard road from Pittenweem to Crail, and for all his business hurry, drawing up to speak good-humouredly with those he met. And now, in his turn, Lindsay is gone also; inhabits only the memories of other men, till these shall follow him; and figures in my reminiscences as my grandfather figured in his.

To-day, again, they have Professor Butcher, and I hear he has a prodigious deal of Greek; and they have Professor Chrystal, who is a man filled with the mathematics. And doubtless these are set-offs. But they cannot change the fact that Professor Blackie has retired, and that Professor Kelland is dead. No man's education is complete or truly liberal who knew not Kelland. There were unutterable lessons in the mere sight of that frail old clerical gentleman, lively as a boy, kind like a fairy godfather, and keeping perfect order in his class by the spell of that very kindness. I have heard him drift into reminiscences in class time, though not for long, and give us glimpses of old-world life in out-of-the-way English parishes when he was young; thus playing the same part as Lindsay — the part of the surviving memory, signalling out of the dark backward and abysm of time the images of perished things. But it was a part that scarce became him; he somehow lacked the means: for all his silver hair and worn face, he was not truly old; and he had too much of the unrest and petulant fire of youth, and too much invincible innocence of mind, to play the veteran well. The time to measure him best, to taste (in the old phrase) his gracious nature, was when he received his class at home. What a pretty simplicity would he then show, trying to amuse us like children with toys; and what an engaging nervousness of manner, as fearing that his efforts might not succeed! Truly he made us all feel like children, and like children embarrassed, but at the same time filled with sympathy for the conscientious, troubled elder-boy who was working so hard to entertain us. A theorist has held the view that there is no feature in man so tell-tale as his spectacles; that the mouth may be compressed and the brow smoothed artificially, but the sheen of the barnacles is diagnostic. And truly it must have been thus with Kelland; for as I still fancy I behold him frisking actively about the platform, pointer in hand, that which I seem to see most clearly is the way his glasses glittered with affection. I never knew but one other man who had (if you will permit the phrase) so kind a spectacle; and that was Dr. Appleton. But the light in his case was tempered and passive; in Kelland's it danced, and changed, and flashed vivaciously among the students, like a perpetual challenge to goodwill.

I cannot say so much about Professor Blackie, for a good reason. Kelland's class I attended, once even gained there a certificate of merit, the only distinction

195

of my University career. But although I am the holder
of a certificate of attendance in the professor's own hand,
I cannot remember to have been present in the Greek
class above a dozen times. Professor Blackie was even
kind enough to remark (more than once) while in the
very act of writing the document above referred to, that
he did not know my face. Indeed, I denied myself
many opportunities; acting upon an extensive and highly
rational system of truantry, which cost me a great deal
of trouble to put in exercise — perhaps as much as would
have taught me Greek — and sent me forth into the
world and the profession of letters with the merest
shadow of an education. But they say it is always a
good thing to have taken pains, and that success is its
own reward, whatever be its nature; so that, perhaps,
even upon this I should plume myself, that no one ever
played the truant with more deliberate care, and none
ever had more certificates for less education. One consequence, however, of my system is that I have much
less to say of Professor Blackie than I had of Professor
Kelland; and as he is still alive, and will long, I hope,
continue to be so, it will not surprise you very much
that I have no intention of saying it.

Meanwhile, how many others have gone — Jenkin,
Hodgson, and I know not who besides; and of that tide
of students that used to throng the arch and blacken the
quadrangle, how many are scattered into the remotest
parts of the earth, and how many more have lain down
beside their fathers in their "resting-graves!" And
again, how many of these last have not found their way
there, all too early, through the stress of education! That
was one thing, at least, from which my truantry protected

me. I am sorry indeed that I have no Greek, but I should be sorrier still if I were dead; nor do I know the name of that branch of knowledge which is worth acquiring at the price of a brain fever. There are many sordid tragedies in the life of the student, above all if he be poor, or drunken, or both; but nothing more moves a wise man's pity than the case of the lad who is in too much hurry to be learned. And so, for the sake of a moral at the end, I will call up one more figure, and have done. A student, ambitious of success by that hot, intemperate manner of study that now grows so common, read night and day for an examination. As he went on, the task became more easy to him, sleep was more easily banished, his brain grew hot and clear and more capacious, the necessary knowledge daily fuller and more orderly. It came to the eve of the trial and he watched all night in his high chamber, reviewing what he knew, and already secure of success. His window looked eastward, and being (as I said) high up, and the house itself standing on a hill, commanded a view over dwindling suburbs to a country horizon. At last my student drew up his blind, and still in quite a jocund humour, looked abroad. Day was breaking, the east was tinging with strange fires, the clouds breaking up for the coming of the sun; and at the sight, nameless terror seized upon his mind. He was sane, his senses were undisturbed; he saw clearly, and knew what he was seeing, and knew that it was normal; but he could neither bear to see it nor find the strength to look away, and fled in panic from his chamber into the enclosure of the street. In the cool air and silence, and among the sleeping houses, his strength was renewed. Nothing troubled him but the memory of what had passed, and an abject fear of its return.

> " Gallo canente, spes redit,
> Aegris salus refunditur,
> Lapsis fides revertitur,"

as they sang of old in Portugal in the Morning Office. But to him that good hour of cockcrow, and the changes of the dawn, had brought panic, and lasting doubt, and such terror as he still shook to think of. He dared not return to his lodging; he could not eat; he sat down, he rose up, he wandered; the city woke about him with its cheerful bustle, the sun climbed overhead; and still he grew but the more absorbed in the distress of his recollection and the fear of his past fear. At the appointed hour, he came to the door of the place of examination; but when he was asked, he had forgotten his name. Seeing him so disordered, they had not the heart to send him away, but gave him a paper and admitted him, still nameless, to the Hall. Vain kindness, vain efforts. He could only sit in a still growing horror, writing nothing, ignorant of all, his mind filled with a single memory of the breaking day and his own intolerable fear. And that same night he was tossing in a brain fever.

People are afraid of war and wounds and dentists, all with excellent reason; but these are not to be compared with such chaotic terrors of the mind as fell on this young man, and made him cover his eyes from the innocent morning. We all have by our bedsides the box of the Merchant Abudah, thank God, securely enough shut; but when a young man sacrifices sleep to labour, let him have a care, for he is playing with the lock.

III. OLD MORTALITY

I

THERE is a certain graveyard, looked upon on the one side by a prison, on the other by the windows of a quiet hotel; below, under a steep cliff, it beholds the traffic of many lines of rail, and the scream of the engine and the shock of meeting buffers mount to it all day long. The aisles are lined with the inclosed sepulchres of families, door beyond door, like houses in a street; and in the morning the shadow of the prison turrets, and of many tall memorials, fall upon the graves. There, in the hot fits of youth, I came to be unhappy. Pleasant incidents are woven with my memory of the place. I here made friends with a certain plain old gentleman, a visitor on sunny mornings, gravely cheerful, who, with one eye upon the place that awaited him, chirped about his youth like winter sparrows; a beautiful housemaid of the hotel once, for some days together, dumbly flirted with me from a window and kept my wild heart flying; and once — she possibly remembers — the wise Eugenia followed me to that austere inclosure. Her hair came down, and in the shelter of the tomb my trembling fingers helped her to repair the braid. But for the most part I went there solitary and, with irrevocable emotion, pored on the names of the

199

forgotten. Name after name, and to each the conventional attributions and the idle dates: a regiment of the unknown that had been the joy of mothers, and had thrilled with the illusions of youth, and at last, in the dim sick-room, wrestled with the pangs of old mortality. In that whole crew of the silenced there was but one of whom my fancy had received a picture; and he, with his comely, florid countenance, bewigged and habited in scarlet, and in his day combining fame and popularity, stood forth, like a taunt, among that company of phantom appellations. It was then possible to leave behind us something more explicit than these severe, monotonous and lying epitaphs; and the thing left, the memory of a painted picture and what we call the immortality of a name, was hardly more desirable than mere oblivion. Even David Hume, as he lay composed beneath that " circular idea," was fainter than a dream; and when the housemaid, broom in hand, smiled and beckoned from the open window, the fame of that bewigged philosopher melted like a raindrop in the sea.

And yet in soberness I cared as little for the housemaid as for David Hume. The interests of youth are rarely frank; his passions, like Noah's dove, come home to roost. The fire, sensibility, and volume of his own nature, that is all that he has learned to recognise. The tumultuary and gray tide of life, the empire of routine, the unrejoicing faces of his elders, fill him with contemptuous surprise; there also he seems to walk among the tombs of spirits; and it is only in the course of years, and after much rubbing with his fellow-men, that he begins by glimpses to see himself from without and his

fellows from within: to know his own for one among
the thousand undenoted countenances of the city street,
and to divine in others the throb of human agony and
hope. In the meantime he will avoid the hospital doors,
the pale faces, the cripple, the sweet whiff of chloroform — for there, on the most thoughtless, the pains of
others are burned home; but he will continue to walk,
in a divine self-pity, the aisles of the forgotten graveyard. The length of man's life, which is endless to the
brave and busy, is scorned by his ambitious thought.
He cannot bear to have come for so little, and to go
again so wholly. He cannot bear, above all, in that
brief scene, to be still idle, and by way of cure, neglects
the little that he has to do. The parable of the talent is
the brief epitome of youth. To believe in immortality
is one thing, but it is first needful to believe in life.
Denunciatory preachers seem not to suspect that they
may be taken gravely and in evil part; that young men
may come to think of time as of a moment, and with
the pride of Satan wave back the inadequate gift. Yet
here is a true peril; this it is that sets them to pace the
graveyard alleys and to read, with strange extremes of
pity and derision, the memorials of the dead.

Books were the proper remedy: books of vivid human import, forcing upon their minds the issues, pleasures, busyness, importance and immediacy of that life
in which they stand; books of smiling or heroic temper,
to excite or to console; books of a large design, shad-
owing the complexity of that game of consequences to
which we all sit down, the hanger-back not least. But
the average sermon flees the point, disporting itself in
that eternity of which we know, and need to know, so

little; avoiding the bright, crowded, and momentous fields of life where destiny awaits us. Upon the average book a writer may be silent; he may set it down to his ill-hap that when his own youth was in the acrid fermentation, he should have fallen and fed upon the cheerless fields of Obermann. Yet to Mr. Arnold, who led him to these pastures, he still bears a grudge. The day is perhaps not far off when people will begin to count *Moll Flanders,* ay, or *The Country Wife,* more wholesome and more pious diet than these guide-books to consistent egoism.

But the most inhuman of boys soon wearies of the inhumanity of Obermann. And even while I still continued to be a haunter of the graveyard, I began insensibly to turn my attention to the grave-diggers, and was weaned out of myself to observe the conduct of visitors. This was dayspring, indeed, to a lad in such great darkness. Not that I began to see men, or to try to see them, from within, nor to learn charity and modesty and justice from the sight; but still stared at them externally from the prison windows of my affectation. Once I remember to have observed two working-women with a baby halting by a grave ; there was something monumental in the grouping, one upright carrying the child, the other with bowed face crouching by her side. A wreath of immortelles under a glass dome had thus attracted them; and, drawing near, I overheard their judgment on that wonder. "Eh! what extravagance!" To a youth afflicted with the callosity of sentiment, this quaint and pregnant saying appeared merely base.

My acquaintance with grave-diggers, considering its length, was unremarkable. One, indeed, whom I found

plying his spade in the red evening, high above Allan
Water and in the shadow of Dunblane Cathedral, told
me of his acquaintance with the birds that still attended
on his labours; how some would even perch about him,
waiting for their prey; and in a true Sexton's Calendar,
how the species varied with the season of the year.
But this was the very poetry of the profession. The
others whom I knew were somewhat dry. A faint flavour of the gardener hung about them, but sophisticated
and disbloomed. They had engagements to keep, not
alone with the deliberate series of the seasons, but with
mankind's clocks and hour-long measurement of time.
And thus there was no leisure for the relishing pinch,
or the hour-long gossip, foot on spade. They were
men wrapped up in their grim business; they liked well
to open long-closed family vaults, blowing in the key
and throwing wide the grating; and they carried in their
minds a calendar of names and dates. It would be "in
fifty-twa" that such a tomb was last opened for "Miss
Jemimy." It was thus they spoke of their past patients —
familiarly but not without respect, like old family ser-
vants. Here is indeed a servant, whom we forget that
we possess; who does not wait at the bright table, or
run at the bell's summons, but patiently smokes his pipe
beside the mortuary fire, and in his faithful memory
notches the burials of our race. To suspect Shakespeare in his maturity of a superficial touch savours of
paradox; yet he was surely in error when he attributed
insensibility to the digger of the grave. But perhaps it
is on Hamlet that the charge should lie; or perhaps the
English sexton differs from the Scotch. The "good-
man delver," reckoning up his years of office, might

have at least suggested other thoughts. It is a pride common among sextons. A cabinet-maker does not count his cabinets, nor even an author his volumes, save when they stare upon him from the shelves; but the grave-digger numbers his graves. He would indeed be something different from human if his solitary open-air and tragic labours left not a broad mark upon his mind. There, in his tranquil aisle, apart from city clamour, among the cats and robins and the ancient effigies and legends of the tomb, he waits the continual passage of his contemporaries, falling like minute drops into eternity. As they fall, he counts them; and this enumeration, which was at first perhaps appalling to his soul, in the process of years and by the kindly influence of habit grows to be his pride and pleasure. There are many common stories telling how he piques himself on crowded cemeteries. But I will rather tell of the old grave-digger of Monkton, to whose unsuffering bedside the minister was summoned. He dwelt in a cottage built into the wall of the churchyard; and through a bull's-eye pane above his bed he could see, as he lay dying, the rank grasses and the upright and recumbent stones. Dr. Laurie was, I think, a Moderate: 'tis certain, at least, that he took a very Roman view of death-bed dispositions; for he told the old man that he had lived beyond man's natural years, that his life had been easy and reputable, that his family had all grown up and been a credit to his care, and that it now behoved him unregretfully to gird his loins and follow the majority. The gravedigger heard him out; then he raised himself upon one elbow, and with the other hand pointed through the window to the scene of his life-long labours.

"Doctor," he said, "I ha'e laid three hunner and fower-score in that kirkyaird; an it had been His wull," indicating Heaven, "I would ha'e likit weel to ha'e made out the fower hunner." But it was not to be; this tragedian of the fifth act had now another part to play; and the time had come when others were to gird and carry him.

II

I would fain strike a note that should be more heroical; but the ground of all youth's suffering, solitude, hysteria, and haunting of the grave, is nothing else than naked, ignorant selfishness. It is himself that he sees dead; those are his virtues that are forgotten; his is the vague epitaph. Pity him but the more, if pity be your cue; for where a man is all pride, vanity, and personal aspiration, he goes through fire unshielded. In every part and corner of our life, to lose oneself is to be gainer; to forget oneself is to be happy; and this poor, laughable and tragic fool has not yet learned the rudiments; himself, giant Prometheus, is still ironed on the peaks of Caucasus. But by and by his truant interests will leave that tortured body, slip abroad and gather flowers. Then shall death appear before him in an altered guise; no longer as a doom peculiar to himself, whether fate's crowning injustice or his own last vengeance upon those who fail to value him; but now as a power that wounds him far more tenderly, not without solemn compensations, taking and giving, bereaving and yet storing up.

The first step for all is to learn to the dregs our own ignoble fallibility. When we have fallen through story after story of our vanity and aspiration, and sit rueful among the ruins, then it is that we begin to measure the stature of our friends: how they stand between us and our own contempt, believing in our best; how, linking us with others, and still spreading wide the influential circle, they weave us in and in with the fabric of contemporary life; and to what petty size they dwarf the virtues and the vices that appeared gigantic in our youth. So that at the last, when such a pin falls out — when there vanishes in the least breath of time one of those rich magazines of life on which we drew for our supply — when he who had first dawned upon us as a face among the faces of the city, and, still growing, came to bulk on our regard with those clear features of the loved and living man, falls in a breath to memory and shadow, there falls along with him a whole wing of the palace of our life.

III

One such face I now remember; one such blank some half a dozen of us labour to dissemble. In his youth he was most beautiful in person, most serene and genial by disposition; full of racy words and quaint thoughts. Laughter attended on his coming. He had the air of a great gentleman, jovial and royal with his equals, and to the poorest student gentle and attentive. Power seemed to reside in him exhaustless; we saw him stoop to play with us, but held him marked for higher destinies; we loved his notice; and I have rarely had my pride more gratified than when he sat at my father's table, my acknowledged friend. So he walked among us, both hands full of gifts, carrying with nonchalance the seeds of a most influential life.

The powers and the ground of friendship is a mystery; but, looking back, I can discern that, in part, we loved the thing he was, for some shadow of what he was to be. For with all his beauty, power, breeding, urbanity and mirth, there was in those days something soulless in our friend. He would astonish us by sallies, witty, innocent and inhumane; and by a misapplied Johnsonian pleasantry, demolish honest sentiment. I can still see and hear him, as he went his way along the lamplit streets, *Là ci darem la mano* on his lips, a noble figure of a youth, but following vanity and incredulous of good; and sure enough, somewhere on the high seas of life, with his health, his hopes, his patrimony and his self-respect, miserably went down.

From this disaster, like a spent swimmer, he came desperately ashore, bankrupt of money and consideration; creeping to the family he had deserted; with broken wing, never more to rise. But in his face there was a light of knowledge that was new to it. Of the wounds of his body he was never healed; died of them gradually, with clear-eyed resignation; of his wounded pride, we knew only from his silence. He returned to that city where he had lorded it in his ambitious youth; lived there alone, seeing few; striving to retrieve the irretrievable; at times still grappling with that mortal frailty that had brought him down; still joying in his friend's successes; his laugh still ready but with kindlier music; and over all his thoughts the shadow of that unalterable law which he had disavowed and which had brought him low. Lastly, when his bodily evils had quite disabled him, he lay a great while dying, still without complaint, still finding interests; to his last step gentle, urbane and with the will to smile.

The tale of this great failure is, to those who remained true to him, the tale of a success. In his youth he took thought for no one but himself; when he came ashore again, his whole armada lost, he seemed to think of none but others. Such was his tenderness for others, such his instinct of fine courtesy and pride, that of that impure passion of remorse he never breathed a syllable; even regret was rare with him, and pointed with a jest. You would not have dreamed, if you had known him then, that this was that great failure, that beacon to young men, over whose fall a whole society had hissed and pointed fingers. Often have we gone to him, red-hot with our own hopeful sorrows, railing on the rose-leaves in our princely bed of life, and he would patiently give ear and wisely counsel; and it was only upon some return of our own thoughts that we were reminded what manner of man this was to whom we disembosomed: a man, by his own fault, ruined; shut out of the garden of his gifts; his whole city of hope both ploughed and salted; silently awaiting the deliverer. Then something took us by the throat; and to see him there, so gentle, patient, brave and pious, oppressed but not cast down, sorrow was so swallowed up in admiration that we could not dare to pity him. Even if the old fault flashed out again, it but awoke our wonder that, in that lost battle, he should have still the energy to fight. He had gone to ruin with a kind of kingly *abandon,* like one who condescended; but once ruined, with the lights all out, he fought as for a kingdom. Most men, finding themselves the authors of their own disgrace, rail the louder against God or destiny. Most men, when they repent, oblige their friends to share the bitterness of that repentance. But he had held an inquest and passed sentence: *mene, mene;* and condemned himself to smiling silence. He had given trouble enough; had earned misfortune amply, and foregone the right to murmur.

Thus was our old comrade, like Samson, careless in his days of strength; but on the coming of adversity, and when that strength was gone that had betrayed him—"for our strength is weakness"—he began to blossom and bring forth. Well, now, he is out of the fight: the burden that he bore thrown down before the great deliverer. We

> " in the vast cathedral leave him:
> God accept him,
> Christ receive him!"

IV

If we go now and look on these innumerable epitaphs, the pathos and the irony are strangely fled. They do not stand merely to the dead, these foolish monuments; they are pillars and legends set up to glorify the difficult but not desperate life of man. This ground is hallowed by the heroes of defeat.

I see the indifferent pass before my friend's last resting-place; pause, with a shrug of pity, marvelling that so rich an argosy had sunk. A pity, now that he is done with suffering, a pity most uncalled for, and an ignorant wonder. Before those who loved him, his memory shines like a reproach; they honour him for silent lessons; they cherish his example; and in what remains before them of their toil, fear to be unworthy of the dead. For this proud man was one of those who prospered in the valley of humiliation; — of whom Bunyan wrote that, "Though Christian had the hard hap to meet in the valley with Apollyon, yet I must tell you, that in former times men have met with angels here; have found pearls here; and have in this place found the words of life."

IV. A COLLEGE MAGAZINE

I

ALL through my boyhood and youth, I was known and pointed out for the pattern of an idler; and yet I was always busy on my own private end, which was to learn to write. I kept always two books in my pocket, one to read, one to write in. As I walked, my mind was busy fitting what I saw with appropriate words; when I sat by the roadside, I would either read, or a pencil and a penny version-book would be in my hand, to note down the features of the scene or commemorate some halting stanzas. Thus I lived with words. And what I thus wrote was for no ulterior use, it was written consciously for practice. It was not so much that I wished to be an author (though I wished that too) as that I had vowed that I would learn to write. That was a proficiency that tempted me; and I practised to acquire it, as men learn to whittle, in a wager with myself. Description was the principal field of my exercise; for to any one with senses there is always something worth describing, and town and country are but one continuous subject. But I worked in other ways also; often accompanied my walks with dramatic dialogues, in which I played many parts; and often exercised myself in writing down conversations from memory.

This was all excellent, no doubt; so were the diaries
I sometimes tried to keep, but always and very speedily discarded, finding them a school of posturing and
melancholy self-deception. And yet this was not the
most efficient part of my training. Good though it was,
it only taught me (so far as I have learned them at all)
the lower and less intellectual elements of the art, the
choice of the essential note and the right word: things
that to a happier constitution had perhaps come by
nature. And regarded as training, it had one grave defect; for it set me no standard of achievement. So that
there was perhaps more profit, as there was certainly
more effort, in my secret labours at home. Whenever
I read a book or a passage that particularly pleased me,
in which a thing was said or an effect rendered with
propriety, in which there was either some conspicuous
force or some happy distinction in the style, I must sit
down at once and set myself to ape that quality. I
was unsuccessful, and I knew it; and tried again, and
was again unsuccessful and always unsuccessful; but
at least in these vain bouts, I got some practice in
rhythm, in harmony, in construction and the co-ordi-
nation of parts. I have thus played the sedulous ape
to Hazlitt, to Lamb, to Wordsworth, to Sir Thomas
Browne, to Defoe, to Hawthorne, to Montaigne, to Bau-
delaire and to Obermann. I remember one of these
monkey tricks, which was called *The Vanity of Morals:*
it was to have had a second part, *The Vanity of Knowledge;* and as I had neither morality nor scholarship,
the names were apt; but the second part was never
attempted, and the first part was written (which is my
reason for recalling it, ghostlike, from its ashes) no less

than three times: first in the manner of Hazlitt, second in the manner of Ruskin, who had cast on me a passing spell, and third, in a laborious pasticcio of Sir Thomas Browne. So with my other works: *Cain,* an epic, was (save the mark!) an imitation of *Sordello: Robin Hood,* a tale in verse, took an eclectic middle course among the fields of Keats, Chaucer and Morris: in *Monmouth,* a tragedy, I reclined on the bosom of Mr. Swinburne; in my innumerable gouty-footed lyrics, I followed many masters; in the first draft of *The King's Pardon,* a tragedy, I was on the trail of no lesser man than John Webster; in the second draft of the same piece, with staggering versatility, I had shifted my allegiance to Congreve, and of course conceived my fable in a less serious vein — for it was not Congreve's verse, it was his exquisite prose, that I admired and sought to copy. Even at the age of thirteen I had tried to do justice to the inhabitants of the famous city of Peebles in the style of the *Book of Snobs.* So I might go on for ever, through all my abortive novels, and down to my later plays, of which I think more tenderly, for they were not only conceived at first under the bracing influence of old Dumas, but have met with resurrections: one, strangely bettered by another hand, came on the stage itself and was played by bodily actors; the other, originally known as *Semiramis: a Tragedy,* I have observed on bookstalls under the *alias* of *Prince Otto.* But enough has been said to show by what arts of impersonation, and in what purely ventriloquial efforts I first saw my words on paper.

That, like it or not, is the way to learn to write; whether I have profited or not, that is the way. It was so Keats learned, and there was never a finer temperament for literature than Keats's; it was so, if we could trace it out, that all men have learned; and that is why a revival of letters is always accompanied or heralded by a cast back to earlier and fresher models. Perhaps I hear some one cry out: But this is not the way to be original! It is not; nor is there any way but to be born so. Nor yet, if you are born original, is there anything in this training that shall clip the wings of your originality. There can be none more original than Montaigne, neither could any be more unlike Cicero; yet no craftsman can fail to see how much the one must have tried in his time to imitate the other. Burns is the very type of a prime force in letters: he was of all men the most imitative. Shakespeare himself, the imperial, proceeds directly from a school. It is only from a school that we can expect to have good writers; it is almost invariably from a school that great writers, these lawless exceptions, issue. Nor is there anything here that should astonish the considerate. Before he can tell what cadences he truly prefers, the student should have tried all that are possible; before he can choose and preserve a fitting key of words, he should long have practised the literary scales; and it is only after years of such gymnastic that he can sit down at last, legions of words swarming to his call, dozens of turns of phrase simultaneously bidding for his choice, and he himself knowing what he wants to do and (within the narrow limit of a man's ability) able to do it.

And it is the great point of these imitations that there still shines beyond the student's reach his inimitable model. Let him try as he please, he is still sure of fail-

ure; and it is a very old and a very true saying that failure is the only highroad to success. I must have had
some disposition to learn; for I clear-sightedly condemned my own performances. I liked doing them
indeed; but when they were done, I could see they
were rubbish. In consequence, I very rarely showed
them even to my friends; and such friends as I chose to
be my confidants I must have chosen well, for they had
the friendliness to be quite plain with me. "Padding,"
said one. Another wrote: "I cannot understand why
you do lyrics so badly." No more could I! Thrice I
put myself in the way of a more authoritative rebuff, by
sending a paper to a magazine. These were returned;
and I was not surprised nor even pained. If they had
not been looked at, as (like all amateurs) I suspected
was the case, there was no good in repeating the experiment; if they had been looked at — well, then I had not
yet learned to write, and I must keep on learning and
living. Lastly, I had a piece of good fortune which is
the occasion of this paper, and by which I was able to
see my literature in print, and to measure experimentally how far I stood from the favour of the public.

II

The Speculative Society is a body of some antiquity,
and has counted among its members Scott, Brougham,
Jeffrey, Horner, Benjamin Constant, Robert Emmet, and
many a legal and local celebrity besides. By an accident, variously explained, it has its rooms in the very
buildings of the University of Edinburgh: a hall, Tur-
key-carpeted, hung with pictures, looking, when lighted

up at night with fire and candle, like some goodly dining-room; a passage-like library, walled with books in
their wire cages; and a corridor with a fireplace, benches,
a table, many prints of famous members, and a mural
tablet to the virtues of a former secretary. Here a member can warm himself and loaf and read; here, in defiance of Senatus-consults, he can smoke. The Senatus
looks askance at these privileges; looks even with a
somewhat vinegar aspect on the whole society; which
argues a lack of proportion in the learned mind, for the
world, we may be sure, will prize far higher this haunt
of dead lions than all the living dogs of the professorate.

I sat one December morning in the library of the Speculative; a very humble-minded youth, though it was a
virtue I never had much credit for; yet proud of my
privileges as a member of the Spec.; proud of the pipe
I was smoking in the teeth of the Senatus; and in particular, proud of being in the next room to three very
distinguished students, who were then conversing beside the corridor fire. One of these has now his name
on the back of several volumes, and his voice, I learn, is
influential in the law courts. Of the death of the second,
you have just been reading what I had to say. And the
third also has escaped out of that battle of life in which
he fought so hard, it may be so unwisely. They were
all three, as I have said, notable students; but this was
the most conspicuous. Wealthy, handsome, ambitious,
adventurous, diplomatic, a reader of Balzac, and of all
men that I have known, the most like to one of Balzac's
characters, he led a life, and was attended by an ill fortune, that could be properly set forth only in the *Comé-
die Humaine*. He had then his eye on Parliament; and

soon after the time of which I write, he made a showy speech at a political dinner, was cried up to heaven next day in the *Courant,* and the day after was dashed lower than earth with a charge of plagiarism in the *Scotsman.* Report would have it (I daresay, very wrongly) that he was betrayed by one in whom he particularly trusted, and that the author of the charge had learned its truth from his own lips.   Thus, at least, he was up one day on a pinnacle, admired and envied by all; and the next, though still but a boy, he was publicly disgraced.   The blow would have broken a less finely tempered spirit; and even him I suppose it rendered reckless; for he took flight to London, and there, in a fast club, disposed of the bulk of his considerable patrimony in the space of one winter.   For years thereafter he lived I know not how; always well dressed, always in good hotels and good society, always with empty pockets.   The charm of his manner may have stood him in good stead; but though my own manners are very agreeable, I have never found in them a source of livelihood; and to ex- plain the miracle of his continued existence, I must fall back upon the theory of the philosopher, that in his case, as in all of the same kind, "there was a suffering rela- tive in the background."   From this genteel eclipse he reappeared upon the scene, and presently sought me out in the character of a generous editor.   It is in this part that I best remember him; tall, slender, with a not un- graceful stoop; looking quite like a refined gentleman, and quite like an urbane adventurer; smiling with an engaging ambiguity; cocking at you one peaked eye- brow with a great appearance of finesse; speaking low and sweet and thick, with a touch of burr; telling strange tales with singular deliberation and, to a patient listener, excellent effect. After all these ups and downs, he seemed still, like the rich student that he was of yore, to breathe of money; seemed still perfectly sure of himself and certain of his end. Yet he was then upon the brink of his last overthrow. He had set himself to found the strangest thing in our society: one of those periodical sheets from which men suppose themselves to learn opinions; in which young gentlemen from the universities are encouraged, at so much a line, to garble facts, insult foreign nations and calumniate private individuals; and which are now the source of glory, so that if a man's name be often enough printed there, he becomes a kind of demigod; and people will pardon him when he talks back and forth, as they do for Mr. Gladstone; and crowd him to suffocation on railway platforms, as they did the other day to General Boulanger; and buy his literary works, as I hope you have just done for me. Our fathers, when they were upon some great enterprise, would sacrifice a life; building, it may be, a favourite slave into the foundations of their palace. It was with his own life that my companion disarmed the envy of the gods. He fought his paper single-handed; trusting no one, for he was something of a cynic; up early and down late, for he was nothing of a sluggard; daily ear-wigging influential men, for he was a master of ingratiation. In that slender and silken fellow there must have been a rare vein of courage, that he should thus have died at his employment; and doubtless ambition spoke loudly in his ear, and doubtless love also, for it seems there was a marriage in his view had he succeeded. But he died, and his paper died after him; and of all this grace, and tact, and courage, it must seem to our blind eyes as if there had come literally nothing.

These three students sat, as I was saying, in the corridor, under the mural tablet that records the virtues of Macbean, the former secretary. We would often smile at that ineloquent memorial, and thought it a poor thing to come into the world at all and leave no more behind one than Macbean. And yet of these three, two are gone and have left less; and this book, perhaps, when it is old and foxy, and some one picks it up in a corner of a book-shop, and glances through it, smiling at the old, graceless turns of speech, and perhaps for the love of *Alma Mater* (which may be still extant and flourishing) buys it, not without haggling, for some pence — this book may alone preserve a memory of James Walter Ferrier and Robert Glasgow Brown.

Their thoughts ran very differently on that December morning; they were all on fire with ambition; and when they had called me in to them, and made me a sharer in their design, I too became drunken with pride and hope. We were to found a University magazine. A pair of little, active brothers—Livingstone by name, great skippers on the foot, great rubbers of the hands, who kept a book-shop over against the University building—had been debauched to play the part of publishers. We four were to be conjunct editors and, what was the main point of the concern, to print our own works; while, by every rule of arithmetic—that flatterer of credulity — the adventure must succeed and bring great profit. Well, well: it was a bright vision. I went home that morning walking upon air. To have been chosen by these three distinguished students was to me

the most unspeakable advance; it was my first draught
of consideration; it reconciled me to myself and to my
fellow-men; and as I steered round the railings at the
Tron, I could not withhold my lips from smiling publicly.   Yet, in the bottom of my heart, I knew that
magazine would be a grim fiasco; I knew it would not
be worth reading; I knew, even if it were, that nobody
would read it; and I kept wondering how I should be
able, upon my compact income of twelve pounds per
annum, payable monthly, to meet my share in the expense.   It was a comfortable thought to me that I had
a father.

The magazine appeared, in a yellow cover which was
the best part of it, for at least it was unassuming; it
ran four months in undisturbed obscurity, and died
without a gasp.   The first number was edited by all
four of us with prodigious bustle; the second fell prin-
cipally into the hands of Ferrier and me; the third I
edited alone; and it has long been a solemn question
who it was that edited the fourth.   It would perhaps
be still more difficult to say who read it.   Poor yellow
sheet, that looked so hopefully in the Livingstones' window!   Poor, harmless paper, that might have gone to
print a *Shakespeare* on, and was instead so clumsily
defaced with nonsense!   And, shall I say, Poor Editors?
I cannot pity myself, to whom it was all pure gain.   It
was no news to me, but only the wholesome confirma-
tion of my judgment, when the magazine struggled
into half-birth, and instantly sickened and subsided into
night.   I had sent a copy to the lady with whom my
heart was at that time somewhat engaged, and who
did all that in her lay to break it; and she, with some

tact, passed over the gift and my cherished contributions in silence. I will not say that I was pleased at this; but I will tell her now, if by any chance she takes up the work of her former servant, that I thought the better of her taste. I cleared the decks after this lost engagement; had the necessary interview with my father, which passed off not amiss; paid over my share of the expense to the two little, active brothers, who rubbed their hands as much, but methought skipped rather less than formerly, having perhaps, these two also, embarked upon the enterprise with some graceful illusions; and then, reviewing the whole episode, I told myself that the time was not yet ripe, nor the man ready; and to work I went again with my penny version-books, having fallen back in one day from the printed author to the manuscript student.

III

From this defunct periodical I am going to reprint one of my own papers. The poor little piece is all tail-foremost. I have done my best to straighten its array, I have pruned it fearlessly, and it remains invertebrate and wordy. No self-respecting magazine would print the thing; and here you behold it in a bound volume, not for any worth of its own, but for the sake of the man whom it purports dimly to represent and some of whose sayings it preserves; so that in this volume of Memories and Portraits, Robert Young, the Swanston gardener, may stand alongside of John Todd, the Swanston shepherd. Not that John and Robert drew very close together in their lives; for John was rough, he smelt of the windy brae; and Robert was gentle, and smacked of the garden in the hollow. Perhaps it is to my shame that I liked John the better of the two; he had grit and dash, and that salt of the Old Adam that pleases men with any savage inheritance of blood; and he was a wayfarer besides, and took my gipsy fancy. But however that may be, and however Robert's profile may be blurred in the boyish sketch that follows, he was a man of a most quaint and beautiful nature, whom, if it were possible to recast a piece of work so old, I should like well to draw again with a maturer touch. And as I think of him and of John, I wonder in what other country two such men would be found dwelling together, in a hamlet of some twenty cottages, in the woody fold of a green hill.

V. AN OLD SCOTCH GARDENER

I THINK I might almost have said the last: somewhere, indeed, in the uttermost glens of the Lam-
mermuir or among the south-western hills there may
yet linger a decrepit representative of this bygone good
fellowship; but as far as actual experience goes, I have
only met one man in my life who might fitly be quoted
in the same breath with Andrew Fairservice, — though
without his vices. He was a man whose very presence
could impart a savour of quaint antiquity to the baldest
and most modern flower-plots. There was a dignity
about his tall stooping form, and an earnestness in his
wrinkled face that recalled Don Quixote; but a Don
Quixote who had come through the training of the
Covenant, and been nourished in his youth on *Walker's
Lives* and *The Hind let Loose.*

Now, as I could not bear to let such a man pass away
with no sketch preserved of his old-fashioned virtues, I
hope the reader will take this as an excuse for the present paper, and judge as kindly as he can the infirmities
of my description. To me, who find it so difficult to
tell the little that I know, he stands essentially as a
genius loci. It is impossible to separate his spare form
and old straw hat from the garden in the lap of the hill,

223

with its rocks overgrown with clematis, its shadowy walks, and the splendid breadth of champaign that one saw from the north-west corner. The garden and gardener seem part and parcel of each other. When I take him from his right surroundings and try to make him appear for me on paper, he looks unreal and phantasmal: the best that I can say may convey some notion to those that never saw him, but to me it will be ever impotent.

The first time that I saw him, I fancy Robert was pretty old already: he had certainly begun to use his years as a stalking horse. Latterly he was beyond all the impudencies of logic, considering a reference to the parish register worth all the reasons in the world. *"I am old and well stricken in years,"* he was wont to say; and I never found any one bold enough to answer the argument. Apart from this vantage that he kept over all who were not yet octogenarian, he had some other drawbacks as a gardener. He shrank the very place he cultivated. The dignity and reduced gentility of his appearance made the small garden cut a sorry figure. He was full of tales of greater situations in his younger days. He spoke of castles and parks with a humbling familiarity. He told of places where under-gardeners had trembled at his looks, where there were meres and swanneries, labyrinths of walk and wildernesses of sad shrubbery in his control, till you could not help feeling that it was condescension on his part to dress your humbler garden plots. You were thrown at once into an invidious position. You felt that you were profiting by the needs of dignity, and that his poverty and not his will consented to your vulgar rule. Involuntarily you compared yourself with the swineherd that made Alfred watch his cakes, or some bloated citizen who may have given his sons and his condescension to the fallen Dionysius. Nor were the disagreeables purely fanciful and metaphysical, for the sway that he exercised over your feelings he extended to your garden, and, through the garden, to your diet. He would trim a hedge, throw away a favourite plant, or fill the most favoured and fertile section of the garden with a vegetable that none of us could eat, in supreme contempt for our opinion. If you asked him to send you in one of your own artichokes, "*That I wull, mem,*" he would say, "*with pleasure, for it is mair blessed to give than to receive.*" Ay, and even when, by extra twisting of the screw, we prevailed on him to prefer our commands to his own inclination, and he went away, stately and sad, professing that "*our wull was his pleasure,*" but yet reminding us that he would do it "*with feelin's,*"—even then, I say, the triumphant master felt humbled in his triumph, felt that he ruled on sufferance only, that he was taking a mean advantage of the other's low estate, and that the whole scene had been one of those "slights that patient merit of the unworthy takes."

In flowers his taste was old-fashioned and catholic; affecting sunflowers and dahlias, wallflowers and roses, and holding in supreme aversion whatsoever was fantastic, new-fashioned or wild. There was one exception to this sweeping ban. Foxgloves, though undoubtedly guilty on the last count, he not only spared, but loved; and when the shrubbery was being thinned, he stayed his hand and dexterously manipulated his bill in order to save every stately stem. In boyhood, as he told me once, speaking in that tone that only actors and the old-fashioned common folk can use nowadays, his heart grew *"proud"* within him when he came on a burn-course among the braes of Manor that shone purple with their graceful trophies; and not all his apprentice-ship and practice for so many years of precise garden-ing had banished these boyish recollections from his heart. Indeed, he was a man keenly alive to the beauty of all that was bygone. He abounded in old stories of his boyhood, and kept pious account of all his former pleasures; and when he went (on a holiday) to visit one of the fabled great places of the earth where he had served before, he came back full of little pre-Raphaelite reminiscences that showed real passion for the past, such as might have shaken hands with Hazlitt or Jean-Jacques.

But however his sympathy with his old feelings might affect his liking for the foxgloves, the very truth was that he scorned all flowers together. They were but garnishings, childish toys, trifling ornaments for ladies' chimney-shelves. It was towards his cauliflowers and peas and cabbage that his heart grew warm. His pref-erence for the more useful growths was such that cab-bages were found invading the flower-plots, and an out-post of savoys was once discovered in the centre of the lawn. He would prelect over some thriving plant with wonderful enthusiasm, piling reminiscence on reminis-cence of former and perhaps yet finer specimens. Yet even then he did not let the credit leave himself. He had, indeed, raised *"finer o' them"*; but it seemed that no one else had been favoured with a like success. All other gardeners, in fact, were mere foils to his own su-

perior attainments; and he would recount, with perfect
soberness of voice and visage, how so and so had won-
dered, and such another could scarcely give credit to his
eyes. Nor was it with his rivals only that he parted
praise and blame. If you remarked how well a plant
was looking, he would gravely touch his hat and thank
you with solemn unction; all credit in the matter falling
to him. If, on the other hand, you called his attention
to some back-going vegetable, he would quote Scripture: *"Paul may plant and Apollos may water";* all
blame being left to Providence, on the score of deficient
rain or untimely frosts.

There was one thing in the garden that shared his
preference with his favourite cabbages and rhubarb, and
that other was the bee-hive. Their sound, their industry, perhaps their sweet product also, had taken hold of
his imagination and heart, whether by way of memory
or no I cannot say, although perhaps the bees too were
linked to him by some recollection of Manor braes and
his country childhood. Nevertheless, he was too chary
of his personal safety or (let me rather say) his personal
dignity to mingle in any active office towards them.
But he could stand by while one of the contemned rivals
did the work for him, and protest that it was quite safe
in spite of his own considerate distance and the cries of
the distressed assistant. In regard to bees, he was
rather a man of word than deed, and some of his most
striking sentences had the bees for text. *" They are indeed wonderfu' creatures, mem,"* he said once. *" They
just mind me o' what the Queen of Sheba said to Solomon — and I think she said it wi' a sigh —' The half of
it hath not been told unto me '."*

As far as the Bible goes he was deeply read. Like the old Covenanters, of whom he was the worthy representative, his mouth was full of sacred quotations; it was the book that he had studied most and thought upon most deeply. To many people in his station the Bible, and perhaps Burns, are the only books of any vital literary merit that they read, feeding themselves, for the rest, on the draff of country newspapers, and the very instructive but not very palatable pabulum of some cheap educational series. This was Robert's position. All day long he had dreamed of the Hebrew stories, and his head had been full of Hebrew poetry and Gospel ethics; until they had struck deep root into his heart, and the very expressions had become a part of him; so that he rarely spoke without some antique idiom or Scripture mannerism that gave a raciness to the merest trivialities of talk. But the influence of the Bible did not stop here. There was more in Robert than quaint phrase and ready store of reference. He was imbued with a spirit of peace and love: he interposed between man and wife: he threw himself between the angry, touching his hat the while with all the ceremony of an usher: he protected the birds from everybody but himself, seeing, I suppose, a great difference between official execution and wanton sport. His mistress telling him one day to put some ferns into his master's particular corner, and adding, "Though, indeed, Robert, he doesn't deserve them, for he wouldn't help me to gather them," "*Eh, mem,*" replies Robert, "*but I wouldnae say that, for I think he's just a most deservin' gentleman.*" Again, two of our friends, who were on intimate terms, and accustomed to use language to each

other, somewhat without the bounds of the parliamentary, happened to differ about the position of a seat in
the garden. The discussion, as was usual when these
two were at it, soon waxed tolerably insulting on both
sides. Every one accustomed to such controversies
several times a day was quietly enjoying this prize-
fight of somewhat abusive wit — every one but Robert,
to whom the perfect good faith of the whole quarrel
seemed unquestionable, and who, after having waited
till his conscience would suffer him to wait no more,
and till he expected every moment that the disputants
would fall to blows, cut suddenly in with tones of
almost tearful entreaty: " *Eh, but, gentlemen, I wad hae
nae mair words about it!*" One thing was noticeable
about Robert's religion: it was neither dogmatic nor
sectarian. He never expatiated (at least, in my hearing) on the doctrines of his creed, and he never condemned anybody else. I have no doubt that he held all
Roman Catholics, Atheists, and Mahometans as consid-
erably out of it; I don't believe he had any sympathy
for Prelacy; and the natural feelings of man must have
made him a little sore about Free-Churchism; but at
least, he never talked about these views, never grew
controversially noisy, and never openly aspersed the
belief or practice of anybody. Now all this is not generally characteristic of Scotch piety; Scotch sects being
churches militant with a vengeance, and Scotch believ-
ers perpetual crusaders the one against the other, and
missionaries the one to the other. Perhaps Robert's
originally tender heart was what made the difference;
or, perhaps, his solitary and pleasant labour among
fruits and flowers had taught him a more sunshiny

creed than those whose work is among the tares of
fallen humanity; and the soft influences of the garden
had entered deep into his spirit,

> " Annihilating all that's made
> To a green thought in a green shade."

But I could go on forever chronicling his golden sayings or telling of his innocent and living piety. I had
meant to tell of his cottage, with the German pipe hung
reverently above the fire, and the shell box that he had
made for his son, and of which he would say patheti-
cally: *" He was real pleased wi' it at first, but I think
he's got a kind o' tired o' it now"*—the son being then
a man of about forty. But I will let all these pass.
"'Tis more significant: he's dead." The earth, that he
had digged so much in his life, was dug out by another
for himself; and the flowers that he had tended drew
their life still from him, but in a new and nearer way.
A bird flew about the open grave, as if it too wished
to honour the obsequies of one who had so often quoted
Scripture in favour of its kind: " Are not two sparrows
sold for one farthing? and yet not one of them falleth to
the ground."

Yes, he is dead. But the kings did not rise in the
place of death to greet him " with taunting proverbs "
as they rose to greet the haughty Babylonian; for in his
life he was lowly, and a peacemaker and a servant of
God.

VI. PASTORAL

TO leave home in early life is to be stunned and quickened with novelties; but when years have come,
it only casts a more endearing light upon the past. As
in those composite photographs of Mr. Galton's, the image of each new sitter brings out but the more clearly
the central features of the race; when once youth has
flown, each new impression only deepens the sense of
nationality and the desire of native places. So may
some cadet of Royal Écossais or the Albany Regiment,
as he mounted guard about French citadels, so may
some officer marching his company of the Scots-Dutch
among the polders, have felt the soft rains of the Hebri-
des upon his brow, or started in the ranks at the remembered aroma of peat-smoke. And the rivers of home are
dear in particular to all men. This is as old as Naaman,
who was jealous for Abana and Pharpar; it is confined
to no race nor country, for I know one of Scottish blood
but a child of Suffolk, whose fancy still lingers about the
lilied lowland waters of that shire. But the streams of
Scotland are incomparable in themselves — or I am only
the more Scottish to suppose so — and their sound and
colour dwell for ever in the memory. How often and
willingly do I not look again in fancy on Tummel, or
Manor, or the talking Airdle, or Dee swirling in its

Lynn; on the bright burn of Kinnaird, or the golden burn that pours and sulks in the den behind Kingussie! I think shame to leave out one of these enchantresses, but the list would grow too long if I remembered all; only I may not forget Allan Water, nor birch-wetting Rogie, nor yet Almond; nor, for all its pollutions, that Water of Leith of the many and well-named mills — Bell's Mills, and Canon Mills, and Silver Mills; nor Redford Burn of pleasant memories; nor yet, for all its smallness, that nameless trickle that springs in the green bosom of Allermuir, and is fed from Halkerside with a perennial teacupful, and threads the moss under the Shearer's Knowe, and makes one pool there, overhung by a rock, where I loved to sit and make bad verses, and is then kidnapped in its infancy by subterranean pipes for the service of the sea-beholding city in the plain. From many points in the moss you may see at one glance its whole course and that of all its tributaries; the geographer of this Lilliput may visit all its corners without sitting down, and not yet begin to be breathed; Shearer's Knowe and Halkerside are but names of adjacent cantons on a single shoulder of a hill, as names are squandered (it would seem to the inexpert, in superfluity) upon these upland sheepwalks; a bucket would receive the whole discharge of the toy river; it would take it an appreciable time to fill your morning bath; for the most part, besides, it soaks unseen through the moss; and yet for the sake of auld lang syne, and the figure of a certain *genius loci*, I am condemned to linger awhile in fancy by its shores; and if the nymph (who cannot be above a span in stature) will but inspire my pen, I would gladly carry the reader along with me.

John Todd, when I knew him, was already "the oldest herd on the Pentlands," and had been all his days faithful to that curlew-scattering, sheep-collecting life. He remembered the droving days, when the drove roads, that now lie green and solitary through the heather, were thronged thoroughfares. He had himself often marched flocks into England, sleeping on the hillsides with his caravan; and by his account it was a rough business not without danger. The drove roads lay apart from habitation; the drovers met in the wilderness, as to-day the deep-sea fishers meet off the banks in the solitude of the Atlantic; and in the one as in the other case rough habits and fist-law were the rule. Crimes were committed, sheep filched, and drovers robbed and beaten; most of which offences had a moorland burial and were never heard of in the courts of justice. John, in those days, was at least once attacked, — by two men after his watch, — and at least once, betrayed by his habitual anger, fell under the danger of the law and was clapped into some rustic prison-house, the doors of which he burst in the night and was no more heard of in that quarter. When I knew him, his life had fallen in quieter places, and he had no cares beyond the dulness of his dogs and the inroads of pedestrians from town. But for a man of his propensity to wrath these were enough; he knew neither rest nor peace, except by snatches; in the gray of the summer morning, and already from far up the hill, he would wake the "toun" with the sound of his shoutings; and in the lambing time, his cries were not yet silenced late at night. This wrathful voice of a man unseen might be said to haunt that quarter of the Pentlands, an audible bogie; and no doubt it added to the fear in which men stood of John a touch of something legendary. For my own part, he was at first my enemy, and I, in my character of a rambling boy, his natural abhorrence. It was long before I saw him near at hand, knowing him only by some sudden blast of bellowing from far above, bidding me "c'way oot amang the sheep." The quietest recesses of the hill harboured this ogre; I skulked in my favourite wilderness like a Cameronian of the Killing Time, and John Todd was my Claverhouse, and his dogs my questing dragoons. Little by little we dropped into civilities; his hail at sight of me began to have less of the ring of a war-slogan; soon, we never met but he produced his snuff-box, which was with him, like the calumet with the Red Indian, a part of the heraldry of peace; and at length, in the ripeness of time, we grew to be a pair of friends, and when I lived alone in these parts in the winter, it was a settled thing for John to "give me a cry" over the garden wall as he set forth upon his evening round, and for me to overtake and bear him company.

That dread voice of his that shook the hills when he was angry, fell in ordinary talk very pleasantly upon the ear, with a kind of honied, friendly whine, not far off singing, that was eminently Scottish. He laughed not very often, and when he did, with a sudden, loud haw-haw, hearty but somehow joyless, like an echo from a rock. His face was permanently set and coloured; ruddy and stiff with weathering; more like a picture than a face; yet with a certain strain and a threat of latent anger in the expression, like that of a man trained too fine and harassed with perpetual vigilance. He spoke in the richest dialect of Scotch I ever heard; the words in themselves were a pleasure and often a surprise to me, so that I often came back from one of our patrols with new acquisitions; and this vocabulary he would handle like a master, stalking a little before me, "beard on shoulder," the plaid hanging loosely about him, the yellow staff clapped under his arm, and guiding me uphill by that devious, tactical ascent which seems peculiar to men of his trade. I might count him with the best talkers; only that talking Scotch and talking English seem incomparable acts. He touched on nothing at least, but he adorned it; when he narrated, the scene was before you; when he spoke (as he did mostly) of his own antique business, the thing took on a colour of romance and curiosity that was surprising. The clans of sheep with their particular territories on the hill, and how, in the yearly killings and purchases, each must be proportionally thinned and strengthened; the midnight busyness of animals, the signs of the weather, the cares of the snowy season, the exquisite stupidity of sheep, the exquisite cunning of dogs: all these he could present so humanly, and with so much old experience and living gusto, that weariness was excluded. And in the midst he would suddenly straighten his bowed back, the stick would fly abroad in demonstration, and the sharp thunder of his voice roll out a long itinerary for the dogs, so that you saw at last the use of that great wealth of names for every knowe and howe upon the hillside; and the dogs, having hearkened with lowered tails and raised faces, would run up their flags again to the masthead and spread themselves upon the indicated circuit. It used to fill me with wonder how they could follow and retain so long a story. But John denied

these creatures all intelligence; they were the constant
butt of his passion and contempt; it was just possible
to work with the like of them, he said,—not more than
possible. And then he would expand upon the subject
of the really good dogs that he had known, and the one
really good dog that he had himself possessed. He had
been offered forty pounds for it; but a good collie was
worth more than that, more than anything, to a "herd";
he did the herd's work for him. "As for the like of
them!" he would cry, and scornfully indicate the scour-
ing tails of his assistants.

Once—I translate John's Lallan, for I cannot do it justice, being born *Britannis in montibus,* indeed, but alas!
inerudito sæculo—once, in the days of his good dog,
he had bought some sheep in Edinburgh, and on the
way out, the road being crowded, two were lost. This
was a reproach to John, and a slur upon the dog; and
both were alive to their misfortune. Word came, after
some days, that a farmer about Braid had found a pair
of sheep; and thither went John and the dog to ask for
restitution. But the farmer was a hard man and stood
upon his rights. "How were they marked?" he asked;
and since John had bought right and left from many
sellers and had no notion of the marks—"Very well,"
said the farmer, "then it's only right that I should keep
them—"Well," said John, "it's a fact that I cannae
tell the sheep; but if my dog can, will ye let me have
them?" The farmer was honest as well as hard, and
besides I daresay he had little fear of the ordeal; so he
had all the sheep upon his farm into one large park, and
turned John's dog into their midst. The hairy man of
business knew his errand well; he knew that John and

he had bought two sheep and (to their shame) lost them about Boroughmuirhead; he knew besides (the Lord knows how, unless by listening) that they were come to Braid for their recovery; and without pause or blunder singled out, first one and then another, the two waifs. It was that afternoon the forty pounds were offered and refused. And the shepherd and his dog — what do I say? the true shepherd and his man — set off together by Fairmilehead in jocund humour, and "smiled to ither" all the way home, with the two recovered ones before them. So far, so good; but intelligence may be abused. The dog, as he is by little man's inferior in mind, is only by little his superior in virtue; and John had another collie tale of quite a different complexion. At the foot of the moss behind Kirk Yetton (Caer Ketton, wise men say) there is a scrog of low wood and a pool with a dam for washing sheep. John was one day lying under a bush in the scrog, when he was aware of a collie on the far hillside skulking down through the deepest of the heather with obtrusive stealth. He knew the dog; knew him for a clever, rising practitioner from quite a distant farm; one whom perhaps he had coveted as he saw him masterfully steering flocks to market. But what did the practitioner so far from home? and why this guilty and secret manœuvring towards the pool? — for it was towards the pool that he was heading. John lay the closer under his bush, and presently saw the dog come forth upon the margin, look all about to see if he were anywhere observed, plunge in and repeatedly wash himself over head and ears, and then (but now openly and with tail in air) strike homeward over the hills. That same night word

was sent his master, and the rising practitioner, shaken
up from where he lay, all innocence before the fire, was
had out to a dykeside and promptly shot; for alas! he
was that foulest of criminals under trust, a sheep-eater;
and it was from the maculation of sheep's blood that he
had come so far to cleanse himself in the pool behind
Kirk Yetton.

A trade that touches nature, one that lies at the foundations of life, in which we have all had ancestors employed, so that on a hint of it ancestral memories revive,
lends itself to literary use, vocal or written.   The fortune of a tale lies not alone in the skill of him that writes,
but as much, perhaps, in the inherited experience of
him who reads; and when I hear with a particular thrill
of things that I have never done or seen, it is one of
that innumerable army of my ancestors rejoicing in past
deeds.   Thus novels begin to touch not the fine *dilet-
tanti* but the gross mass of mankind, when they leave
off to speak of parlours and shades of manner and still-
born niceties of motive, and begin to deal with fighting,
sailoring, adventure, death or child-birth; and thus ancient out-door crafts and occupations, whether Mr. Hardy
wields the shepherd's crook or Count Tolstoi swings
the scythe, lift romance into a near neighbourhood with
epic.   These aged things have on them the dew of
man's morning; they lie near, not so much to us, the
semi-artificial flowerets, as to the trunk and aboriginal
taproot of the race.   A thousand interests spring up in
the process of the ages, and a thousand perish; that is
now an eccentricity or a lost art which was once the
fashion of an empire; and those only are perennial matters that rouse us to-day, and that roused men in all

epochs of the past. There is a certain critic, not indeed
of execution but of matter, whom I dare be known to set
before the best: a certain low-browed, hairy gentleman,
at first a percher in the fork of trees, next (as they re-
late) a dweller in caves, and whom I think I see squat-
ting in cave-mouths, of a pleasant afternoon, to munch
his berries — his wife, that accomplished lady, squat-
ting by his side: his name I never heard, but he is often
described as Probably Arboreal, which may serve for
recognition. Each has his own tree of ancestors, but
at the top of all sits Probably Arboreal; in all our veins
there run some minims of his old, wild, tree-top blood;
our civilised nerves still tingle with his rude terrors and
pleasures; and to that which would have moved our
common ancestor, all must obediently thrill.

We have not so far to climb to come to shepherds;
and it may be I had one for an ascendant who has
largely moulded me. But yet I think I owe my taste
for that hillside business rather to the art and interest of
John Todd. He it was that made it live for me, as the
artist can make all things live. It was through him the
simple strategy of massing sheep upon a snowy evening, with its attendant scampering of earnest, shaggy
aides-de-camp, was an affair that I never wearied of
seeing, and that I never weary of recalling to mind: the
shadow of the night darkening on the hills, inscrutable
black blots of snow shower moving here and there like
night already come, huddles of yellow sheep and dart-
ings of black dogs upon the snow, a bitter air that took
you by the throat, unearthly harpings of the wind along
the moors; and for centre piece to all these features and
influences, John winding up the brae, keeping his cap-

tain's eye upon all sides, and breaking, ever and again, into a spasm of bellowing that seemed to make the evening bleaker. It is thus that I still see him in my mind's eye, perched on a hump of the declivity not far from Halkerside, his staff in airy flourish, his great voice taking hold upon the hills and echoing terror to the lowlands; I, meanwhile, standing somewhat back, until the fit should be over, and, with a pinch of snuff, my friend relapse into his easy, even conversation.

VII. THE MANSE

I HAVE named, among many rivers that make music in my memory, that dirty Water of Leith. Often and often I desire to look upon it again; and the choice of a point of view is easy to me. It should be at a certain water-door, embowered in shrubbery. The river is there dammed back for the service of the flour-mill just below, so that it lies deep and darkling, and the sand slopes into brown obscurity with a glint of gold; and it has but newly been recruited by the borrowings of the snuff-mill just above, and these, tumbling merrily in, shake the pool to its black heart, fill it with drowsy eddies, and set the curded froth of many other mills solemnly steering to and fro upon the surface. Or so it was when I was young; for change, and the masons, and the pruning-knife, have been busy; and if I could hope to repeat a cherished experience, it must be on many and impossible conditions. I must choose, as well as the point of view, a certain moment in my growth, so that the scale may be exaggerated, and the trees on the steep opposite side may seem to climb to heaven, and the sand by the water-door, where I am standing, seem as low as Styx. And I must choose the season also, so that the valley may be brimmed like a cup with sunshine and the songs of birds; — and the year of grace, so that when I turn to leave the riverside I may find the old manse and its inhabitants unchanged.

It was a place in that time like no other: the garden cut into provinces by a great hedge of beech, and overlooked by the church and the terrace of the churchyard, where the tombstones were thick, and after nightfall "spunkies" might be seen to dance, at least by children; flower-plots lying warm in sunshine; laurels and the great yew making elsewhere a pleasing horror of shade; the smell of water rising from all round, with an added tang of paper-mills; the sound of water everywhere, and the sound of mills — the wheel and the dam singing their alternate strain; the birds on every bush and from every corner of the overhanging woods pealing out their notes until the air throbbed with them; and in the midst of this, the manse. I see it, by the standard of my childish stature, as a great and roomy house. In truth, it was not so large as I supposed, nor yet so convenient, and, standing where it did, it is difficult to suppose that it was healthful. Yet a large family of stalwart sons and tall daughters was housed and reared, and came to man and womanhood in that nest of little chambers; so that the face of the earth was peppered with the children of the manse, and letters with outlandish stamps became familiar to the local postman, and the walls of the little chambers brightened with the wonders of the East. The dullest could see this was a house that had a pair of hands in divers foreign places: a well-beloved house — its image fondly dwelt on by many travellers.

Here lived an ancestor of mine, who was a herd of

men. I read him, judging with older criticism the report of childish observation, as a man of singular simplicity of nature; unemotional, and hating the display
of what he felt; standing contented on the old ways; a
lover of his life and innocent habits to the end. We
children admired him: partly for his beautiful face and
silver hair, for none more than children are concerned
for beauty and, above all, for beauty in the old; partly
for the solemn light in which we beheld him once a
week, the observed of all observers, in the pulpit. But
his strictness and distance, the effect, I now fancy, of
old age, slow blood, and settled habit, oppressed us
with a kind of terror. When not abroad, he sat much
alone, writing sermons or letters to his scattered family
in a dark and cold room with a library of bloodless books
— or so they seemed in those days, although I have
some of them now on my own shelves and like well
enough to read them; and these lonely hours wrapped
him in the greater gloom for our imaginations. But the
study had a redeeming grace in many Indian pictures,
gaudily coloured and dear to young eyes. I cannot depict (for I have no such passions now) the greed with
which I beheld them; and when I was once sent in to
say a psalm to my grandfather, I went, quaking indeed
with fear, but at the same time glowing with hope that,
if I said it well, he might reward me with an Indian
picture.

> " Thy foot He'll not let slide, nor will
> He slumber that thee keeps,"

it ran: a strange conglomerate of the unpronouncea-
ble, a sad model to set in childhood before one who was

himself to be a versifier, and a task in recitation that really merited reward. And I must suppose the old man thought so too, and was either touched or amused by the performance; for he took me in his arms with most unwonted tenderness, and kissed me, and gave me a little kindly sermon for my psalm; so that, for that day, we were clerk and parson. I was struck by this reception into so tender a surprise that I forgot my disappointment. And indeed the hope was one of those that childhood forges for a pastime, and with no design upon reality. Nothing was more unlikely than that my grandfather should strip himself of one of those pictures, love-gifts and reminders of his absent sons; nothing more unlikely than that he should bestow it upon me. He had no idea of spoiling children, leaving all that to my aunt; he had fared hard himself, and blubbered under the rod in the last century; and his ways were still Spartan for the young. The last word I heard upon his lips was in this Spartan key. He had over-walked in the teeth of an east wind, and was now near the end of his many days. He sat by the dining-room fire, with his white hair, pale face and bloodshot eyes, a somewhat awful figure; and my aunt had given him a dose of our good old Scotch medicine, Dr. Gregory's powder. Now that remedy, as the work of a near kinsman of Rob Roy himself, may have a savour of romance for the imagination; but it comes uncouthly to the palate. The old gentleman had taken it with a wry face; and that being accomplished, sat with perfect simplicity, like a child's, munching a "barley-sugar kiss." But when my aunt, having the canister open in her hands, proposed to let me share in the sweets, he interfered at once. I had had no Gregory; then I should have no barley-sugar kiss: so he decided with a touch of irritation. And just then the phaeton coming opportunely to the kitchen door — for such was our unlordly fashion — I was taken for the last time from the presence of my grandfather.

Now I often wonder what I have inherited from this old minister. I must suppose, indeed, that he was fond of preaching sermons, and so am I, though I never heard it maintained that either of us loved to hear them. He sought health in his youth in the Isle of Wight, and I have sought it in both hemispheres; but whereas he found and kept it, I am still on the quest. He was a great lover of Shakespeare, whom he read aloud, I have been told, with taste; well, I love my Shakespeare also, and am persuaded I can read him well, though I own I never have been told so. He made embroidery, designing his own patterns; and in that kind of work I never made anything but a kettle-holder in Berlin wool, and an odd garter of knitting, which was as black as the chimney before I had done with it. He loved port, and nuts, and porter; and so do I, but they agreed better with my grandfather, which seems to me a breach of contract. He had chalk-stones in his fingers; and these, in good time, I may possibly inherit, but I would much rather have inherited his noble presence. Try as I please, I cannot join myself on with the reverend doctor; and all the while, no doubt, and even as I write the phrase, he moves in my blood, and whispers words to me, and sits efficient in the very knot and centre of my being. In his garden, as I played there, I learned the love of mills—or had I an ancestor a miller?—and a kindness for the neighbourhood of graves, as homely things not without their poetry— or had I an ancestor a sexton? But what of the garden where he played himself?—for that, too, was a scene of my education. Some part of me played there in the eighteenth century, and ran races under the green avenue at Pilrig; some part of me trudged up Leith Walk, which was still a country place, and sat on the High School benches, and was thrashed, perhaps, by Dr. Adam. The house where I spent my youth was not yet thought upon; but we made holiday parties among the cornfields on its site, and ate strawberries and cream near by at a gardener's. All this I had forgotten; only my grandfather remembered and once reminded me. I have forgotten, too, how we grew up, and took orders, and went to our first Ayrshire parish, and fell in love with and married a daughter of Burns's Dr. Smith—"Smith opens out his cauld harangues." I have forgotten, but I was there all the same, and heard stories of Burns at first hand.

And there is a thing stranger than all that; for this *homunculus* or part-man of mine that walked about the eighteenth century with Dr. Balfour in his youth, was in the way of meeting other *homunculos* or part-men, in the persons of my other ancestors. These were of a lower order, and doubtless we looked down upon them duly. But as I went to college with Dr. Balfour, I may have seen the lamp and oil man taking down the shutters from his shop beside the Tron;— we may have had a rabbit-hutch or a bookshelf made for us by a certain carpenter in I know not what wynd of the old, smoky city; or, upon some holiday excursion, we may have looked into the windows of a cottage in a flower-garden and seen a certain weaver plying his shuttle.   And these were all kinsmen of mine upon the other side; and from the eyes of the lamp and oil man one-half of my unborn father, and one-quarter of myself, looked out upon us as we went by to college. Nothing of all this would cross the mind of the young student, as he posted up the Bridges with trim, stockinged legs, in that city of cocked hats and good Scotch still unadulterated.   It would not cross his mind that he should have a daughter; and the lamp and oil man, just then beginning, by a not unnatural metastasis, to bloom into a lighthouse-engineer, should have a grandson; and that these two, in the fulness of time, should wed; and some portion of that student himself should survive yet a year or two longer in the person of their child.

But our ancestral adventures are beyond even the arithmetic of fancy; and it is the chief recommendation of long pedigrees, that we can follow backward the careers of our *homunculi* and be reminded of our antenatal lives.   Our conscious years are but a moment in the history of the elements that build us.   Are you a bank-clerk, and do you live at Peckham?   It was not always so.   And though to-day I am only a man of letters, either tradition errs or I was present when there landed at St. Andrews a French barber-surgeon, to tend the health and the beard of the great Cardinal Beaton; I have shaken a spear in the Debatable Land and shouted the slogan of the Elliots; I was present when a skipper, plying from Dundee, smuggled Jacobites to France after the '15; I was in a West India merchant's office, perhaps next door to Bailie Nichol Jarvie's, and managed the business of a plantation in St. Kitt's; I was with my engineer-grandfather (the son-in-law of the lamp and oil man) when he sailed north about Scotland on the famous cruise that gave us the *Pirate* and the *Lord of the Isles;* I was with him, too, on the Bell Rock, in the fog, when the *Smeaton* had drifted from her moorings, and the Aberdeen men, pick in hand, had seized upon the only boats, and he must stoop and lap sea-water before his tongue could utter audible words; and once more with him when the Bell Rock beacon took a "thrawe," and his workmen fled into the tower, then nearly finished, and he sat unmoved reading in his Bible — or affecting to read — till one after another slunk back with confusion of countenance to their engineer. Yes, parts of me have seen life, and met adventures, and sometimes met them well. And away in the still cloudier past, the threads that make me up can be traced by fancy into the bosoms of thousands and millions of ascendants: Picts who rallied round Macbeth and the old (and highly preferable) system of descent by females, fleërs from before the legions of Agricola, marchers in Pannonian morasses, star-gazers on Chaldæan plateaus; and, furthest of all, what face is this that fancy can see peering through the disparted branches? What sleeper in green tree-tops, what muncher of nuts, concludes my pedigree? Probably arboreal in his habits. . . .

And I know not which is the more strange, that I should carry about with me some fibres of my minister-grandfather; or that in him, as he sat in his cool study, grave, reverend, contented gentleman, there was an aboriginal frisking of the blood that was not his; tree-top memories, like undeveloped negatives, lay dormant in his mind; tree-top instincts awoke and were trod down; and Probably Arboreal (scarce to be distinguished from a monkey) gambolled and chattered in the brain of the old divine.

VIII. MEMOIRS OF AN ISLET

THOSE who try to be artists use, time after time, the matter of their recollections, setting and resetting little coloured memories of men and scenes, rigging up (it may be) some especial friend in the attire of a buccaneer, and decreeing armies to manœuvre, or murder to be done, on the playground of their youth. But the memories are a fairy gift which cannot be worn out in using. After a dozen services in various tales, the little sunbright pictures of the past still shine in the mind's eye with not a lineament defaced, not a tint impaired. *Glück und Unglück wird Gesang*, if Goethe pleases; yet only by endless avatars, the original reembodying after each. So that a writer, in time, begins to wonder at the perdurable life of these impressions; begins, perhaps, to fancy that he wrongs them when he weaves them in with fiction; and looking back on them with ever-growing kindness, puts them at last, substantive jewels, in a setting of their own.

One or two of these pleasant spectres I think I have laid. I used one but the other day: a little eyot of dense, freshwater sand, where I once waded deep in butterburrs, delighting to hear the song of the river on both sides, and to tell myself that I was indeed and at last upon an island. Two of my puppets lay there a summer's day, hearkening to the shearers at work in riverside fields and to the drums of the gray old garrison upon the neighbouring hill. And this was, I think, done rightly: the place was rightly peopled — and now belongs not to me but to my puppets — for a time at least. In time, perhaps, the puppets will grow faint; the original memory swim up instant as ever; and I shall once more lie in bed, and see the little sandy isle in Allan Water as it is in nature, and the child (that once was me) wading there in butterburrs; and wonder at the instancy and virgin freshness of that memory; and be pricked again, in season and out of season, by the desire to weave it into art.

There is another isle in my collection, the memory of which besieges me. I put a whole family there, in one of my tales; and later on, threw upon its shores, and condemned to several days of rain and shellfish on its tumbled boulders, the hero of another. The ink is not yet faded; the sound of the sentences is still in my mind's ear; and I am under a spell to write of that island again.

I

The little isle of Earraid lies close in to the south-west corner of the Ross of Mull: the sound of Iona on one side, across which you may see the isle and church of Columba; the open sea to the other, where you shall be able to mark, on a clear, surfy day, the breakers running white on many sunken rocks. I first saw it, or first remember seeing it, framed in the round bull's-eye of a cabin port, the sea lying smooth along its shores like the waters of a lake, the colourless, clear light of the early morning making plain its heathery and rocky hummocks. There stood upon it, in these days, a single rude house of uncemented stones, approached by a pier of wreckwood. It must have been very early, for it was then summer, and in summer, in that latitude, day scarcely withdraws; but even at that hour the house was making a sweet smoke of peats which came to me over the bay, and the bare-legged daughters of the cotter were wading by the pier. The same day we visited the shores of the isle in the ship's boats; rowed deep into Fiddler's Hole, sounding as we went, and having taken stock of all possible accommodations, pitched on the northern inlet as the scene of operations. For it was no accident that had brought the lighthouse steamer to anchor in the Bay of Earraid. Fifteen miles away to seaward, a certain black rock stood environed by the Atlantic rollers, the outpost of the Torran reefs. Here was a tower to be built, and a star lighted, for the conduct of seamen. But as the rock was small, and hard of access, and far from land, the work would be one of years; and my father was now looking for a shore station, where the stones might be quarried and dressed, the men live, and the tender, with some degree of safety, lie at anchor.

I saw Earraid next from the stern thwart of an Iona lugger, Sam Bough and I sitting there cheek by jowl, with our feet upon our baggage, in a beautiful, clear, northern summer eve. And behold! there was now a pier of stone, there were rows of sheds, railways, travelling-cranes, a street of cottages, an iron house for the resident engineer, wooden bothies for the men, a stage where the courses of the tower were put together experimentally, and behind the settlement a great gash in the hillside where granite was quarried. In the bay, the steamer lay at her moorings. All day long there hung about the place the music of chinking tools; and even in the dead of night, the watchman carried his lantern to and fro in the dark settlement, and could light the pipe of any midnight muser. It was, above all, strange to see Earraid on the Sunday, when the sound of the tools ceased and there fell a crystal quiet. All about the green compound men would be sauntering in their Sunday's best, walking with those lax joints of the reposing toiler, thoughtfully smoking, talking small, as if in honour of the stillness, or hearkening to the wailing of the gulls. And it was strange to see our Sabbath services, held, as they were, in one of the bothies, with Mr. Brebner reading at a table, and the congregation perched about in the double tier of sleeping bunks; and to hear the singing of the psalms, "the chapters," the inevitable Spurgeon's sermon, and the old, eloquent lighthouse prayer.

In fine weather, when by the spy-glass on the hill the sea was observed to run low upon the reef, there would be a sound of preparation in the very early morning; and before the sun had risen from behind Ben More, the tender would steam out of the bay. Over fifteen sea-miles of the great blue Atlantic rollers she ploughed her way, trailing at her tail a brace of wallowing stone-lighters. The open ocean widened upon either board, and the hills of the mainland began to go down on the horizon, before she came to her unhomely destination, and lay-to at last where the rock clapped its

black head above the swell, with the tall iron barrack
on its spider legs, and the truncated tower, and the
cranes waving their arms, and the smoke of the engine-
fire rising in the mid-sea. An ugly reef is this of the
Dhu Heartach; no pleasant assemblage of shelves, and
pools, and creeks, about which a child might play for a
whole summer without weariness, like the Bell Rock
or the Skerryvore, but one oval nodule of black-trap,
sparsely bedabbled with an inconspicuous fucus, and
alive in every crevice with a dingy insect between a
slater and a bug. No other life was there but that of
sea-birds, and of the sea itself, that here ran like a mill-
race, and growled about the outer reef for ever, and
ever and again, in the calmest weather, roared and
spouted on the rock itself. Times were different upon
Dhu Heartach when it blew, and the night fell dark, and
the neighbour lights of Skerryvore and Rhu-val were
quenched in fog, and the men sat prisoned high up in
their iron drum, that then resounded with the lashing of
the sprays. Fear sat with them in their sea-beleaguered
dwelling; and the colour changed in anxious faces when
some greater billow struck the barrack, and its pillars
quivered and sprang under the blow. It was then that
the foreman builder, Mr. Goodwillie, whom I see before
me still in his rock-habit of undecipherable rags, would
get his fiddle down and strike up human minstrelsy
amid the music of the storm. But it was in sunshine
only that I saw Dhu-Heartach; and it was in sunshine,
or the yet lovelier summer afterglow, that the steamer
would return to Earraid, ploughing an enchanted sea;
the obedient lighters, relieved of their deck cargo, riding in her wake more quietly; and the steersman upon

each, as she rose on the long swell, standing tall and dark against the shining west.

II

But it was in Earraid itself that I delighted chiefly. The lighthouse settlement scarce encroached beyond its fences; over the top of the first brae the ground was all virgin, the world all shut out, the face of things unchanged by any of man's doings.   Here was no living presence, save for the limpets on the rocks, for some old, gray, rain-beaten ram that I might rouse out of a ferny den betwixt two boulders, or for the haunting and the piping of the gulls.   It was older than man; it was found so by incoming Celts, and seafaring Norsemen, and Columba's priests.   The earthy savour of the bog plants, the rude disorder of the boulders, the inimitable seaside brightness of the air, the brine and the iodine, the lap of the billows among the weedy reefs, the sudden springing up of a great run of dashing surf along the sea-front of the isle, all that I saw and felt my predecessors must have seen and felt with scarce a difference.   I steeped myself in open air and in past ages.

> " Delightful would it be to me to be in *Uchd Ailiun*
>   On the pinnacle of a rock,
> That I might often see
>   The face of the ocean;
> That I might hear the song of the wonderful birds,
>   Source of happiness;
> That I might hear the thunder of the crowding waves
>   Upon the rocks:
> At times at work without compulsion—
>   This would be delightful;
> At times plucking dulse from the rocks;
>   At times at fishing."

So, about the next island of Iona, sang Columba himself twelve hundred years before. And so might I have sung of Earraid.

And all the while I was aware that this life of seabathing and sun-burning was for me but a holiday. In that year cannon were roaring for days together on French battlefields; and I would sit in my isle (I call it mine, after the use of lovers) and think upon the war, and the loudness of these far-away battles, and the pain of the men's wounds, and the weariness of their marching. And I would think too of that other war which is as old as mankind, and is indeed the life of man: the unsparing war, the grinding slavery of competition; the toil of seventy years, dear-bought bread, precarious honour, the perils and pitfalls, and the poor rewards. It was a long look forward; the future summoned me as with trumpet calls, it warned me back as with a voice of weeping and beseeching; and I thrilled and trembled on the brink of life, like a childish bather on the beach.

There was another young man on Earraid in these days, and we were much together, bathing, clambering on the boulders, trying to sail a boat and spinning round instead in the oily whirlpools of the roost. But the most part of the time we spoke of the great uncharted desert of our futures; wondering together what should there befall us; hearing with surprise the sound of our own voices in the empty vestibule of youth. As far, and as hard, as it seemed then to look forward to the grave, so far it seems now to look backward upon these emotions; so hard to recall justly that loath submission, as of the sacrificial bull, with which we stooped our necks under the yoke of destiny. I met my old companion but the

other day; I cannot tell of course what he was thinking; but, upon my part, I was wondering to see us both
so much at home, and so composed and sedentary in
the world; and how much we had gained, and how
much we had lost, to attain to that composure; and
which had been upon the whole our best estate: when
we sat there prating sensibly like men of some experience, or when we shared our timorous and hopeful
counsels in a western islet.

IX. THOMAS STEVENSON

CIVIL ENGINEER

THE death of Thomas Stevenson will mean not very much to the general reader. His service to mankind took on forms of which the public knows little and understands less. He came seldom to London, and then only as a task, remaining always a stranger and a convinced provincial; putting up for years at the same hotel where his father had gone before him; faithful for long to the same restaurant, the same church, and the same theatre, chosen simply for propinquity; steadfastly refusing to dine out. He had a circle of his own, indeed, at home; few men were more beloved in Edinburgh, where he breathed an air that pleased him; and wherever he went, in railway carriages or hotel smoking-rooms, his strange, humorous vein of talk, and his transparent honesty, raised him up friends and admirers. But to the general public and the world of London, except about the parliamentary committee-rooms, he remained unknown. All the time, his lights were in every part of the world, guiding the mariner; his firm were consulting engineers to the Indian, the New Zealand, and the Japanese Lighthouse Boards, so that Edinburgh was a world centre for that branch of applied science; in Germany, he had been called "the Nestor of lighthouse illumination;" even in France, where his claims were long denied, he was at last, on the occasion of the late Exposition, recognised and medalled. And to show by one instance the inverted nature of his reputation, comparatively small at home, yet filling the world, a friend of mine was this winter on a visit to the Spanish main, and was asked by a Peruvian if he "knew Mr. Stevenson the author, because his works were much esteemed in Peru?" My friend supposed the reference was to the writer of tales; but the Peruvian had never heard of *Dr. Jekyll;* what he had in his eye, what was esteemed in Peru, were the volumes of the engineer.

Thomas Stevenson was born at Edinburgh in the year 1818, the grandson of Thomas Smith, first engineer to the Board of Northern Lights, son of Robert Stevenson, brother of Alan and David; so that his nephew, David Alan Stevenson, joined with him at the time of his death in the engineership, is the sixth of the family who has held, successively or conjointly, that office. The Bell Rock, his father's great triumph, was finished before he was born; but he served under his brother Alan in the building of Skerryvore, the noblest of all extant deep-sea lights; and, in conjunction with his Brother David, he added two — the Chickens and Dhu Heartach — to that small number of man's extreme outposts in the ocean. Of shore lights, the two brothers last named erected no fewer than twenty-seven; of beacons,[1] about twenty-five. Many harbours were successfully carried out: one, the harbour of Wick, the chief disaster of my

[1] In Dr. Murray's admirable new dictionary, I have remarked a flaw *sub voce* Beacon. In its express, technical sense, a beacon may be defined as "a founded, artificial sea-mark, not lighted."

father's life, was a failure; the sea proved too strong for man's arts; and after expedients hitherto unthought of, and on a scale hyper-cyclopean, the work must be deserted, and now stands a ruin in that bleak, God-forsaken bay, ten miles from John-o'-Groat's. In the improvement of rivers the brothers were likewise in a large way of practice over both England and Scotland, nor had any British engineer anything approaching their experience.

It was about this nucleus of his professional labours that all my father's scientific inquiries and inventions centred; these proceeded from, and acted back upon, his daily business. Thus it was as a harbour engineer that he became interested in the propagation and reduction of waves; a difficult subject in regard to which he has left behind him much suggestive matter and some valuable approximate results. Storms were his sworn adversaries, and it was through the study of storms that he approached that of meteorology at large. Many who knew him not otherwise, knew — perhaps have in their gardens — his louvre-boarded screen for instruments. But the great achievement of his life was, of course, in optics as applied to lighthouse illumination. Fresnel had done much; Fresnel had settled the fixed light apparatus on a principle that still seems unimprovable; and when Thomas Stevenson stepped in and brought to a comparable perfection the revolving light, a not unnatural jealousy and much painful controversy rose in France. It had its hour; and, as I have told already, even in France it has blown by. Had it not, it would have mattered the less, since all through his life my father continued to justify his claim by fresh advances.

New apparatus for lights in new situations was continually being designed with the same unwearied search after perfection, the same nice ingenuity of means; and though the holophotal revolving light perhaps still remains his most elegant contrivance, it is difficult to give it the palm over the much later condensing system, with its thousand possible modifications. The number and the value of these improvements entitle their author to the name of one of mankind's benefactors. In all parts of the world a safer landfall awaits the mariner. Two things must be said: and, first, that Thomas Stevenson was no mathematician. Natural shrewdness, a sentiment of optical laws, and a great intensity of consideration led him to just conclusions; but to calculate the necessary formulæ for the instruments he had conceived was often beyond him, and he must fall back on the help of others, notably on that of his cousin and lifelong intimate friend, *emeritus* Professor Swan, of St. Andrews, and his later friend, Professor P. G. Tait. It is a curious enough circumstance, and a great encouragement to others, that a man so ill equipped should have succeeded in one of the most abstract and arduous walks of applied science. The second remark is one that applies to the whole family, and only particularly to Thomas Stevenson from the great number and importance of his inventions: holding as the Stevensons did a Government appointment, they regarded their original work as something due already to the nation, and none of them has ever taken out a patent. It is another cause of the comparative obscurity of the name: for a patent not only brings in money, it infallibly spreads reputation; and my father's instruments enter anonymously into a hundred light-rooms, and are passed anonymously over in a hundred reports, where the least considerable patent would stand out and tell its author's story.

But the life-work of Thomas Stevenson remains; what we have lost, what we now rather try to recall, is the friend and companion. He was a man of a somewhat antique strain: with a blended sternness and softness that was wholly Scottish and at first somewhat bewildering; with a profound essential melancholy of disposition and (what often accompanies it) the most humorous geniality in company; shrewd and childish; passionately attached, passionately prejudiced; a man of many extremes, many faults of temper, and no very stable foothold for himself among life's troubles. Yet he was a wise adviser; many men, and these not inconsiderable, took counsel with him habitually. "I sat at his feet," writes one of these, "when I asked his advice, and when the broad brow was set in thought and the firm mouth said his say, I always knew that no man could add to the worth of the conclusion." He had excellent taste, though whimsical and partial; collected old furniture and delighted specially in sunflowers long before the days of Mr. Wilde; took a lasting pleasure in prints and pictures; was a devout admirer of Thomson of Duddingston at a time when few shared the taste; and though he read little, was constant to his favourite books. He had never any Greek; Latin he happily re-taught himself after he had left school, where he was a mere consistent idler: happily, I say, for Lactantius, Vossius, and Cardinal Bona were his chief authors. The first he must have read for twenty years uninterruptedly, keeping it near him in his study, and carrying it in his bag

on journeys. Another old theologian, Brown of Wam-
phray, was often in his hands. When he was indis-
posed, he had two books, *Guy Mannering* and *The
Parent's Assistant*, of which he never wearied. He was
a strong Conservative, or, as he preferred to call himself,
a Tory; except in so far as his views were modified by
a hot-headed chivalrous sentiment for women. He was
actually in favour of a marriage law under which any
woman might have a divorce for the asking, and no
man on any ground whatever; and the same sentiment
found another expression in a Magdalen Mission in
Edinburgh, founded and largely supported by himself.
This was but one of the many channels of his public
generosity; his private was equally unstrained. The
Church of Scotland, of which he held the doctrines
(though in a sense of his own) and to which he bore
a clansman's loyalty, profited often by his time and
money; and though, from a morbid sense of his own
unworthiness, he would never consent to be an office-
bearer, his advice was often sought, and he served the
Church on many committees. What he perhaps valued
highest in his work were his contributions to the defence of Christianity; one of which, in particular, was
praised by Hutchinson Stirling and reprinted at the re-
quest of Professor Crawford.

His sense of his own unworthiness I have called morbid; morbid, too, were his sense of the fleetingness of
life and his concern for death. He had never accepted
the conditions of man's life or his own character; and
his inmost thoughts were ever tinged with the Celtic
melancholy. Cases of conscience were sometimes griev-
ous to him, and that delicate employment of a scien-

tific witness cost him many qualms. But he found respite from these troublesome humours in his work, in his lifelong study of natural science, in the society of those he loved, and in his daily walks, which now would carry him far into the country with some congenial friend, and now keep him dangling about the town from one old book-shop to another, and scraping romantic acquaintance with every dog that passed. His talk, compounded of so much sterling sense and so much freakish humour, and clothed in language so apt, droll, and emphatic, was a perpetual delight to all who knew him before the clouds began to settle on his mind. His use of language was both just and picturesque; and when at the beginning of his illness he began to feel the ebbing of this power, it was strange and painful to hear him reject one word after another as inadequate, and at length desist from the search and leave his phrase unfinished rather than finish it without propriety. It was perhaps another Celtic trait that his affections and emotions, passionate as these were, and liable to passionate ups and downs, found the most eloquent expression both in words and gestures. Love, anger, and indignation shone through him and broke forth in imagery, like what we read of Southern races. For all these emotional extremes, and in spite of the melancholy ground of his character, he had upon the whole a happy life; nor was he less fortunate in his death, which at the last came to him unaware.

X. TALK AND TALKERS

"Sir, we had a good talk."— JOHNSON.

"As we must account for every idle word, so we must for every idle silence."— FRANKLIN.

I

THERE can be no fairer ambition than to excel in talk; to be affable, gay, ready, clear and welcome; to have a fact, a thought, or an illustration, pat to every subject; and not only to cheer the flight of time among our intimates, but bear our part in that great international congress, always sitting, where public wrongs are first declared, public errors first corrected, and the course of public opinion shaped, day by day, a little nearer to the right. No measure comes before Parliament but it has been long ago prepared by the grand jury of the talkers; no book is written that has not been largely composed by their assistance. Literature in many of its branches is no other than the shadow of good talk; but the imitation falls far short of the original in life, freedom and effect. There are always two to a talk, giving and taking, comparing experience and according conclusions. Talk is fluid, tentative, continually "in further search and progress;" while written words remain fixed, become idols even to the writer, found wooden dogmatisms, and preserve flies of obvious error

in the amber of the truth. Last and chief, while literature, gagged with linsey-woolsey, can only deal with a
fraction of the life of man, talk goes fancy free and may
call a spade a spade. Talk has none of the freezing immunities of the pulpit. It cannot, even if it would, become merely æsthetic or merely classical like literature.
A jest intervenes, the solemn humbug is dissolved in
laughter, and speech runs forth out of the contemporary
groove into the open fields of nature, cheery and cheer-
ing, like schoolboys out of school. And it is in talk
alone that we can learn our period and ourselves. In
short, the first duty of a man is to speak; that is his
chief business in this world; and talk, which is the harmonious speech of two or more, is by far the most accessible of pleasures. It costs nothing in money; it is
all profit; it completes our education, founds and fosters
our friendships, and can be enjoyed at any age and in
almost any state of health.

The spice of life is battle; the friendliest relations are
still a kind of contest; and if we would not forego all
that is valuable in our lot, we must continually face some
other person, eye to eye, and wrestle a fall whether in
love or enmity. It is still by force of body, or power of
character or intellect, that we attain to worthy pleasures.
Men and women contend for each other in the lists of
love, like rival mesmerists; the active and adroit decide
their challenges in the sports of the body; and the sedentary sit down to chess or conversation. All sluggish
and pacific pleasures are, to the same degree, solitary
and selfish; and every durable bond between human
beings is founded in or heightened by some element of
competition. Now, the relation that has the least root

in matter is undoubtedly that airy one of friendship; and hence, I suppose, it is that good talk most commonly arises among friends. Talk is, indeed, both the scene and instrument of friendship. It is in talk alone that the friends can measure strength, and enjoy that amicable counter-assertion of personality which is the gauge of relations and the sport of life.

A good talk is not to be had for the asking. Humours must first be accorded in a kind of overture or prologue; hour, company and circumstance be suited; and then, at a fit juncture, the subject, the quarry of two heated minds, spring up like a deer out of the wood. Not that the talker has any of the hunter's pride, though he has all and more than all his ardour. The genuine artist follows the stream of conversation as an angler follows the windings of a brook, not dallying where he fails to "kill." He trusts implicitly to hazard; and he is rewarded by continual variety, continual pleasure, and those changing prospects of the truth that are the best of education. There is nothing in a subject, so called, that we should regard it as an idol, or follow it beyond the promptings of desire. Indeed, there are few subjects; and so far as they are truly talkable, more than the half of them may be reduced to three: that I am I, that you are you, and that there are other people dimly understood to be not quite the same as either. Wherever talk may range, it still runs half the time on these eternal lines. The theme being set, each plays on himself as on an instrument; asserts and justifies himself; ransacks his brain for instances and opinions, and brings them forth new-minted, to his own surprise and the admiration of his adversary. All natural talk is a festival of ostentation; and by the laws of the game each accepts and fans the vanity of the other. It is from that reason that we venture to lay ourselves so open, that we dare to be so warmly eloquent, and that we swell in each other's eyes to such a vast proportion. For talkers, once launched, begin to overflow the limits of their ordinary selves, tower up to the height of their secret pretensions, and give themselves out for the heroes, brave, pious, musical and wise, that in their most shining moments they aspire to be. So they weave for themselves with words and for a while inhabit a palace of delights, temple at once and theatre, where they fill the round of the world's dignities, and feast with the gods, exulting in Kudos. And when the talk is over, each goes his way, still flushed with vanity and admiration, still trailing clouds of glory; each declines from the height of his ideal orgie, not in a moment, but by slow declension. I remember, in the *entr'acte* of an afternoon performance, coming forth into the sunshine, in a beautiful green, gardened corner of a romantic city; and as I sat and smoked, the music moving in my blood, I seemed to sit there and evaporate *The Flying Dutchman* (for it was that I had been hearing) with a wonderful sense of life, warmth, well-being and pride; and the noises of the city, voices, bells and marching feet, fell together in my ears like a symphonious orchestra. In the same way, the excitement of a good talk lives for a long while after in the blood, the heart still hot within you, the brain still simmering, and the physical earth swimming around you with the colours of the sunset.

Natural talk, like ploughing, should turn up a large

surface of life, rather than dig mines into geological strata. Masses of experience, anecdote, incident, cross-lights, quotation, historical instances, the whole flotsam and jetsam of two minds forced in and in upon the matter in hand from every point of the compass, and from every degree of mental elevation and abasement — these are the material with which talk is fortified, the food on which the talkers thrive. Such argument as is proper to the exercise should still be brief and seizing. Talk should proceed by instances; by the apposite, not the expository. It should keep close along the lines of humanity, near the bosoms and businesses of men, at the level where history, fiction and experience intersect and illuminate each other. I am I, and You are You, with all my heart; but conceive how these lean proposi-tions change and brighten when, instead of words, the actual you and I sit cheek by jowl, the spirit housed in the live body, and the very clothes uttering voices to corroborate the story in the face. Not less surprising is the change when we leave off to speak of generalities — the bad, the good, the miser, and all the characters of Theophrastus — and call up other men, by anecdote or instance, in their very trick and feature; or trading on a common knowledge, toss each other famous names, still glowing with the hues of life. Communication is no longer by words, but by the instancing of whole biographies, epics, systems of philosophy, and epochs of history, in bulk. That which is understood excels that which is spoken in quantity and quality alike; ideas thus figured and personified, change hands, as we may say, like coin; and the speakers imply without effort the most obscure and intricate thoughts. Strangers who have a large common ground of reading will, for this reason, come the sooner to the grapple of genuine converse. If they know Othello and Napoleon, Consuelo and Clarissa Harlowe, Vautrin and Steenie Steenson, they can leave generalities and begin at once to speak by figures.

Conduct and art are the two subjects that arise most frequently and that embrace the widest range of facts. A few pleasures bear discussion for their own sake, but only those which are most social or most radically human; and even these can only be discussed among their devotees. A technicality is always welcome to the expert, whether in athletics, art or law; I have heard the best kind of talk on technicalities from such rare and happy persons as both know and love their business. No human being ever spoke of scenery for above two minutes at a time, which makes me suspect we hear too much of it in literature. The weather is regarded as the very nadir and scoff of conversational topics. And yet the weather, the dramatic element in scenery, is far more tractable in language, and far more human both in import and suggestion than the stable features of the landscape. Sailors and shepherds, and the people generally of coast and mountain, talk well of it; and it is often excitingly presented in literature. But the tendency of all living talk draws it back and back into the common focus of humanity. Talk is a creature of the street and market-place, feeding on gossip; and its last resort is still in a discussion on morals. That is the heroic form of gossip; heroic in virtue of its high pretensions; but still gossip, because it turns on personalities. You can keep no men long, nor Scotchmen at all, off moral or theological discussion. These are to all the world what law is to lawyers; they are everybody's technicalities; the medium through which all consider life, and the dialect in which they express their judgments. I knew three young men who walked together daily for some two months in a solemn and beautiful forest and in cloudless summer weather; daily they talked with unabated zest, and yet scarce wandered that whole time beyond two subjects — theology and love. And perhaps neither a court of love nor an assembly of divines would have granted their premises or welcomed their conclusions.

Conclusions, indeed, are not often reached by talk any more than by private thinking. That is not the profit. The profit is in the exercise, and above all in the experience; for when we reason at large on any subject, we review our state and history in life. From time to time, however, and specially, I think, in talking art, talk becomes effective, conquering like war, widening the boundaries of knowledge like an exploration. A point arises; the question takes a problematical, a baffling, yet a likely air; the talkers begin to feel lively presentiments of some conclusion near at hand; towards this they strive with emulous ardour, each by his own path, and struggling for first utterance; and then one leaps upon the summit of that matter with a shout, and almost at the same moment the other is beside him; and behold they are agreed. Like enough, the progress is illusory, a mere cat's cradle having been wound and unwound out of words. But the sense of joint discovery is none the less giddy and inspiriting. And in the life of the talker such triumphs, though imaginary, are neither few nor far apart; they are attained with speed and pleasure, in the hour of mirth; and by the nature of the process, they are always worthily shared.

There is a certain attitude, combative at once and deferential, eager to fight yet most averse to quarrel, which marks out at once the talkable man. It is not eloquence, not fairness, not obstinacy, but a certain proportion of all of these that I love to encounter in my amicable adversaries. They must not be pontiffs holding doctrine, but huntsmen questing after elements of truth. Neither must they be boys to be instructed, but fellow-teachers with whom I may wrangle and agree on equal terms. We must reach some solution, some shadow of consent; for without that, eager talk becomes a torture. But we do not wish to reach it cheaply, or quickly, or without the tussle and effort wherein pleasure lies.

The very best talker, with me, is one whom I shall call Spring-Heel'd Jack. I say so, because I never knew any one who mingled so largely the possible ingredients of converse. In the Spanish proverb, the fourth man necessary to compound a salad, is a madman to mix it: Jack is that madman. I know not which is more remarkable; the insane lucidity of his conclusions, the humorous eloquence of his language, or his power of method, bringing the whole of life into the focus of the subject treated, mixing the conversational salad like a drunken god. He doubles like the serpent, changes and flashes like the shaken kaleidoscope, transmigrates bodily into the views of others, and so, in the twinkling of an eye and with a heady rapture, turns questions inside out and flings them empty before you on the ground, like a triumphant conjuror. It is my common practice when a piece of conduct puzzles me, to attack it in the presence of Jack with such grossness, such partiality and such wearing iteration, as at length shall spur him up in its defence. In a moment he transmigrates, dons the required character, and with moonstruck philosophy justifies the act in question. I can fancy nothing to compare with the *vim* of these impersonations, the strange scale of language, flying from Shakespeare to Kant, and from Kant to Major Dyngwell —

> " As fast as a musician scatters sounds
> Out of an instrument — "

the sudden, sweeping generalisations, the absurd irrelevant particularities, the wit, wisdom, folly, humour, eloquence and bathos, each startling in its kind, and yet all luminous in the admired disorder of their combination. A talker of a different calibre, though belonging to the same school, is Burly. Burly is a man of a great presence; he commands a larger atmosphere, gives the impression of a grosser mass of character than most men. It has been said of him that his presence could be felt in a room you entered blindfold; and the same, I think, has been said of other powerful constitutions condemned to much physical inaction, There is something boisterous and piratic in Burly's manner of talk which suits well enough with this impression. He will roar you down, he will bury his face in his hands, he will undergo passions of revolt and agony; and meanwhile his attitude of mind is really both conciliatory and receptive; and after Pistol has been out-Pistol'd, and the welkin rung for hours, you begin to perceive a certain subsidence in

273

these spring torrents, points of agreement issue, and you end arm-in-arm, and in a glow of mutual admiration. The outcry only serves to make your final union the more unexpected and precious. Throughout there has been perfect sincerity, perfect intelligence, a desire to hear although not always to listen, and an unaffected eagerness to meet concessions. You have, with Burly, none of the dangers that attend debate with Spring-Heel'd Jack; who may at any moment turn his powers of transmigration on yourself, create for you a view you never held, and then furiously fall on you for holding it. These, at least, are my two favourites, and both are loud, copious, intolerant talkers. This argues that I myself am in the same category; for if we love talking at all, we love a bright, fierce adversary, who will hold his ground, foot by foot, in much our own manner, sell his attention dearly, and give us our full measure of the dust and exertion of battle. Both these men can be beat from a position, but it takes six hours to do it; a high and hard adventure, worth attempting. With both you can pass days in an enchanted country of the mind, with people, scenery and manners of its own; live a life apart, more arduous, active and glowing than any real existence; and come forth again when the talk is over, as out of a theatre or a dream, to find the east wind still blowing and the chimney-pots of the old battered city still around you. Jack has the far finer mind, Burly the far more honest; Jack gives us the animated poetry, Burly the romantic prose, of similar themes; the one glances high like a meteor and makes a light in darkness; the other, with many changing hues of fire, burns at the sea-level, like a conflagration;

but both have the same humour and artistic interests,
the same unquenched ardour in pursuit, the same gusts
of talk and thunderclaps of contradiction.

Cockshot[1] is a different article, but vastly entertaining, and has been meat and drink to me for many a long
evening. His manner is dry, brisk and pertinacious,
and the choice of words not much. The point about
him is his extraordinary readiness and spirit. You can
propound nothing but he has either a theory about it
ready-made, or will have one instantly on the stocks,
and proceed to lay its timbers and launch it in your
presence. "Let me see," he will say. "Give me a
moment. I *should* have some theory for that." A
blither spectacle than the vigour with which he sets
about the task, it were hard to fancy. He is possessed
by a demoniac energy, welding the elements for his
life, and bending ideas, as an athlete bends a horseshoe,
with a visible and lively effort. He has, in theorising,
a compass, an art; what I would call the synthetic
gusto; something of a Herbert Spencer, who should
see the fun of the thing. You are not bound, and no
more is he, to place your faith in these brand-new opinions. But some of them are right enough, durable even
for life; and the poorest serve for a cock-shy—as when
idle people, after picnics, float a bottle on a pond and
have an hour's diversion ere it sinks. Whichever they
are, serious opinions or humours of the moment, he
still defends his ventures with indefatigable wit and
spirit, hitting savagely himself, but taking punishment
like a man. He knows and never forgets that people
talk, first of all, for the sake of talking; conducts him-

1 The late Fleeming Jenkin.

self in the ring, to use the old slang, like a thorough
"glutton," and honestly enjoys a telling facer from his
adversary. Cockshot is bottled effervescency, the sworn
foe of sleep. Three-in-the-morning Cockshot, says a
victim. His talk is like the driest of all imaginable dry
champagnes. Sleight of hand and inimitable quickness
are the qualities by which he lives. Athelred, on the
other hand, presents you with the spectacle of a sincere and somewhat slow nature thinking aloud. He is
the most unready man I ever knew to shine in conversation. You may see him sometimes wrestle with a
refractory jest for a minute or two together, and perhaps fail to throw it in the end. And there is something singularly engaging, often instructive, in the
simplicity with which he thus exposes the process as
well as the result, the works as well as the dial of the
clock. Withal he has his hours of inspiration. Apt
words come to him as if by accident, and, coming from
deeper down, they smack the more personally, they
have the more of fine old crusted humanity, rich in
sediment and humour. There are sayings of his in
which he has stamped himself into the very grain of
the language; you would think he must have worn the
words next his skin and slept with them. Yet it is not
as a sayer of particular good things that Athelred is
most to be regarded, rather as the stalwart woodman
of thought. I have pulled on a light cord often enough,
while he has been wielding the broad-axe; and between
us, on this unequal division, many a specious fallacy
has fallen. I have known him to battle the same question night after night for years, keeping it in the reign
of talk, constantly applying it and re-applying it to life

with humorous or grave intention, and all the while, never hurrying, nor flagging, nor taking an unfair advantage of the facts. Jack at a given moment, when arising, as it were, from the tripod, can be more radiantly just to those from whom he differs; but then the tenor of his thoughts is even calumnious; while Athelred, slower to forge excuses, is yet slower to condemn, and sits over the welter of the world, vacillating but still judicial, and still faithfully contending with his doubts.

Both the last talkers deal much in points of conduct and religion studied in the "dry light" of prose. Indirectly and as if against his will the same elements from time to time appear in the troubled and poetic talk of Opalstein. His various and exotic knowledge, complete although unready sympathies, and fine, full, discriminative flow of language, fit him out to be the best of talkers; so perhaps he is with some, not *quite* with me—*proxime accessit*, I should say. He sings the praises of the earth and the arts, flowers and jewels, wine and music, in a moonlight, serenading manner, as to the light guitar; even wisdom comes from his tongue like singing; no one is, indeed, more tuneful in the upper notes. But even while he sings the song of the Sirens, he still hearkens to the barking of the Sphinx. Jarring Byronic notes interrupt the flow of his Horatian humours. His mirth has something of the tragedy of the world for its perpetual background; and he feasts like Don Giovanni to a double orchestra, one lightly sounding for the dance, one pealing Beethoven in the distance. He is not truly reconciled either with life or with himself; and this instant war in his members sometimes divides the man's attention. He does not always, perhaps not often, frankly surrender himself in conversation. He brings into the talk other thoughts than those which he expresses; you are conscious that he keeps an eye on something else, that he does not shake off the world, nor quite forget himself. Hence arise occasional disappointments; even an occasional unfairness for his companions, who find themselves one day giving too much, and the next, when they are wary out of season, giving perhaps too little. Purcel is in another class from any I have mentioned. He is no debater, but appears in conversation, as occasion rises, in two distinct characters, one of which I admire and fear, and the other love. In the first, he is radiantly civil and rather silent, sits on a high, courtly hilltop, and from that vantage-ground drops you his remarks like favours. He seems not to share in our sublunary contentions; he wears no sign of interest; when on a sudden there falls in a crystal of wit, so polished that the dull do not perceive it, but so right that the sensitive are silenced. True talk should have more body and blood, should be louder, vainer and more declaratory of the man; the true talker should not hold so steady an advantage over whom he speaks with; and that is one reason out of a score why I prefer my Purcel in his second character, when he unbends into a strain of graceful gossip, singing like the fireside kettle. In these moods he has an elegant homeliness that rings of the true Queen Anne. I know another person who attains, in his moments, to the insolence of a Restoration comedy, speaking, I declare, as Congreve wrote; but that is a sport of nature, and scarce falls under the rubric, for there is none, alas! to give him answer.

One last remark occurs: It is the mark of genuine conversation that the sayings can scarce be quoted with their full effect beyond the circle of common friends. To have their proper weight they should appear in a biography, and with the portrait of the speaker. Good talk is dramatic; it is like an impromptu piece of acting where each should represent himself to the greatest advantage; and that is the best kind of talk where each speaker is most fully and candidly himself, and where, if you were to shift the speeches round from one to another, there would be the greatest loss in significance and perspicuity. It is for this reason that talk depends so wholly on our company. We should like to introduce Falstaff and Mercutio, or Falstaff and Sir Toby; but Falstaff in talk with Cordelia seems even painful. Most of us, by the Protean quality of man, can talk to some degree with all; but the true talk, that strikes out all the slumbering best of us, comes only with the peculiar brethren of our spirits, is founded as deep as love in the constitution of our being, and is a thing to relish with all our energy, while yet we have it, and to be grateful for for ever.

XI. TALK AND TALKERS[1]

II

IN the last paper there was perhaps too much about
mere debate; and there was nothing said at all about
that kind of talk which is merely luminous and restful,
a higher power of silence, the quiet of the evening shared
by ruminating friends. There is something, aside from
personal preference, to be alleged in support of this
omission. Those who are no chimney-cornerers, who
rejoice in the social thunderstorm, have a ground in
reason for their choice. They get little rest indeed; but
restfulness is a quality for cattle; the virtues are all active, life is alert, and it is in repose that men prepare
themselves for evil. On the other hand, they are
bruised into a knowledge of themselves and others;
they have in a high degree the fencer's pleasure in dexterity displayed and proved; what they get they get
upon life's terms, paying for it as they go; and once the
talk is launched, they are assured of honest dealing from
an adversary eager like themselves. The aboriginal
man within us, the cave-dweller, still lusty as when he
fought tooth and nail for roots and berries, scents this
kind of equal battle from afar; it is like his old primæval
days upon the crags, a return to the sincerity of savage

1 This sequel was called forth by an excellent article in *The Spectator*.

life from the comfortable fictions of the civilised. And if it be delightful to the Old Man, it is none the less profitable to his younger brother, the conscientious gentleman. I feel never quite sure of your urbane and smiling coteries; I fear they indulge a man's vanities in silence, suffer him to encroach, encourage him on to be an ass, and send him forth again, not merely contemned for the moment, but radically more contemptible than when he entered. But if I have a flushed, blustering fellow for my opposite, bent on carrying a point, my vanity is sure to have its ears rubbed, once at least, in the course of the debate. He will not spare me when we differ; he will not fear to demonstrate my folly to my face.

For many natures there is not much charm in the still, chambered society, the circle of bland countenances, the digestive silence, the admired remark, the flutter of affectionate approval. They demand more atmosphere and exercise; "a gale upon their spirits," as our pious ancestors would phrase it; to have their wits well breathed in an uproarious Valhalla. And I suspect that the choice, given their character and faults, is one to be defended. The purely wise are silenced by facts; they talk in a clear atmosphere, problems lying around them like a view in nature; if they can be shown to be somewhat in the wrong, they digest the reproof like a thrashing, and make better intellectual blood. They stand corrected by a whisper; a word or a glance reminds them of the great eternal law. But it is not so with all. Others in conversation seek rather contact with their fellow-men than increase of knowledge or clarity of thought. The drama, not the philosophy, of life is the sphere of their intellectual activity. Even when they pursue truth, they desire as much as possible of what we may call human scenery along the road they follow. They dwell in the heart of life; the blood sounding in their ears, their eyes laying hold of what delights them with a brutal avidity that makes them blind to all besides, their interest riveted on people, living, loving, talking, tangible people. To a man of this description, the sphere of argument seems very pale and ghostly. By a strong expression, a perturbed countenance, floods of tears, an insult which his conscience obliges him to swallow, he is brought round to knowledge which no syllogism would have conveyed to him. His own experience is so vivid, he is so superlatively conscious of himself, that if, day after day, he is allowed to hector and hear nothing but approving echoes, he will lose his hold on the soberness of things and take himself in earnest for a god. Talk might be to such an one the very way of moral ruin; the school where he might learn to be at once intolerable and ridiculous.

This character is perhaps commoner than philosophers suppose. And for persons of that stamp to learn much by conversation, they must speak with their superiors, not in intellect, for that is a superiority that must be proved, but in station. If they cannot find a friend to bully them for their good, they must find either an old man, a woman, or some one so far below them in the artificial order of society, that courtesy may be particularly exercised.

The best teachers are the aged. To the old our mouths are always partly closed; we must swallow our obvious retorts and listen. They sit above our heads,

on life's raised daïs, and appeal at once to our respect
and pity. A flavour of the old school, a touch of something different in their manner — which is freer and
rounder, if they come of what is called a good family,
and often more timid and precise if they are of the middle class — serves, in these days, to accentuate the difference of age and add a distinction to gray hairs. But
their superiority is founded more deeply than by outward marks or gestures. They are before us in the
march of man; they have more or less solved the irking
problem; they have battled through the equinox of life;
in good and evil they have held their course; and now,
without open shame, they near the crown and harbour.
It may be we have been struck with one of fortune's
darts; we can scarce be civil, so cruelly is our spirit
tossed. Yet long before we were so much as thought
upon, the like calamity befell the old man or woman
that now, with pleasant humour, rallies us upon our in-
attention, sitting composed in the holy evening of man's
life, in the clear shining after rain. We grow ashamed
of our distresses, new and hot and coarse, like villain-
ous roadside brandy; we see life in aerial perspective,
under the heavens of faith; and out of the worst, in the
mere presence of contented elders, look forward and
take patience. Fear shrinks before them " like a thing
reproved," not the flitting and ineffectual fear of death,
but the instant, dwelling terror of the responsibilities
and revenges of life. Their speech, indeed, is timid;
they report lions in the path; they counsel a meticulous
footing; but their serene, marred faces are more eloquent
and tell another story. Where they have gone, we will
go also, not very greatly fearing; what they have en-

dured unbroken, we also, God helping us, will make a shift to bear.

Not only is the presence of the aged in itself remedial, but their minds are stored with antidotes, wisdom's simples, plain considerations overlooked by youth. They have matter to communicate, be they never so stupid. Their talk is not merely literature, it is great literature; classic in virtue of the speaker's detachment, studded, like a book of travel, with things we should not otherwise have learnt. In virtue, I have said, of the speaker's detachment, — and this is why, of two old men, the one who is not your father speaks to you with the more sensible authority; for in the paternal relation the oldest have lively interests and remain still young. Thus I have known two young men great friends; each swore by the other's father; the father of each swore by the other lad; and yet each pair of parent and child were perpetually by the ears. This is typical: it reads like the germ of some kindly comedy.

The old appear in conversation in two characters: the critically silent and the garrulous anecdotic. The last is perhaps what we look for; it is perhaps the more instructive. An old gentleman, well on in years, sits handsomely and naturally in the bow-window of his age, scanning experience with reverted eye; and chirping and smiling, communicates the accidents and reads the lesson of his long career. Opinions are strengthened, indeed, but they are also weeded out in the course of years. What remains steadily present to the eye of the retired veteran in his hermitage, what still ministers to his content, what still quickens his old honest heart — these are "the real long-lived things"

that Whitman tells us to prefer. Where youth agrees
with age, not where they differ, wisdom lies; and it is
when the young disciple finds his heart to beat in tune
with his grey-bearded teacher's that a lesson may be
learned. I have known one old gentleman, whom I
may name, for he is now gathered to his stock—Robert
Hunter, Sheriff of Dumbarton, and author of an excellent law-book still re-edited and republished. Whether
he was originally big or little is more than I can guess.
When I knew him he was all fallen away and fallen in;
crooked and shrunken; buckled into a stiff waistcoat
for support; troubled by ailments, which kept him
hobbling in and out of the room; one foot gouty; a
wig for decency, not for deception, on his head; close
shaved, except under his chin—and for that he never
failed to apologise, for it went sore against the traditions
of his life. You can imagine how he would fare in a
novel by Miss Mather; yet this rag of a Chelsea veteran
lived to his last year in the plenitude of all that is best
in man, brimming with human kindness, and staunch
as a Roman soldier under his manifold infirmities. You
could not say that he had lost his memory, for he would
repeat Shakespeare and Webster and Jeremy Taylor and
Burke by the page together; but the parchment was
filled up, there was no room for fresh inscriptions, and
he was capable of repeating the same anecdote on
many successive visits. His voice survived in its full
power, and he took a pride in using it. On his last
voyage as Commissioner of Lighthouses, he hailed a
ship at sea and made himself clearly audible without a
speaking trumpet, ruffling the while with a proper
vanity in his achievement. He had a habit of eking

out his words with interrogative hems, which was puzzling and a little wearisome, suited ill with his appearance, and seemed a survival from some former stage of bodily portliness. Of yore, when he was a great pedestrian and no enemy to good claret, he may have pointed with these minute guns his allocutions to the bench. His humour was perfectly equable, set beyond the reach of fate; gout, rheumatism, stone and gravel might have combined their forces against that frail tabernacle, but when I came round on Sunday evening, he would lay aside Jeremy Taylor's *Life of Christ* and greet me with the same open brow, the same kind formality of manner. His opinions and sympathies dated the man almost to a decade. He had begun life, under his mother's influence, as an admirer of Junius, but on maturer knowledge had transferred his admiration to Burke. He cautioned me, with entire gravity, to be punctilious in writing English; never to forget that I was a Scotchman, that English was a foreign tongue, and that if I attempted the colloquial, I should certainly be shamed: the remark was apposite, I suppose, in the days of David Hume. Scott was too new for him; he had known the author — known him, too, for a Tory; and to the genuine classic a contemporary is always something of a trouble. He had the old, serious love of the play; had even, as he was proud to tell, played a certain part in the history of Shakespearian revivals, for he had successfully pressed on Murray, of the old Edinburgh Theatre, the idea of producing Shakespeare's fairy pieces with great scenic display. A moderate in religion, he was much struck in the last years of his life by a conversation with two young lads, revivalists.

"H'm," he would say — "new to me. I have had — h'm — no such experience." It struck him, not with pain, rather with a solemn philosophic interest, that he, a Christian as he hoped, and a Christian of so old a standing, should hear these young fellows talking of his own subject, his own weapons that he had fought the battle of life with, — " and — h'm — not understand." In this wise and graceful attitude he did justice to himself and others, reposed unshaken in his old beliefs, and recognised their limits without anger or alarm. His last recorded remark, on the last night of his life, was after he had been arguing against Calvinism with his minister and was interrupted by an intolerable pang. "After all," he said, " of all the 'isms, I know none so bad as rheumatism." My own last sight of him was some time before, when we dined together at an inn; he had been on circuit, for he stuck to his duties like a chief part of his existence; and I remember it as the only occasion on which he ever soiled his lips with slang — a thing he loathed. We were both Roberts; and as we took our places at table, he addressed me with a twinkle: " We are just what you would call two bob." He offered me port, I remember, as the proper milk of youth; spoke of "twenty-shilling notes;" and throughout the meal was full of old-world pleasantry and quaintness, like an ancient boy on a holiday. But what I recall chiefly was his confession that he had never read *Othello* to an end. Shakespeare was his continual study. He loved nothing better than to display his knowledge and memory by adducing parallel passages from Shakespeare, passages where the same word was employed, or the same idea differently treated. But *Othello* had beaten him. "That noble gentleman and that noble lady — h'm — too painful for me." The same night the hoardings were covered with posters, "Burlesque of *Othello*," and the contrast blazed up in my mind like a bonfire. An unforgettable look it gave me into that kind man's soul. His acquaintance was indeed a liberal and pious education. All the humanities were taught in that bare dining-room beside his gouty footstool. He was a piece of good advice; he was himself the instance that pointed and adorned his various talk. Nor could a young man have found elsewhere a place so set apart from envy, fear, discontent, or any of the passions that debase; a life so honest and composed; a soul like an ancient violin, so subdued to harmony, responding to a touch in music — as in that dining-room, with Mr. Hunter chatting at the eleventh hour, under the shadow of eternity, fearless and gentle.

The second class of old people are not anecdotic; they are rather hearers than talkers, listening to the young with an amused and critical attention. To have this sort of intercourse to perfection, I think we must go to old ladies. Women are better hearers than men, to begin with; they learn, I fear in anguish, to bear with the tedious and infantile vanity of the other sex; and we will take more from a woman than even from the oldest man in the way of biting comment. Biting comment is the chief part, whether for profit or amusement, in this business. The old lady that I have in my eye is a very caustic speaker, her tongue, after years of practice, in absolute command, whether for silence or attack. If she chance to dislike you, you will be tempted to curse the malignity of age. But if you chance to please even slightly, you will be listened to with a particular laughing grace of sympathy, and from time to time chastised, as if in play, with a parasol as heavy as a pole-axe. It requires a singular art, as well as the vantage-ground of age, to deal these stunning corrections among the coxcombs of the young. The pill is disguised in sugar of wit; it is administered as a compliment — if you had not pleased, you would not have been censured; it is a personal affair — a hyphen, a *trait d'union*, between you and your censor; age's philandering, for her pleasure and your good. Incontestably the young man feels very much of a fool; but he must be a perfect Malvolio, sick with self-love, if he cannot take an open buffet and still smile. The correction of silence is what kills; when you know you have transgressed, and your friend says nothing and avoids your eye. If a man were made of gutta-percha, his heart would quail at such a moment. But when the word is out, the worst is over; and a fellow with any good-humour at all may pass through a perfect hail of witty criticism, every bare place on his soul hit to the quick with a shrewd missile, and reappear, as if after a dive, tingling with a fine moral reaction, and ready, with a shrinking readiness, one-third loath, for a repetition of the discipline.

There are few women, not well sunned and ripened, and perhaps toughened, who can thus stand apart from a man and say the true thing with a kind of genial cruelty. Still there are some — and I doubt if there be any man who can return the compliment. The class of man represented by Vernon Whitford in *The Egoist* says, indeed, the true thing, but he says it stockishly. Vernon is a noble fellow, and makes, by the way, a noble and instructive contrast to Daniel Deronda; his conduct is the conduct of a man of honour; but we agree with him, against our consciences, when he remorsefully considers "its astonishing dryness." He is the best of men, but the best of women manage to combine all that and something more. Their very faults assist them; they are helped even by the falseness of their position in life. They can retire into the fortified camp of the proprieties. They can touch a subject and suppress it. The most adroit employ a somewhat elaborate reserve as a means to be frank, much as they wear gloves when they shake hands. But a man has the full responsibility of his freedom, cannot evade a question, can scarce be silent without rudeness, must answer for his words upon the moment, and is not seldom left face to face with a damning choice, between the more or less dishonourable wriggling of Deronda and the downright woodenness of Vernon Whitford.

But the superiority of women is perpetually menaced; they do not sit throned on infirmities like the old; they are suitors as well as sovereigns; their vanity is engaged, their affections are too apt to follow; and hence much of the talk between the sexes degenerates into something unworthy of the name. The desire to please, to shine with a certain softness of lustre and to draw a fascinating picture of oneself, banishes from conversation all that is sterling and most of what is humorous. As soon as a strong current of mutual admiration begins to flow, the human interest triumphs entirely over the intellectual, and the commerce of words, consciously or not, becomes secondary to the commercing of eyes. But even where this ridiculous danger is avoided, and a man and woman converse equally and honestly, something in their nature or their education falsifies the strain. An instinct prompts them to agree; and where that is impossible, to agree to differ. Should they neglect the warning, at the first suspicion of an argument, they find themselves in different hemispheres. About any point of business or conduct, any actual affair demanding settlement, a woman will speak and listen, hear and answer arguments, not only with natural wisdom, but with candour and logical honesty. But if the subject of debate be something in the air, an abstraction, an excuse for talk, a logical Aunt Sally, then may the male debater instantly abandon hope; he may employ reason, adduce facts, be supple, be smiling, be angry, all shall avail him nothing; what the woman said first, that (unless she has forgotten it) she will repeat at the end. Hence, at the very junctures when a talk between men grows brighter and quicker and begins to promise to bear fruit, talk between the sexes is menaced with dissolution. The point of difference, the point of interest, is evaded by the brilliant woman, under a shower of irrelevant conversational rockets; it is bridged by the discreet woman with a rustle of silk, as she passes smoothly forward to the nearest point of safety. And this sort of prestidigitation, juggling the dangerous topic out of sight until it can be reintroduced with safety in an altered shape, is a piece of tactics among the true drawing-room queens.

The drawing-room is, indeed, an artificial place; it is so by our choice and for our sins. The subjection of women; the ideal imposed upon them from the cradle, and worn, like a hair-shirt, with so much constancy; their motherly, superior tenderness to man's vanity and self-importance; their managing arts — the arts of a civilised slave among good-natured barbarians — are all painful ingredients and all help to falsify relations. It is not till we get clear of that amusing artificial scene that genuine relations are founded, or ideas honestly compared. In the garden, on the road or the hillside, or *tête-à-tête* and apart from interruptions, occasions arise when we may learn much from any single woman; and nowhere more often than in married life. Marriage is one long conversation, chequered by disputes. The disputes are valueless; they but ingrain the difference; the heroic heart of woman prompting her at once to nail her colours to the mast. But in the intervals, almost unconsciously and with no desire to shine, the whole material of life is turned over and over, ideas are struck out and shared, the two persons more and more adapt their notions one to suit the other, and in process of time, without sound of trumpet, they conduct each other into new worlds of thought.

XII. THE CHARACTER OF DOGS

THE civilisation, the manners, and the morals of dog-kind are to a great extent subordinated to those of his ancestral master, man. This animal, in many ways so superior, has accepted a position of inferiority, shares the domestic life, and humours the caprices of the tyrant. But the potentate, like the British in India, pays small regard to the character of his willing client, judges him with listless glances, and condemns him in a byword. Listless have been the looks of his admirers, who have exhausted idle terms of praise, and buried the poor soul below exaggerations. And yet more idle and, if possible, more unintelligent has been the attitude of his express detractors; those who are very fond of dogs "but in their proper place"; who say "poo' fellow, poo' fellow," and are themselves far poorer; who whet the knife of the vivisectionist or heat his oven; who are not ashamed to admire "the creature's instinct"; and flying far beyond folly, have dared to resuscitate the theory of animal machines. The "dog's instinct" and the "automaton-dog," in this age of psychology and science, sound like strange anachronisms. An automaton he certainly is; a machine working independently of his control, the heart like the mill-wheel, keeping all in motion, and the consciousness, like a person shut in the mill garret, enjoying the view out of the window and shaken by the thunder of the stones; an automaton in one corner of which a living spirit is confined: an automaton like man. Instinct again he certainly possesses. Inherited aptitudes are his, inherited frailties. Some things he at once views and understands, as though he were awakened from a sleep, as though he came "trailing clouds of glory." But with him, as with man, the field of instinct is limited; its utterances are obscure and occasional; and about the far larger part of life both the dog and his master must conduct their steps by deduction and observation.

The leading distinction between dog and man, after and perhaps before the different duration of their lives, is that the one can speak and that the other cannot. The absence of the power of speech confines the dog in the development of his intellect. It hinders him from many speculations, for words are the beginning of metaphysic. At the same blow it saves him from many superstitions, and his silence has won for him a higher name for virtue than his conduct justifies. The faults of the dog are many. He is vainer than man, singularly greedy of notice, singularly intolerant of ridicule, suspicious like the deaf, jealous to the degree of frenzy, and radically devoid of truth. The day of an intelligent small dog is passed in the manufacture and the laborious communication of falsehood; he lies with his tail, he lies with his eye, he lies with his protesting paw; and when he rattles his dish or scratches at the door his purpose is other than appears. But he has some apology to offer for the vice. Many of the signs which form his dialect have come to bear an arbitrary meaning, clearly understood both by his master and himself; yet when a new want arises he must either invent a new vehicle of meaning or wrest an old one to a different purpose; and this necessity frequently recurring must tend to lessen his idea of the sanctity of symbols. Meanwhile the dog is clear in his own conscience, and draws, with a human nicety, the distinction between formal and essential truth. Of his punning perversions, his legitimate dexterity with symbols, he is even vain; but when he has told and been detected in a lie, there is not a hair upon his body but confesses guilt. To a dog of gentlemanly feeling theft and falsehood are disgraceful vices. The canine, like the human, gentleman demands in his misdemeanours Montaigne's *"je ne sais quoi de généreux."* He is never more than half ashamed of having barked or bitten; and for those faults into which he has been led by the desire to shine before a lady of his race, he retains, even under physical correction, a share of pride. But to be caught lying, if he understands it, instantly uncurls his fleece.

Just as among dull observers he preserves a name for truth, the dog has been credited with modesty. It is amazing how the use of language blunts the faculties of man — that because vainglory finds no vent in words, creatures supplied with eyes have been unable to detect a fault so gross and obvious. If a small spoiled dog were suddenly to be endowed with speech, he would prate interminably, and still about himself; when we had friends, we should be forced to lock him in a garret; and what with his whining jealousies and his foible for falsehood, in a year's time he would have gone

295

far to weary out our love. I was about to compare him to Sir Willoughby Patterne, but the Patternes have a manlier sense of their own merits; and the parallel, besides, is ready. Hans Christian Andersen, as we behold him in his startling memoirs, thrilling from top to toe with an excruciating vanity, and scouting even along the street for shadows of offence — here was the talking dog.

It is just this rage for consideration that has betrayed the dog into his satellite position as the friend of man. The cat, an animal of franker appetites, preserves his independence. But the dog, with one eye ever on the audience, has been wheedled into slavery, and praised and patted into the renunciation of his nature. Once he ceased hunting and became man's plate-licker, the Rubicon was crossed. Thenceforth he was a gentleman of leisure; and except the few whom we keep working, the whole race grew more and more self-conscious, mannered and affected. The number of things that a small dog does naturally is strangely small. Enjoying better spirits and not crushed under material cares, he is far more theatrical than average man. His whole life, if he be a dog of any pretension to gallantry, is spent in a vain show, and in the hot pursuit of admiration. Take out your puppy for a walk, and you will find the little ball of fur clumsy, stupid, bewildered, but natural. Let but a few months pass, and when you repeat the process you will find nature buried in convention. He will do nothing plainly; but the simplest processes of our material life will all be bent into the forms of an elaborate and mysterious etiquette. Instinct, says the fool, has awakened. But it is not so.

Some dogs — some, at the very least — if they be kept separate from others, remain quite natural; and these, when at length they meet with a companion of experience, and have the game explained to them, distinguish themselves by the severity of their devotion to its rules. I wish I were allowed to tell a story which would radiantly illuminate the point; but men, like dogs, have an elaborate and mysterious etiquette. It is their bond of sympathy that both are the children of convention.

The person, man or dog, who has a conscience is eternally condemned to some degree of humbug; the sense of the law in their members fatally precipitates either towards a frozen and affected bearing. And the converse is true; and in the elaborate and conscious manners of the dog, moral opinions and the love of the ideal stand confessed. To follow for ten minutes in the street some swaggering, canine cavalier, is to receive a lesson in dramatic art and the cultured conduct of the body; in every act and gesture you see him true to a refined conception; and the dullest cur, beholding him, pricks up his ear and proceeds to imitate and parody that charming ease. For to be a high-mannered and high-minded gentleman, careless, affable, and gay, is the inborn pretension of the dog. The large dog, so much lazier, so much more weighed upon with matter, so majestic in repose, so beautiful in effort, is born with the dramatic means to wholly represent the part. And it is more pathetic and perhaps more instructive to consider the small dog in his conscientious and imperfect efforts to outdo Sir Philip Sidney. For the ideal of the dog is feudal and religious; the ever-present polytheism, the whip-bearing Olympus of mankind, rules them on the one hand; on the other, their singular difference of size and strength among themselves effectually prevents the appearance of the democratic notion. Or we might more exactly compare their society to the curious spectacle presented by a school — ushers, monitors, and big and little boys — qualified by one circumstance, the introduction of the other sex. In each, we should observe a somewhat similar tension of manner, and somewhat similar points of honour. In each the larger animal keeps a contemptuous good humour; in each the smaller annoys him with wasp-like impudence, certain of practical immunity; in each we shall find a double life producing double characters, and an excursive and noisy heroism combined with a fair amount of practical timidity. I have known dogs, and I have known school heroes that, set aside the fur, could hardly have been told apart; and if we desire to understand the chivalry of old, we must turn to the school playfields or the dungheap where the dogs are trooping.

Woman, with the dog, has been long enfranchised. Incessant massacre of female innocents has changed the proportions of the sexes and perverted their relations. Thus, when we regard the manners of the dog, we see a romantic and monogamous animal, once perhaps as delicate as the cat, at war with impossible conditions. Man has much to answer for; and the part he plays is yet more damnable and parlous than Corin's in the eyes of Touchstone. But his intervention has at least created an imperial situation for the rare surviving ladies. In that society they reign without a rival: conscious queens; and in the only instance of a canine wife-beater that has ever fallen under my notice, the criminal was somewhat

excused by the circumstances of his story. He is a little, very alert, well-bred, intelligent Skye, as black as
a hat, with a wet bramble for a nose and two cairn-
gorms for eyes. To the human observer, he is decidedly
well-looking; but to the ladies of his race he seems ab-
horrent. A thorough elaborate gentleman, of the plume
and sword-knot order, he was born with a nice sense
of gallantry to women. He took at their hands the
most outrageous treatment; I have heard him bleating
like a sheep, I have seen him streaming blood, and his
ear tattered like a regimental banner; and yet he would
scorn to make reprisals. Nay more, when a human
lady upraised the contumelious whip against the very
dame who had been so cruelly misusing him, my little
great-heart gave but one hoarse cry and fell upon the
tyrant tooth and nail. This is the tale of a soul's tragedy. After three years of unavailing chivalry, he suddenly, in one hour, threw off the yoke of obligation;
had he been Shakespeare he would then have written
Troilus and Cressida to brand the offending sex; but
being only a little dog, he began to bite them. The
surprise of the ladies whom he attacked indicated the
monstrosity of his offence; but he had fairly beaten off
his better angel, fairly committed moral suicide; for almost in the same hour, throwing aside the last rags of
decency, he proceeded to attack the aged also. The fact
is worth remark, showing, as it does, that ethical laws
are common both to dogs and men; and that with both
a single deliberate violation of the conscience loosens all.
"But while the lamp holds on to burn," says the para-
phrase, "the greatest sinner may return." I have been
cheered to see symptoms of effectual penitence in my

sweet ruffian; and by the handling that he accepted un-
complainingly the other day from an indignant fair one,
I begin to hope the period of *Sturm und Drang* is
closed.

All these little gentlemen are subtle casuists. The
duty to the female dog is plain; but where competing
duties rise, down they will sit and study them out, like
Jesuit confessors. I knew another little Skye, somewhat plain in manner and appearance, but a creature
compact of amiability and solid wisdom. His family
going abroad for a winter, he was received for that
period by an uncle in the same city. The winter over,
his own family home again, and his own house (of
which he was very proud) reopened, he found himself
in a dilemma between two conflicting duties of loyalty
and gratitude. His old friends were not to be neglected, but it seemed hardly decent to desert the new.
This was how he solved the problem. Every morning,
as soon as the door was opened, off posted Coolin to
his uncle's, visited the children in the nursery, saluted
the whole family, and was back at home in time for
breakfast and his bit of fish. Nor was this done without a sacrifice on his part, sharply felt; for he had to
forego the particular honour and jewel of his day — his
morning's walk with my father. And, perhaps from
this cause, he gradually wearied of and relaxed the practice, and at length returned entirely to his ancient habits. But the same decision served him in another and
more distressing case of divided duty, which happened
not long after. He was not at all a kitchen dog, but the
cook had nursed him with unusual kindness during the
distemper; and though he did not adore her as he

adored my father—although (born snob) he was critically conscious of her position as "only a servant"—
he still cherished for her a special gratitude. Well, the
cook left, and retired some streets away to lodgings of
her own; and there was Coolin in precisely the same
situation with any young gentleman who has had the
inestimable benefit of a faithful nurse. The canine
conscience did not solve the problem with a pound of
tea at Christmas. No longer content to pay a flying
visit, it was the whole forenoon that he dedicated to his
solitary friend. And so, day by day, he continued to
comfort her solitude until (for some reason which I
could never understand and cannot approve) he was
kept locked up to break him of the graceful habit. Here,
it is not the similarity, it is the difference, that is worthy
of remark; the clearly marked degrees of gratitude
and the proportional duration of his visits. Anything
further removed from instinct it were hard to fancy ;
and one is even stirred to a certain impatience with
a character so destitute of spontaneity, so passionless
in justice, and so priggishly obedient to the voice of
reason.

There are not many dogs like this good Coolin, and
not many people. But the type is one well marked,
both in the human and the canine family. Gallantry
was not his aim, but a solid and somewhat oppressive
respectability. He was a sworn foe to the unusual and
the conspicuous, a praiser of the golden mean, a kind
of city uncle modified by Cheeryble. And as he was
precise and conscientious in all the steps of his own
blameless course, he looked for the same precision and
an even greater gravity in the bearing of his deity, **my**

father. It was no sinecure to be Coolin's idol: he was exacting like a rigid parent; and at every sign of levity in the man whom he respected, he announced loudly the death of virtue and the proximate fall of the pillars of the earth.

I have called him a snob; but all dogs are so, though in varying degrees. It is hard to follow their snobbery among themselves; for though I think we can perceive distinctions of rank, we cannot grasp what is the criterion. Thus in Edinburgh, in a good part of the town, there were several distinct societies or clubs that met in the morning to — the phrase is technical — to "rake the backets" in a troop. A friend of mine, the master of three dogs, was one day surprised to observe that they had left one club and joined another; but whether it was a rise or a fall, and the result of an invitation or an expulsion, was more than he could guess. And this illustrates pointedly our ignorance of the real life of dogs, their social ambitions and their social hierarchies. At least, in their dealings with men they are not only conscious of sex, but of the difference of station. And that in the most snobbish manner; for the poor man's dog is not offended by the notice of the rich, and keeps all his ugly feeling for those poorer or more ragged than his master. And again, for every station they have an ideal of behaviour, to which the master, under pain of derogation, will do wisely to conform. How often has not a cold glance of an eye informed me that my dog was disappointed; and how much more gladly would he not have taken a beating than to be thus wounded in the seat of piety!

I knew one disrespectable dog. He was far liker a

302

cat; cared little or nothing for men, with whom he merely coexisted as we do with cattle, and was entirely devoted to the art of poaching. A house would not hold him, and to live in a town was what he refused. He led, I believe, a life of troubled but genuine pleasure, and perished beyond all question in a trap. But this was an exception, a marked reversion to the ancestral type; like the hairy human infant. The true dog of the nineteenth century, to judge by the remainder of my fairly large acquaintance, is in love with respectability. A street-dog was once adopted by a lady. While still an Arab, he had done as Arabs do, gambolling in the mud, charging into butchers' stalls, a cat-hunter, a sturdy beggar, a common rogue and vagabond; but with his rise into society he laid aside these inconsistent pleasures. He stole no more, he hunted no more cats; and conscious of his collar, he ignored his old companions. Yet the canine upper class was never brought to recognize the upstart, and from that hour, except for human countenance, he was alone. Friendless, shorn of his sports and the habits of a lifetime, he still lived in a glory of happiness, content with his acquired respectability, and with no care but to support it solemnly. Are we to condemn or praise this self-made dog? We praise his human brother. And thus to conquer vicious habits is as rare with dogs as with men. With the more part, for all their scruple-mongering and moral thought, the vices that are born with them remain invincible throughout; and they live all their years, glorying in their virtues, but still the slaves of their defects. Thus the sage Coolin was a thief to the last; among a thousand peccadilloes, a whole goose and a whole cold leg of mutton lay upon his conscience; but Woggs,[1] whose soul's shipwreck in the matter of gallantry I have recounted above, has only twice been known to steal, and has often nobly conquered the temptation. The eighth is his favourite commandment. There is something painfully human in these unequal virtues and mortal frailties of the best. Still more painful is the bearing of those "stammering professors" in the house of sickness and under the terror of death. It is beyond a doubt to me that, somehow or other, the dog connects together, or confounds, the uneasiness of sickness and the consciousness of guilt. To the pains of the body he often adds the tortures of the conscience; and at these times his haggard protestations form, in regard to the human deathbed, a dreadful parody or parallel.

I once supposed that I had found an inverse relation between the double etiquette which dogs obey; and that those who were most addicted to the showy street life among other dogs were less careful in the practice of home virtues for the tyrant man. But the female dog, that mass of carneying affections, shines equally in either sphere; rules her rough posse of attendant swains with unwearying tact and gusto; and with her master and mistress pushes the arts of insinuation to their crowning point. The attention of man and the regard of other dogs flatter (it would thus appear) the same sensibility; but perhaps, if we could read the canine heart, they would be found to flatter it in very

[1] Walter, Watty, Woggy, Woggs, Wogg, and lastly Bogue; under which last name he fell in battle some twelve months ago. Glory was his aim and he attained it ; for his icon, by the hand of Caldecott, now lies among the treasures of the nation.

different degrees. Dogs live with man as courtiers round a monarch, steeped in the flattery of his notice and enriched with sinecures. To push their favour in this world of pickings and caresses is, perhaps, the business of their lives; and their joys may lie outside. I am in despair at our persistent ignorance. I read in the lives of our companions the same processes of reason, the same antique and fatal conflicts of the right against the wrong, and of unbitted nature with too rigid custom; I see them with our weaknesses, vain, false, inconstant against appetite, and with our one stalk of virtue, devoted to the dream of an ideal; and yet, as they hurry by me on the street with tail in air, or come singly to solicit my regard, I must own the secret purport of their lives is still inscrutable to man. Is man the friend, or is he the patron only? Have they indeed forgotten nature's voice? or are those moments snatched from courtiership when they touch noses with the tinker's mongrel, the brief reward and pleasure of their artificial lives? Doubtless, when man shares with his dog the toils of a profession and the pleasures of an art, as with the shepherd or the poacher, the affection warms and strengthens till it fills the soul. But doubtless, also, the masters are, in many cases, the object of a merely interested cultus, sitting aloft like Louis Quatorze, giving and receiving flattery and favour; and the dogs, like the majority of men, have but foregone their true existence and become the dupes of their ambition.

XIII. "A PENNY PLAIN AND TWOPENCE COLOURED"

THESE words will be familiar to all students of Skelt's Juvenile Drama. That national monument, after having changed its name to Park's, to Webb's, to Redington's, and last of all to Pollock's, has now become, for the most part, a memory. Some of its pillars, like Stonehenge, are still afoot, the rest clean vanished. It may be the Museum numbers a full set; and Mr. Ionides perhaps, or else her gracious Majesty, may boast their great collections; but to the plain private person they are become, like Raphaels, unattainable. I have, at different times, possessed *Aladdin, The Red Rover, The Blind Boy, The Old Oak Chest, The Wood Dæmon, Jack Sheppard, The Miller and his Men, Der Freischütz, The Smuggler, The Forest of Bondy, Robin Hood, The Waterman, Richard I., My Poll and my Partner Joe, The Inchcape Bell* (imperfect), and *Three-Fingered Jack, the Terror of Jamaica;* and I have assisted others in the illumination of *The Maid of the Inn* and *The Battle of Waterloo.* In this roll-call of stirring names you read the evidences of a happy childhood; and though not half of them are still to be procured of any living stationer, in the mind of their once happy owner all survive, kaleidoscopes of changing pictures, echoes of the past.

There stands, I fancy, to this day (but now how fallen!) a certain stationer's shop at a corner of the wide thoroughfare that joins the city of my childhood with the sea. When, upon any Saturday, we made a party to behold the ships, we passed that corner; and since in those days I loved a ship as a man loves Burgundy or daybreak, this of itself had been enough to hallow it. But there was more than that. In the Leith Walk window, all the year round, there stood displayed a theatre in working order, with a "forest set," a "combat," and a few "robbers carousing" in the slides; and below and about, dearer tenfold to me! the plays themselves, those budgets of romance, lay tumbled one upon another. Long and often have I lingered there with empty pockets. One figure, we shall say, was visible in the first plate of characters, bearded, pistol in hand, or drawing to his ear the clothyard arrow; I would spell the name: was it Macaire, or Long Tom Coffin, or Grindoff, 2d dress? O, how I would long to see the rest! how — if the name by chance were hidden — I would wonder in what play he figured, and what immortal legend justified his attitude and strange apparel! And then to go within, to announce yourself as an intending purchaser, and, closely watched, be suffered to undo those bundles and breathlessly devour those pages of gesticulating villains, epileptic combats, bosky forests, palaces and war-ships, frowning fortresses and prison vaults — it was a giddy joy. That shop, which was dark and smelt of Bibles, was a loadstone rock for all that bore the name of boy. They could not pass it by, nor, having entered, leave it. It was a place besieged; the shopmen, like the Jews

307

rebuilding Salem, had a double task. They kept us at
the stick's end, frowned us down, snatched each play
out of our hand ere we were trusted with another;
and, incredible as it may sound, used to demand of
us upon our entrance, like banditti, if we came with
money or with empty hand. Old Mr. Smith himself,
worn out with my eternal vacillation, once swept the
treasures from before me, with the cry: "I do not
believe, child, that you are an intending purchaser at
all!" These were the dragons of the garden; but for
such joys of paradise we could have faced the Terror
of Jamaica himself. Every sheet we fingered was another lightning glance into obscure, delicious story; it
was like wallowing in the raw stuff of story-books. I
know nothing to compare with it save now and then in
dreams, when I am privileged to read in certain unwrit
stories of adventure, from which I awake to find the
world all vanity. The *crux* of Buridan's donkey was
as nothing to the uncertainty of the boy as he handled
and lingered and doated on these bundles of delight;
there was a physical pleasure in the sight and touch of
them which he would jealously prolong; and when at
length the deed was done, the play selected, and the
impatient shopman had brushed the rest into the gray
portfolio, and the boy was forth again, a little late for
dinner, the lamps springing into light in the blue winter's even, and *The Miller,* or *The Rover,* or some
kindred drama clutched against his side—on what gay
feet he ran, and how he laughed aloud in exultation!
I can hear that laughter still. Out of all the years of
my life, I can recall but one home-coming to compare
with these, and that was on the night when I brought

back with me the *Arabian Entertainments* in the fat, old, double-columned volume with the prints. I was just well into the story of the Hunchback, I remember, when my clergyman-grandfather (a man we counted pretty stiff) came in behind me. I grew blind with terror. But instead of ordering the book away, he said he envied me. Ah, well he might!

The purchase and the first half-hour at home, that was the summit. Thenceforth the interest declined by little and little. The fable, as set forth in the play-book, proved to be not worthy of the scenes and characters: what fable would not? Such passages as: "Scene 6. The Hermitage. Night set scene. Place back of scene 1, No. 2, at back of stage and hermitage, Fig. 2, out of set piece, R. H. in a slanting direction"—such passages, I say, though very practical, are hardly to be called good reading. Indeed, as literature, these dramas did not much appeal to me. I forget the very outline of the plots. Of *The Blind Boy,* beyond the fact that he was a most injured prince and once, I think, abducted, I know nothing. And *The Old Oak Chest,* what was it all about? that proscript (1st dress), that prodigious number of banditti, that old woman with the broom, and the magnificent kitchen in the third act (was it in the third?)—they are all fallen in a deliquium, swim faintly in my brain, and mix and vanish.

I cannot deny that joy attended the illumination; nor can I quite forgive that child who, wilfully foregoing pleasure, stoops to "twopence coloured." With crimson lake (hark to the sound of it—crimson lake!—the horns of elf-land are not richer on the ear)—with crimson lake and Prussian blue a certain purple is to be compounded which, for cloaks especially, Titian could not equal. The latter colour with gamboge, a hated name although an exquisite pigment, supplied a green of such a savoury greenness that to-day my heart regrets it. Nor can I recall without a tender weakness the very aspect of the water where I dipped my brush. Yes, there was pleasure in the painting. But when all was painted, it is needless to deny it, all was spoiled. You might, indeed, set up a scene or two to look at; but to cut the figures out was simply sacrilege; nor could any child twice court the tedium, the worry, and the long-drawn disenchantment of an actual performance. Two days after the purchase the honey had been sucked. Parents used to complain; they thought I wearied of my play. It was not so: no more than a person can be said to have wearied of his dinner when he leaves the bones and dishes; I had got the marrow of it and said grace.

Then was the time to turn to the back of the play-book and to study that enticing double file of names, where poetry, for the true child of Skelt, reigned happy and glorious like her Majesty the Queen. Much as I have travelled in these realms of gold, I have yet seen, upon that map or abstract, names of El Dorados that still haunt the ear of memory, and are still but names. *The Floating Beacon* — why was that denied me ? or *The Wreck Ashore ? Sixteen-String Jack,* whom I did not even guess to be a highwayman, troubled me awake and haunted my slumbers; and there is one sequence of three from that enchanted calendar that I still at times recall, like a loved verse of poetry: *Lodoiska, Silver Palace, Echo of Westminster Bridge.* Names, bare names, are surely more to children than we poor, grown-up, obliterated fools remember.

The name of Skelt itself has always seemed a part and parcel of the charm of his productions. It may be different with the rose, but the attraction of this paper drama sensibly declined when Webb had crept into the rubric: a poor cuckoo, flaunting in Skelt's nest. And now we have reached Pollock, sounding deeper gulfs. Indeed, this name of Skelt appears so stagey and piratic, that I will adopt it boldly to design these qualities. Skeltery, then, is a quality of much art. It is even to be found, with reverence be it said, among the works of nature. The stagey is its generic name; but it is an old, insular, home-bred staginess; not French, domestically British; not of to-day, but smacking of O. Smith, Fitzball, and the great age of melodrama: a peculiar fragrance haunting it; uttering its unimportant message in a tone of voice that has the charm of fresh antiquity. I will not insist upon the art of Skelt's purveyors. These wonderful characters that once so thrilled our soul with their bold attitude, array of deadly engines and incomparable costume, to-day look somewhat pallidly; the extreme hard favour of the heroine strikes me, I had almost said with pain; the villain's scowl no longer thrills me like a trumpet; and the scenes themselves, those once unparalleled landscapes, seem the efforts of a prentice hand. So much of fault we find; but on the other side the impartial critic rejoices to remark the presence of a great unity of gusto; of those direct clap-trap appeals, which a man is dead and buriable when he fails to answer; of the footlight glamour, the ready-made, bare-faced, transpontine picturesque, a thing not one with cold reality, but how much dearer to the mind!

The scenery of Skeltdom — or, shall we say, the kingdom of Transpontus? — had a prevailing character. Whether it set forth Poland as in *The Blind Boy,* or Bohemia with *The Miller and his Men,* or Italy with *The Old Oak Chest,* still it was Transpontus. A botanist could tell it by the plants. The hollyhock was all pervasive, running wild in deserts; the dock was common, and the bending reed; and overshadowing these were poplar, palm, potato tree, and *Quercus Skeltica* — brave growths. The caves were all embowelled in the Surreyside formation; the soil was all betrodden by the light pump of T. P. Cooke. Skelt, to be sure, had yet another, an oriental string: he held the gorgeous east in fee; and in the new quarter of Hyères, say, in the garden of the Hotel des Isles d'Or, you may behold these blessed visions realised. But on these I will not dwell; they were an outwork; it was in the occidental scenery that Skelt was all himself. It had a strong flavour of England; it was a sort of indigestion of England and drop-scenes, and I am bound to say was charming. How the roads wander, how the castle sits upon the hill, how the sun eradiates from behind the cloud, and how the congregated clouds themselves uproll, as stiff as bolsters! Here is the cottage interior, the usual first flat, with the cloak upon the nail, the rosaries of onions, the gun and powder-horn and corner-cupboard; here is the inn (this drama must be nautical, I foresee Captain Luff and Bold Bob Bowsprit) with the red curtain, pipes, spittoons, and eight-day clock; and there again is that impressive dungeon with the chains, which was so dull to colour. England, the hedgerow elms, the thin brick houses, windmills, glimpses of the navigable Thames — England, when at last I came to visit it, was only Skelt made evident: to cross the border was, for the Scotsman, to come home to Skelt; there was the inn-sign and there the horse-trough, all foreshadowed in the faithful Skelt. If, at the ripe age of fourteen years, I bought a certain cudgel, got a friend to load it, and thenceforward walked the tame ways of the earth my own ideal, radiating pure romance — still I was but a puppet in the hand of Skelt; the original of that regretted bludgeon, and surely the antitype of all the bludgeon kind, greatly improved from Cruikshank, had adorned the hand of Jonathan Wild, pl. I. "This is mastering me," as Whitman cries, upon some lesser provocation. What am I? what are life, art, letters, the world, but what my Skelt has made them? He stamped himself upon my immaturity. The world was plain before I knew him, a poor penny world; but soon it was all coloured with romance. If I go to the theatre to see a good old melodrama, 'tis but Skelt a little faded. If I visit a bold scene in nature, Skelt would have been bolder; there had been certainly a castle on that mountain, and the hollow tree — that set piece — I seem to miss it in the foreground. Indeed, out of this cut-and-dry, dull, swaggering, obtrusive and infantile art, I seem to have learned the very spirit of my life's enjoyment; met there the shadows of the characters I was to read about and love in a late future; got the romance of *Der Freischütz* long ere I was to hear of Weber or the mighty Formes; acquired a gallery of scenes and characters with which, in the silent theatre of the brain, I might enact all novels and romances; and took from these rude cuts an enduring and transforming pleasure. Reader — and yourself?

A word of moral: it appears that B. Pollock, late J. Redington, No. 73 Hoxton Street, not only publishes twenty-three of these old stage favourites, but owns the necessary plates and displays a modest readiness to issue other thirty-three. If you love art, folly, or the bright eyes of children, speed to Pollock's, or to Clarke's of Garrick Street. In Pollock's list of publicanda I perceive a pair of my ancient aspirations: *Wreck Ashore* and *Sixteen-String Jack;* and I cherish the belief that when these shall see once more the light of day, B. Pollock will remember this apologist. But, indeed, I have a dream at times that is not all a dream. I seem to myself to wander in a ghostly street — E. W., I think, the postal district — close below the fool's-cap of St. Paul's, and yet within easy hearing of the echo of the Abbey bridge. There in a dim shop, low in the roof and smelling strong of glue and footlights, I find myself in quaking treaty with great Skelt himself, the aboriginal, all dusty from the tomb. I buy, with what a choking heart — I buy them all, all but the pantomimes; I pay my mental money, and go forth; and lo ! the packets are dust.

XIV. A GOSSIP ON A NOVEL OF DUMAS'S

THE books that we re-read the oftenest are not always those that we admire the most; we choose and we revisit them for many and various reasons, as we choose and revisit human friends. One or two of Scott's novels, Shakespeare, Molière, Montaigne, *The Egoist,* and the *Vicomte de Bragelonne,* form the inner circle of my intimates. Behind these comes a good troop of dear acquaintances; *The Pilgrim's Progress* in the front rank, *The Bible in Spain* not far behind. There are besides a certain number that look at me with reproach as I pass them by on my shelves: books that I once thumbed and studied: houses which were once like home to me, but where I now rarely visit. I am on these sad terms (and blush to confess it) with Wordsworth, Horace, Burns and Hazlitt. Last of all, there is the class of book that has its hour of brilliancy — glows, sings, charms, and then fades again into insignificance until the fit return. Chief of those who thus smile and frown on me by turns, I must name Virgil and Herrick, who, were they but

" Their sometime selves the same throughout the year,"

must have stood in the first company with the six names of my continual literary intimates. To these six, incongruous as they seem, I have long been faithful, and hope to be faithful to the day of death. I have never read the whole of Montaigne, but I do not like to be long without reading some of him, and my delight in what I do read never lessens. Of Shakespeare I have read all but *Richard III., Henry VI., Titus Andronicus,* and *All's Well that Ends Well;* and these, having already made all suitable endeavour, I now know that I shall never read — to make up for which unfaithfulness I could read much of the rest for ever. Of Molière — surely the next greatest name of Christendom — I could tell a very similar story; but in a little corner of a little essay these princes are too much out of place, and I prefer to pay my fealty and pass on. How often I have read *Guy Mannering, Rob Roy,* or *Redgauntlet,* I have no means of guessing, having begun young. But it is either four or five times that I have read *The Egoist,* and either five or six that I have read the *Vicomte de Bragelonne.*

Some, who would accept the others, may wonder that I should have spent so much of this brief life of ours over a work so little famous as the last. And, indeed, I am surprised myself; not at my own devotion, but the coldness of the world. My acquaintance with the *Vicomte* began, somewhat indirectly, in the year of grace 1863, when I had the advantage of studying certain illustrated dessert plates in a hotel at Nice. The name of d'Artagnan in the legends I already saluted like an old friend, for I had met it the year before in a work of Miss Yonge's. My first perusal was in one of those pirated editions that swarmed at that time out of Brussels, and ran to such a troop of neat and dwarfish vol-

umes. I understood but little of the merits of the book;
my strongest memory is of the execution of d'Eyméric
and Lyodot — a strange testimony to the dulness of a
boy, who could enjoy the rough-and-tumble in the
Place de Grêve, and forget d'Artagnan's visits to the two
financiers. My next reading was in winter-time, when
I lived alone upon the Pentlands. I would return in the
early night from one of my patrols with the shepherd;
a friendly face would meet me in the door, a friendly re-
triever scurry upstairs to fetch my slippers; and I would
sit down with the *Vicomte* for a long, silent, solitary
lamp-light evening by the fire. And yet I know not
why I call it silent, when it was enlivened with such a
clatter of horse-shoes, and such a rattle of musketry,
and such a stir of talk; or why I call those evenings
solitary in which I gained so many friends. I would
rise from my book and pull the blind aside, and see the
snow and the glittering hollies chequer a Scotch garden, and the winter moonlight brighten the white hills.
Thence I would turn again to that crowded and sunny
field of life in which it was so easy to forget myself,
my cares, and my surroundings: a place busy as a city,
bright as a theatre, thronged with memorable faces, and
sounding with delightful speech. I carried the thread
of that epic into my slumbers, I woke with it unbroken,
I rejoiced to plunge into the book again at breakfast, it
was with a pang that I must lay it down and turn to
my own labours; for no part of the world has ever
seemed to me so charming as these pages, and not even
my friends are quite so real, perhaps quite so dear, as
d'Artagnan.

Since then I have been going to and fro at very brief

intervals in my favourite book; and I have now just
risen from my last (let me call it my fifth) perusal, having liked it better and admired it more seriously than
ever. Perhaps I have a sense of ownership, being so
well known in these six volumes. Perhaps I think that
d'Artagnan delights to have me read of him, and Louis
Quatorze is gratified, and Fouquet throws me a look,
and Aramis, although he knows I do not love him, yet
plays to me with his best graces, as to an old patron of
the show. Perhaps, if I am not careful, something may
befall me like what befell George IV. about the battle of
Waterloo, and I may come to fancy the *Vicomte* one of
the first, and Heaven knows the best, of my own works.
At least, I avow myself a partisan; and when I compare
the popularity of the *Vicomte* with that of *Monte Cristo,*
or its own elder brother, the *Trois Mousquetaires,* I
confess I am both pained and puzzled.

To those who have already made acquaintance with
the titular hero in the pages of *Vingt Ans Après,* perhaps the name may act as a deterrent. A man might
well stand back if he supposed he were to follow, for
six volumes, so well-conducted, so fine-spoken, and
withal so dreary a cavalier as Bragelonne. But the fear
is idle. I may be said to have passed the best years of
my life in these six volumes, and my acquaintance with
Raoul has never gone beyond a bow; and when he, who
has so long pretended to be alive, is at last suffered to
pretend to be dead, I am sometimes reminded of a saying in an earlier volume: *"Enfin, dit Miss Stewart,"* —
and it was of Bragelonne she spoke — *" enfin il a fait
quelquechose: c'est, ma foi! bien heureux."* I am reminded of it, as I say; and the next moment, when

Athos dies of his death, and my dear d'Artagnan bursts into his storm of sobbing, I can but deplore my flippancy.

Or perhaps it is La Vallière that the reader of *Vingt Ans Après* is inclined to flee. Well, he is right there too, though not so right. Louise is no success. Her creator has spared no pains; she is well-meant, not ill-designed, sometimes has a word that rings out true; sometimes, if only for a breath, she may even engage our sympathies. But I have never envied the King his triumph. And so far from pitying Bragelonne for his defeat, I could wish him no worse (not for lack of malice, but imagination) than to be wedded to that lady. Madame enchants me; I can forgive that royal minx her most serious offences; I can thrill and soften with the King on that memorable occasion when he goes to upbraid and remains to flirt; and when it comes to the *"Allons, aimez-moi donc,"* it is my heart that melts in the bosom of de Guiche. Not so with Louise. Readers cannot fail to have remarked that what an author tells us of the beauty or the charm of his creatures goes for nought; that we know instantly better; that the heroine cannot open her mouth but what, all in a moment, the fine phrases of preparation fall from round her like the robes from Cinderella, and she stands before us, self-betrayed, as a poor, ugly, sickly wench, or perhaps a strapping market-woman. Authors, at least, know it well; a heroine will too often start the trick of "getting ugly;" and no disease is more difficult to cure. I said authors; but indeed I had a side eye to one author in particular, with whose works I am very well acquainted, though I cannot read them, and who has spent many vigils in this cause, sitting beside his ailing puppets and (like a magician) wearying his art to restore them to youth and beauty. There are others who ride too high for these misfortunes. Who doubts the loveliness of Rosalind? Arden itself was not more lovely. Who ever questioned the perennial charm of Rose Jocelyn, Lucy Desborough, or Clara Middleton? fair women with fair names, the daughters of George Meredith. Elizabeth Bennet has but to speak, and I am at her knees. Ah! these are the creators of desirable women. They would never have fallen in the mud with Dumas and poor La Vallière. It is my only consolation that not one of all of them, except the first, could have plucked at the moustache of d'Artagnan.

Or perhaps, again, a proportion of readers stumble at the threshold. In so vast a mansion there were sure to be back stairs and kitchen offices where no one would delight to linger; but it was at least unhappy that the vestibule should be so badly lighted; and until, in the seventeenth chapter, d'Artagnan sets off to seek his friends, I must confess, the book goes heavily enough. But, from thenceforward, what a feast is spread! Monk kidnapped; d'Artagnan enriched; Mazarin's death; the ever delectable adventure of Belle Isle, wherein Aramis outwits d'Artagnan, with its epilogue (vol. v. chap. xxviii.), where d'Artagnan regains the moral superiority; the love adventures at Fontainebleau, with St. Aignan's story of the dryad and the business of de Guiche, de Wardes, and Manicamp; Aramis made general of the Jesuits; Aramis at the bastille; the night talk in the forest of Sénart; Belle Isle again, with the death of Porthos; and last, but not least, the taming of d'Artagnan the untamable, under the lash of the young King. What other novel has such epic variety and nobility of incident? often, if you will, impossible; often of the order of an Arabian story; and yet all based in human nature. For if you come to that, what novel has more human nature? not studied with the microscope, but seen largely, in plain daylight, with the natural eye? What novel has more good sense, and gaiety, and wit, and unflagging, admirable literary skill? Good souls, I suppose, must sometimes read it in the blackguard travesty of a translation. But there is no style so untranslatable; light as a whipped trifle, strong as silk; wordy like a village tale; pat like a general's despatch; with every fault, yet never tedious; with no merit, yet inimitably right. And, once more, to make an end of commendations, what novel is inspired with a more unstrained or a more wholesome morality?

Yes; in spite of Miss Yonge, who introduced me to the name of d'Artagnan only to dissuade me from a nearer knowledge of the man, I have to add morality. There is no quite good book without a good morality; but the world is wide, and so are morals. Out of two people who have dipped into Sir Richard Burton's *Thousand and One Nights,* one shall have been offended by the animal details; another to whom these were harmless, perhaps even pleasing, shall yet have been shocked in his turn by the rascality and cruelty of all the characters. Of two readers, again, one shall have been pained by the morality of a religious memoir, one by that of the *Vicomte de Bragelonne.* And the point is that neither need be wrong. We shall always shock each other both in life and art; we cannot get the sun into our pictures, nor the abstract right (if there be such a thing) into our books; enough if, in the one, there glimmer some hint of the great light that blinds us from heaven; enough, if, in the other, there shine, even upon foul details, a spirit of magnanimity. I would scarce send to the *Vicomte* a reader who was in quest of what we may call puritan morality. The ventripotent mulatto, the great eater, worker, earner and waster, the man of much and witty laughter, the man of the great heart and alas! of the doubtful honesty, is a figure not yet clearly set before the world; he still awaits a sober and yet genial portrait; but with whatever art that may be touched, and whatever indulgence, it will not be the portrait of a precisian. Dumas was certainly not thinking of himself, but of Planchet, when he put into the mouth of d'Artagnan's old servant this excellent profession: *"Monsieur, j'étais une de ces bonnes pâtes d'hommes que Dieu a fait pour s'animer pendant un certain temps et pour trouver bonnes toutes choses qui accompagnent leur séjour sur la terre."* He was thinking, as I say, of Planchet, to whom the words are aptly fitted; but they were fitted also to Planchet's creator; and perhaps this struck him as he wrote, for observe what follows: *"D'Artagnan s'assit alors près de la fenêtre, et, cette philosophie de Planchet lui ayant paru solide, il y rêva."* In a man who finds all things good, you will scarce expect much zeal for negative virtues: the active alone will have a charm for him; abstinence, however wise, however kind, will always seem to such a judge entirely mean and partly impious. So with Dumas. Chastity is not near his heart; nor yet, to his own sore cost, that virtue of frugality which is the armour of the

artist.   Now, in the *Vicomte,* he had much to do with
the contest of Fouquet and Colbert.   Historic justice
should be all upon the side of Colbert, of official honesty, and fiscal competence.   And Dumas knew it well:
three times at least he shows his knowledge; once it is
but flashed upon us and received with the laughter of
Fouquet himself, in the jesting controversy in the gardens of Saint Mandé; once it is touched on by Aramis
in the forest of Sénart; in the end, it is set before us
clearly in one dignified speech of the triumphant Colbert.
But in Fouquet, the waster, the lover of good cheer and
wit and art, the swift transactor of much business,
*"l'homme de bruit, l'homme de plaisir, l'homme qui
n'est que parceque les autres sont,"* Dumas saw something of himself and drew the figure the more tenderly.
It is to me even touching to see how he insists on Fouquet's honour; not seeing, you might think, that un-
flawed honour is impossible to spendthrifts; but rather,
perhaps, in the light of his own life, seeing it too well,
and clinging the more to what was left.   Honour can
survive a wound; it can live and thrive without a member.   The man rebounds from his disgrace; he begins
fresh foundations on the ruins of the old; and when his
sword is broken, he will do valiantly with his dagger.
So it is with Fouquet in the book; so it was with Dumas
on the battlefield of life.

To cling to what is left of any damaged quality is
virtue in the man; but perhaps to sing its praises is
scarcely to be called morality in the writer.   And it is
elsewhere, it is in the character of d'Artagnan, that we
must look for that spirit of morality, which is one of the
chief merits of the book, makes one of the main joys of

its perusal, and sets it high above more popular rivals. Athos, with the coming of years, has declined too much into the preacher, and the preacher of a sapless creed; but d'Artagnan has mellowed into a man so witty, rough, kind and upright, that he takes the heart by storm. There is nothing of the copy-book about his virtues, nothing of the drawing-room in his fine, natural civility; he will sail near the wind; he is no district visitor — no Wesley or Robespierre; his conscience is void of all refinement whether for good or evil; but the whole man rings true like a good sovereign. Readers who have approached the *Vicomte*, not across country, but by the legitimate, five-volumed avenue of the *Mousquetaires* and *Vingt Ans Après*, will not have forgotten d'Artagnan's ungentlemanly and perfectly improbable trick upon Milady. What a pleasure it is, then, what a reward, and how agreeable a lesson, to see the old captain humble himself to the son of the man whom he had personated! Here, and throughout, if I am to choose virtues for myself or my friends, let me choose the virtues of d'Artagnan. I do not say there is no character as well drawn in Shakespeare; I do say there is none that I love so wholly. There are many spiritual eyes that seem to spy upon our actions — eyes of the dead and the absent, whom we imagine to behold us in our most private hours, and whom we fear and scruple to offend: our witnesses and judges. And among these, even if you should think me childish, I must count my d'Artagnan — not d'Artagnan of the memoirs whom Thackeray pretended to prefer — a preference, I take the freedom of saying, in which he stands alone; not the d'Artagnan of flesh and blood, but him of the ink and paper; not Nature's, but Dumas's. And this is the particular crown and triumph of the artist — not to be true merely, but to be lovable; not simply to convince, but to enchant.

There is yet another point in the *Vicomte* which I find incomparable. I can recall no other work of the imagination in which the end of life is represented with so nice a tact. I was asked the other day if Dumas made me laugh or cry. Well, in this my late fifth reading of the *Vicomte*, I did laugh once at the small Coquelin de Volière business, and was perhaps a thought surprised at having done so: to make up for it, I smiled continually. But for tears, I do not know. If you put a pistol to my throat, I must own the tale trips upon a very airy foot — within a measurable distance of unreality; and for those who like the big guns to be discharged and the great passions to appear authentically, it may even seem inadequate from first to last. Not so to me; I cannot count that a poor dinner, or a poor book, where I meet with those I love; and, above all, in this last volume, I find a singular charm of spirit. It breathes a pleasant and a tonic sadness, always brave, never hysterical. Upon the crowded, noisy life of this long tale, evening gradually falls; and the lights are extinguished, and the heroes pass away one by one. One by one they go, and not a regret embitters their departure; the young succeed them in their places, Louis Quatorze is swelling larger and shining broader, another generation and another France dawn on the horizon; but for us and these old men whom we have loved so long the inevitable end draws near and is welcome. To read this well is to anticipate experience. Ah, if only when

325

these hours of the long shadows fall for us in reality and not in figure, we may hope to face them with a mind as quiet!

But my paper is running out; the siege guns are firing on the Dutch frontier; and I must say adieu for the fifth time to my old comrade fallen on the field of glory. *Adieu* — rather *au revoir!* Yet a sixth time, dearest d'Artagnan, we shall kidnap Monk and take horse together for Belle Isle.

XV. A GOSSIP ON ROMANCE

IN anything fit to be called by the name of reading,
the process itself should be absorbing and voluptu-
ous; we should gloat over a book, be rapt clean out of
ourselves, and rise from the perusal, our mind filled
with the busiest, kaleidoscopic dance of images, incapable of sleep or of continuous thought. The words, if
the book be eloquent, should run thenceforward in our
ears like the noise of breakers, and the story, if it be a
story, repeat itself in a thousand coloured pictures to
the eye. It was for this last pleasure that we read so
closely, and loved our books so dearly, in the bright,
troubled period of boyhood. Eloquence and thought,
character and conversation, were but obstacles to brush
aside as we dug blithely after a certain sort of incident,
like a pig for truffles. For my part, I liked a story to
begin with an old wayside inn where, "towards the close
of the year 17—," several gentlemen in three-cocked
hats were playing bowls. A friend of mine preferred
the Malabar coast in a storm, with a ship beating to
windward, and a scowling fellow of Herculean proportions striding along the beach; he, to be sure, was a
pirate. This was further afield than my home-keeping
fancy loved to travel, and designed altogether for a larger
canvas than the tales that I affected. Give me a highwayman and I was full to the brim; a Jacobite would

do, but the highwayman was my favourite dish. I can still hear that merry clatter of the hoofs along the moonlit lane; night and the coming of day are still related in my mind with the doings of John Rann or Jerry Abershaw; and the words "postchaise," the "great North road," "ostler," and "nag" still sound in my ears like poetry. One and all, at least, and each with his particular fancy, we read story-books in childhood, not for eloquence or character or thought, but for some quality of the brute incident. That quality was not mere bloodshed or wonder. Although each of these was welcome in its place, the charm for the sake of which we read depended on something different from either. My elders used to read novels aloud; and I can still remember four different passages which I heard, before I was ten, with the same keen and lasting pleasure. One I discovered long afterwards to be the admirable opening of *What will he Do with It:* it was no wonder I was pleased with that. The other three still remain unidentified. One is a little vague; it was about a dark, tall house at night, and people groping on the stairs by the light that escaped from the open door of a sickroom. In another, a lover left a ball, and went walking in a cool, dewy park, whence he could watch the lighted windows and the figures of the dancers as they moved. This was the most sentimental impression I think I had yet received, for a child is somewhat deaf to the sentimental. In the last, a poet, who had been tragically wrangling with his wife, walked forth on the sea-beach on a tempestuous night and witnessed the horrors of a wreck.[1] Different

[1] Since traced by many obliging correspondents to the gallery of Charles Kingsley.

as they are, all these early favourites have a common note — they have all a touch of the romantic.

Drama is the poetry of conduct, romance the poetry of circumstance. The pleasure that we take in life is of two sorts — the active and the passive. Now we are conscious of a great command over our destiny; anon we are lifted up by circumstance, as by a breaking wave, and dashed we know not how into the future. Now we are pleased by our conduct, anon merely pleased by our surroundings. It would be hard to say which of these modes of satisfaction is the more effective, but the latter is surely the more constant. Conduct is three parts of life, they say; but I think they put it high. There is a vast deal in life and letters both which is not immoral, but simply a-moral; which either does not regard the human will at all, or deals with it in obvious and healthy relations; where the interest turns, not upon what a man shall choose to do, but on how he manages to do it; not on the passionate slips and hesitations of the conscience, but on the problems of the body and of the practical intelligence, in clean, open-air adventure, the shock of arms or the diplomacy of life. With such material as this it is impossible to build a play, for the serious theatre exists solely on moral grounds, and is a standing proof of the dissemination of the human conscience. But it is possible to build, upon this ground, the most joyous of verses, and the most lively, beautiful, and buoyant tales.

One thing in life calls for another; there is a fitness in events and places. The sight of a pleasant arbour puts it in our mind to sit there. One place suggests work, another idleness, a third early rising and long rambles in the dew. The effect of night, of any flowing water, of lighted cities, of the peep of day, of ships, of the open ocean, calls up in the mind an army of anonymous desires and pleasures. Something, we feel, should happen; we know not what, yet we proceed in quest of it. And many of the happiest hours of life fleet by us in this vain attendance on the genius of the place and moment. It is thus that tracts of young fir, and low rocks that reach into deep soundings, particularly torture and delight me. Something must have happened in such places, and perhaps ages back, to members of my race; and when I was a child I tried in vain to invent appropriate games for them, as I still try, just as vainly, to fit them with the proper story. Some places speak distinctly. Certain dank gardens cry aloud for a murder; certain old houses demand to be haunted; certain coasts are set apart for shipwreck. Other spots again seem to abide their destiny, suggestive and impenetrable, "miching mallecho." The inn at Burford Bridge, with its arbours and green garden and silent, eddying river—though it is known already as the place where Keats wrote some of his *Endymion* and Nelson parted from his Emma—still seems to wait the coming of the appropriate legend. Within these ivied walls, behind these old green shutters, some further business smoulders, waiting for its hour. The old Hawes Inn at the Queen's Ferry makes a similar call upon my fancy. There it stands, apart from the town, beside the pier, in a climate of its own, half inland, half marine—in front, the ferry bubbling with the tide and the guardship swinging to her anchor; behind, the old garden with the trees. Americans seek it already for the sake

330

of Lovel and Oldbuck, who dined there at the beginning of the *Antiquary*. But you need not tell me —
that is not all; there is some story, unrecorded or not
yet complete, which must express the meaning of that
inn more fully. So it is with names and faces; so it is
with incidents that are idle and inconclusive in themselves, and yet seem like the beginning of some quaint
romance, which the all-careless author leaves untold.
How many of these romances have we not seen determine at their birth; how many people have met us
with a look of meaning in their eye, and sunk at once
into trivial acquaintances; to how many places have we
not drawn near, with express intimations — "here my
destiny awaits me" — and we have but dined there and
passed on! I have lived both at the Hawes and Burford in a perpetual flutter, on the heels, as it seemed, of
some adventure that should justify the place; but
though the feeling had me to bed at night and called
me again at morning in one unbroken round of pleasure and suspense, nothing befell me in either worth
remark. The man or the hour had not yet come; but
some day, I think, a boat shall put off from the Queen's
Ferry, fraught with a dear cargo, and some frosty night
a horseman, on a tragic errand, rattle with his whip
upon the green shutters of the inn at Burford.[1]

Now, this is one of the natural appetites with which
any lively literature has to count. The desire for knowledge, I had almost added the desire for meat, is not
more deeply seated than this demand for fit and strik-

---

[1] Since the above was written I have tried to launch the boat with
my own hands in *Kidnapped*. Some day, perhaps, I may try a rattle at the shutters.

ing incident. The dullest of clowns tells, or tries to tell, himself a story, as the feeblest of children uses invention in his play; and even as the imaginative grown person, joining in the game, at once enriches it with many delightful circumstances, the great creative writer shows us the realisation and the apotheosis of the day-dreams of common men. His stories may be nourished with the realities of life, but their true mark is to satisfy the nameless longings of the reader, and to obey the ideal laws of the day-dream. The right kind of thing should fall out in the right kind of place; the right kind of thing should follow; and not only the characters talk aptly and think naturally, but all the circumstances in a tale answer one to another like notes in music. The threads of a story come from time to time together and make a picture in the web; the characters fall from time to time into some attitude to each other or to nature, which stamps the story home like an illustration. Crusoe recoiling from the footprint, Achilles shouting over against the Trojans, Ulysses bending the great bow, Christian running with his fingers in his ears, these are each culminating moments in the legend, and each has been printed on the mind's eye forever. Other things we may forget; we may forget the words, although they are beautiful; we may forget the author's comment, although perhaps it was ingenious and true; but these epoch-making scenes, which put the last mark of truth upon a story and fill up, at one blow, our capacity for sympathetic pleasure, we so adopt into the very bosom of our mind that neither time nor tide can efface or weaken the impression. This, then, is the plastic part of literature: to embody character, thought, or emotion in some act or attitude that shall be remarkably striking to the mind's eye. This is the highest and hardest thing to do in words; the thing which, once accomplished, equally delights the schoolboy and the sage, and makes, in its own right, the quality of epics. Compared with this, all other purposes in literature, except the purely lyrical or the purely philosophic, are bastard in nature, facile of execution, and feeble in result. It is one thing to write about the inn at Burford, or to describe scenery with the word-painters; it is quite another to seize on the heart of the suggestion and make a country famous with a legend. It is one thing to remark and to dissect, with the most cutting logic, the complications of life, and of the human spirit; it is quite another to give them body and blood in the story of Ajax or of Hamlet. The first is literature, but the second is something besides, for it is likewise art.

English people of the present day[1] are apt, I know not why, to look somewhat down on incident, and reserve their admiration for the clink of teaspoons and the accents of the curate. It is thought clever to write a novel with no story at all, or at least with a very dull one. Reduced even to the lowest terms, a certain interest can be communicated by the art of narrative; a sense of human kinship stirred; and a kind of monotonous fitness, comparable to the words and air of *Sandy's Mull,* preserved among the infinitesimal occurrences recorded. Some people work, in this manner, with even a strong touch. Mr. Trollope's inimitable clergymen naturally arise to the mind in this connection. But even Mr. Trollope does not confine himself to chronicling small

[1] 1882.

beer. Mr. Crawley's collision with the Bishop's wife, Mr. Melnette dallying in the deserted banquet-room, are typical incidents, epically conceived, fitly embodying a crisis. Or again look at Thackeray. If Rawdon Crawley's blow were not delivered, *Vanity Fair* would cease to be a work of art. That scene is the chief ganglion of the tale; and the discharge of energy from Rawdon's fist is the reward and consolation of the reader. The end of *Esmond* is a yet wider excursion from the author's customary fields; the scene at Castlewood is pure Dumas; the great and wily English borrower has here borrowed from the great, unblushing French thief; as usual, he has borrowed admirably well, and the breaking of the sword rounds off the best of all his books with a manly, martial note. But perhaps nothing can more strongly illustrate the necessity for marking incident than to compare the living fame of *Robinson Crusoe* with the discredit of *Clarissa Harlowe*. *Clarissa* is a book of a far more startling import, worked out, on a great canvas, with inimitable courage and unflagging art. It contains wit, character, passion, plot, conversations full of spirit and insight, letters sparkling with unstrained humanity; and if the death of the heroine be somewhat frigid and artificial, the last days of the hero strike the only note of what we now call Byronism, between the Elizabethans and Byron himself. And yet a little story of a shipwrecked sailor, with not a tenth part of the style nor a thousandth part of the wisdom, exploring none of the arcana of humanity and deprived of the perennial interest of love, goes on from edition to edition, ever young, while *Clarissa* lies upon the shelves unread. A friend of mine, a Welsh blacksmith, was twenty-five years old and could neither read nor write, when he heard a chapter of *Robinson* read aloud in a farm kitchen. Up to that moment he had sat content, huddled in his ignorance, but he left that farm another man. There were day-dreams, it appeared, divine day-dreams, written and printed and bound, and to be bought for money and enjoyed at pleasure. Down he sat that day, painfully learned to read Welsh, and returned to borrow the book. It had been lost, nor could he find another copy but one that was in English. Down he sat once more, learned English, and at length, and with entire delight, read *Robinson*. It is like the story of a love-chase. If he had heard a letter from *Clarissa,* would he have been fired with the same chivalrous ardour? I wonder. Yet *Clarissa* has every quality that can be shown in prose, one alone excepted — pictorial or picture-making romance. While *Robinson* depends, for the most part and with the overwhelming majority of its readers, on the charm of circumstance.

In the highest achievements of the art of words, the dramatic and the pictorial, the moral and romantic interest, rise and fall together by a common and organic law. Situation is animated with passion, passion clothed upon with situation. Neither exists for itself, but each inheres indissolubly with the other. This is high art; and not only the highest art possible in words, but the highest art of all, since it combines the greatest mass and diversity of the elements of truth and pleasure. Such are epics, and the few prose tales that have the epic weight. But as from a school of works, aping the creative, incident and romance are ruthlessly discarded, so may character and drama be omitted or subordinated to romance. There is one book, for example, more generally loved than Shakespeare, that captivates in childhood, and still delights in age — I mean the *Arabian Nights* — where you shall look in vain for moral or for intellectual interest. No human face or voice greets us among that wooden crowd of kings and genies, sorcerers and beggarmen. Adventure, on the most naked terms, furnishes forth the entertainment and is found enough. Dumas approaches perhaps nearest of any modern to these Arabian authors in the purely material charm of some of his romances. The early part of *Monte Cristo*, down to the finding of the treasure, is a piece of perfect story-telling; the man never breathed who shared these moving incidents without a tremor; and yet Faria is a thing of packthread and Dantès little more than a name. The sequel is one long-drawn error, gloomy, bloody, unnatural and dull; but as for these early chapters, I do not believe there is another volume extant where you can breathe the same unmingled atmosphere of romance. It is very thin and light, to be sure, as on a high mountain; but it is brisk and clear and sunny in proportion. I saw the other day, with envy, an old and a very clever lady setting forth on a second or third voyage into *Monte Cristo*. Here are stories which powerfully affect the reader, which can be reperused at any age, and where the characters are no more than puppets. The bony fist of the showman visibly propels them; their springs are an open secret; their faces are of wood, their bellies filled with bran; and yet we thrillingly partake of their adventures. And the point may be illustrated still further. The last interview between Lucy and Richard Feverel is pure drama; more than that, it is the strongest scene, since Shakespeare, in the English tongue. Their first meeting by the river, on the other hand, is pure romance; it has nothing to do with character; it might happen to any other boy and maiden, and be none the less delightful for the change. And yet I think he would be a bold man who should choose between these passages. Thus, in the same book, we may have two scenes, each capital in its order: in the one, human passion, deep calling unto deep, shall utter its genuine voice; in the second, according circumstances, like instruments in tune, shall build up a trivial but desirable incident, such as we love to prefigure for ourselves; and in the end, in spite of the critics, we may hesitate to give the preference to either. The one may ask more genius—I do not say it does; but at least the other dwells as clearly in the memory.

True romantic art, again, makes a romance of all things. It reaches into the highest abstraction of the ideal; it does not refuse the most pedestrian realism. *Robinson Crusoe* is as realistic as it is romantic: both qualities are pushed to an extreme, and neither suffers. Nor does romance depend upon the material importance of the incidents. To deal with strong and deadly elements, banditti, pirates, war and murder, is to conjure with great names, and, in the event of failure, to double the disgrace. The arrival of Haydn and Consuelo at the Canon's villa is a very trifling incident; yet we may read a dozen boisterous stories from beginning to end, and not receive so fresh and stirring an impression of adventure. It was the scene of Crusoe at the wreck, if I remember rightly, that so bewitched my blacksmith. Nor is the fact surprising. Every single article the castaway recovers from the hulk is "a joy for ever" to the man who reads of them. They are the things that should be found, and the bare enumeration stirs the blood. I found a glimmer of the same interest the other day in a new book, *The Sailor's Sweetheart*, by Mr. Clark Russell. The whole business of the brig *Morning Star* is very rightly felt and spiritedly written; but the clothes, the books and the money satisfy the reader's mind like things to eat. We are dealing here with the old cut-and-dry, legitimate interest of treasure trove. But even treasure trove can be made dull. There are few people who have not groaned under the plethora of goods that fell to the lot of the *Swiss Family Robinson,* that dreary family. They found article after article, creature after creature, from milk kine to pieces of ordnance, a whole consignment; but no informing taste had presided over the selection, there was no smack or relish in the invoice; and these riches left the fancy cold. The box of goods in Verne's *Mysterious Island* is another case in point: there was no gusto and no glamour about that; it might have come from a shop. But the two hundred and seventy-eight Australian sovereigns on board the *Morning Star* fell upon me like a surprise that I had expected; whole vistas of secondary stories, besides the one in hand, radiated forth from that discovery, as they radiate from a striking particular in life; and I was made for the moment as happy as a reader has the right to be.

To come at all at the nature of this quality of romance, we must bear in mind the peculiarity of our attitude to any art. No art produces illusion; in the theatre we never forget that we are in the theatre; and while we read a story, we sit wavering between two minds, now merely clapping our hands at the merit of the performance, now condescending to take an active part in fancy with the characters. This last is the triumph of romantic story-telling: when the reader consciously plays at being the hero, the scene is a good scene. Now in character-studies the pleasure that we take is critical; we watch, we approve, we smile at incongruities, we are moved to sudden heats of sympathy with courage, suffering or virtue. But the characters are still themselves, they are not us; the more clearly they are depicted, the more widely do they stand away from us, the more imperiously do they thrust us back into our place as a spectator. I cannot identify myself with Rawdon Crawley or with Eugène de Rastignac, for I have scarce a hope or fear in common with them. It is not character but incident that woos us out of our reserve. Something happens as we desire to have it happen to ourselves; some situation, that we have long dallied with in fancy, is realised in the story with enticing and appropriate details. Then we forget the characters; then we push the hero aside; then we plunge into the tale in our own person and bathe in fresh experience; and then, and then only, do we say we have been reading a romance. It is not only pleasurable things that we imagine in our day-dreams; there are lights in which we are willing to contemplate even the idea of our own death; ways in which it seems as if it would amuse us to be cheated, wounded or calumniated. It is thus possible to construct a story, even of

tragic import, in which every incident, detail and trick
of circumstance shall be welcome to the reader's
thoughts. Fiction is to the grown man what play is
to the child; it is there that he changes the atmosphere
and tenor of his life; and when the game so chimes
with his fancy that he can join in it with all his heart,
when it pleases him with every turn, when he loves to
recall it and dwells upon its recollection with entire delight, fiction is called romance.

Walter Scott is out and away the king of the roman-
tics. *The Lady of the Lake* has no indisputable claim to
be a poem beyond the inherent fitness and desirability
of the tale. It is just such a story as a man would make
up for himself, walking, in the best health and temper,
through just such scenes as it is laid in. Hence it is that
a charm dwells undefinable among these slovenly verses,
as the unseen cuckoo fills the mountains with his note;
hence, even after we have flung the book aside, the
scenery and adventures remain present to the mind, a
new and green possession, not unworthy of that beautiful name, *The Lady of the Lake*, or that direct, romantic opening,— one of the most spirited and poetical in
literature,—"The stag at eve had drunk his fill." The
same strength and the same weaknesses adorn and dis-
figure the novels. In that ill-written, ragged book, *The
Pirate*, the figure of Cleveland — cast up by the sea on
the resounding foreland of Dunrossness — moving, with
the blood on his hands and the Spanish words on his
tongue, among the simple islanders — singing a sere-
nade under the window of his Shetland mistress — is
conceived in the very highest manner of romantic invention. The words of his song, "Through groves of

palm," sung in such a scene and by such a lover, clench, as in a nutshell, the emphatic contrast upon which the tale is built. In *Guy Mannering*, again, every incident is delightful to the imagination; and the scene when Harry Bertram lands at Ellangowan is a model instance of romantic method.

" 'I remember the tune well,' he says, 'though I cannot guess what should at present so strongly recall it to my memory.' He took his flageolet from his pocket and played a simple melody. Apparently the tune awoke the corresponding associations of a damsel. . . She immediately took up the song —

> " ' Are these the links of Forth, she said;
> Or are they the crooks of Dee,
> Or the bonny woods of Warroch Head
> That I so fain would see?'

" 'By heaven!' said Bertram, 'it is the very ballad.' "

On this quotation two remarks fall to be made. First, as an instance of modern feeling for romance, this famous touch of the flageolet and the old song is selected by Miss Braddon for omission. Miss Braddon's idea of a story, like Mrs. Todgers's idea of a wooden leg, were something strange to have expounded. As a matter of personal experience, Meg's appearance to old Mr. Bertram on the road, the ruins of Derncleugh, the scene of the flageolet, and the Dominie's recognition of Harry, are the four strong notes that continue to ring in the mind after the book is laid aside. The second point is still more curious. The reader will observe a mark of excision in the passage as quoted by me. Well, here is how it runs in the original: "a damsel, who, close behind a fine spring about half-way down the descent, and which had once supplied the castle with water, was engaged in bleaching linen." A man who gave in such copy would be discharged from the staff of a daily paper. Scott has forgotten to prepare the reader for the presence of the "damsel"; he has forgotten to mention the spring and its relation to the ruin; and now, face to face with his omission, instead of trying back and starting fair, crams all this matter, tail foremost, into a single shambling sentence. It is not merely bad English, or bad style; it is abominably bad narrative besides.

Certainly the contrast is remarkable; and it is one that throws a strong light upon the subject of this paper. For here we have a man of the finest creative instinct touching with perfect certainty and charm the romantic junctures of his story; and we find him utterly careless, almost, it would seem, incapable, in the technical matter of style, and not only frequently weak, but frequently wrong in points of drama. In character parts, indeed, and particularly in the Scotch, he was delicate, strong and truthful; but the trite, obliterated features of too many of his heroes have already wearied two generations of readers. At times his characters will speak with something far beyond propriety with a true heroic note; but on the next page they will be wading wearily forward with an ungrammatical and undramatic rigmarole of words. The man who could conceive and write the character of Elspeth of the Craigburnfoot, as Scott has conceived and written it, had not only splendid romantic, but splendid tragic gifts. How comes it, then, that he could so often fob us off with languid, inarticulate twaddle ?

It seems to me that the explanation is to be found in the very quality of his surprising merits. As his books are play to the reader, so were they play to him. He conjured up the romantic with delight, but he had hardly patience to describe it. He was a great day-dreamer, a seer of fit and beautiful and humorous visions, but hardly a great artist; hardly, in tne manful sense, an artist at all. He pleased himself, and so he pleases us. Of the pleasures of his art he tasted fully; but of its toils and vigils and distresses never man knew less. A great romantic — an idle child.

XVI. A HUMBLE REMONSTRANCE[1]

I

WE have recently[2] enjoyed a quite peculiar pleasure: hearing, in some detail, the opinions,
about the art they practise, of Mr. Walter Besant and
Mr. Henry James; two men certainly of very different
calibre: Mr. James so precise of outline, so cunning of
fence, so scrupulous of finish, and Mr. Besant so genial,
so friendly, with so persuasive and humorous a vein of
whim: Mr. James the very type of the deliberate artist,
Mr. Besant the impersonation of good nature. That
such doctors should differ will excite no great surprise;
but one point in which they seem to agree fills me, I
confess, with wonder. For they are both content to
talk about the "art of fiction;" and Mr. Besant, wax-
ing exceedingly bold, goes on to oppose this so-called
"art of fiction" to the "art of poetry." By the art of
poetry he can mean nothing but the art of verse, an art
of handicraft, and only comparable with the art of
prose. For that heat and height of sane emotion which
we agree to call by the name of poetry, is but a liber-
tine and vagrant quality; present, at times, in any art,

[1] This paper, which does not otherwise fit the present volume, is reprinted here as the proper continuation of the last.

[2] 1884.

344

more often absent from them all; too seldom present in the prose novel, too frequently absent from the ode and epic. Fiction is in the same case; it is no substantive art, but an element which enters largely into all the arts but architecture. Homer, Wordsworth, Phidias, Hogarth, and Salvini, all deal in fiction; and yet I do not suppose that either Hogarth or Salvini, to mention but these two, entered in any degree into the scope of Mr. Besant's interesting lecture or Mr. James's charming essay. The art of fiction, then, regarded as a definition, is both too ample and too scanty. Let me suggest another; let me suggest that what both Mr. James and Mr. Besant had in view was neither more nor less than the art of narrative.

But Mr. Besant is anxious to speak solely of "the modern English novel," the stay and bread-winner of Mr. Mudie; and in the author of the most pleasing novel on that roll, *All Sorts and Conditions of Men,* the desire is natural enough. I can conceive then, that he would hasten to propose two additions, and read thus: the art of *fictitious* narrative *in prose.*

Now the fact of the existence of the modern English novel is not to be denied; materially, with its three volumes, leaded type, and gilded lettering, it is easily distinguishable from other forms of literature; but to talk at all fruitfully of any branch of art, it is needful to build our definitions on some more fundamental ground than binding. Why, then, are we to add "in prose?" *The Odyssey* appears to me the best of romances; *The Lady of the Lake* to stand high in the second order; and Chaucer's tales and prologues to contain more of the matter and art of the modern English novel than the whole treasury of Mr. Mudie. Whether a narrative be written in blank verse or the Spenserian stanza, in the long period of Gibbon or the chipped phrase of Charles Reade, the principles of the art of narrative must be equally observed. The choice of a noble and swelling style in prose affects the problem of narration in the same way, if not to the same degree, as the choice of measured verse; for both imply a closer synthesis of events, a higher key of dialogue, and a more picked and stately strain of words. If you are to refuse *Don Juan,* it is hard to see why you should include *Zanoni* or (to bracket works of very different value) *The Scarlet Letter;* and by what discrimination are you to open your doors to *The Pilgrim's Progress* and close them on *The Faery Queen?* To bring things closer home, I will here propound to Mr. Besant a conundrum. A narrative called *Paradise Lost* was written in English verse by one John Milton; what was it then? It was next translated by Chateaubriand into French prose; and what was it then? Lastly, the French translation was, by some inspired compatriot of George Gilfillan (and of mine) turned bodily into an English novel; and, in the name of clearness, what was it then?

But, once more, why should we add "fictitious?" The reason why is obvious. The reason why not, if something more recondite, does not want for weight. The art of narrative, in fact, is the same, whether it is applied to the selection and illustration of a real series of events or of an imaginary series. Boswell's *Life of Johnson* (a work of cunning and inimitable art) owes its success to the same technical manœuvres as (let us say) *Tom Jones :* the clear conception of certain characters of

man, the choice and presentation of certain incidents out
of a great number that offered, and the invention (yes
invention) and preservation of a certain key in dialogue.
In which these things are done with the more art — in
which with the greater air of nature — readers will differently judge. Boswell's is, indeed, a very special case,
and almost a generic; but it is not only in Boswell, it is
in every biography with any salt of life, it is in every
history where events and men, rather than ideas, are
presented — in Tacitus, in Carlyle, in Michelet, in Macaulay — that the novelist will find many of his own
methods most conspicuously and adroitly handled. He
will find besides that he, who is free — who has the
right to invent or steal a missing incident, who has the
right, more precious still, of wholesale omission — is
frequently defeated, and, with all his advantages, leaves
a less strong impression of reality and passion. Mr.
James utters his mind with a becoming fervour on the
sanctity of truth to the novelist; on a more careful examination truth will seem a word of very debatable
propriety, not only for the labours of the novelist, but
for those of the historian. No art — to use the daring
phrase of Mr. James — can successfully " compete with
life;" and the art that seeks to do so is condemned to
perish *montibus aviis*. Life goes before us, infinite in
complication; attended by the most various and surprising meteors; appealing at once to the eye, to the
ear, to the mind — the seat of wonder, to the touch —
so thrillingly delicate, and to the belly — so imperious
when starved. It combines and employs in its mani-
festation the method and material, not of one art only,
but of all the arts. Music is but an arbitrary trifling

with a few of life's majestic chords; painting is but a shadow of its pageantry of light and colour; literature does but drily indicate that wealth of incident, of moral obligation, of virtue, vice, action, rapture and agony, with which it teems. To "compete with life," whose sun we cannot look upon, whose passions and diseases waste and slay us — to compete with the flavour of wine, the beauty of the dawn, the scorching of fire, the bitterness of death and separation — here is, indeed, a projected escalade of heaven; here are, indeed, labours for a Hercules in a dress coat, armed with a pen and a dictionary to depict the passions, armed with a tube of superior flake-white to paint the portrait of the insufferable sun. No art is true in this sense: none can "compete with life:" not even history, built indeed of indisputable facts, but these facts robbed of their vivacity and sting; so that even when we read of the sack of a city or the fall of an empire, we are surprised, and justly commend the author's talent, if our pulse be quickened. And mark, for a last differentia, that this quickening of the pulse is, in almost every case, purely agreeable; that these phantom reproductions of experience, even at their most acute, convey decided pleasure; while experience itself, in the cockpit of life, can torture and slay.

What, then, is the object, what the method, of an art, and what the source of its power? The whole secret is that no art does "compete with life." Man's one method, whether he reasons or creates, is to half-shut his eyes against the dazzle and confusion of reality. The arts, like arithmetic and geometry, turn away their eyes from the gross, coloured and mobile nature at our feet, and regard instead a certain figmentary abstraction.

Geometry will tell us of a circle, a thing never seen in nature; asked about a green circle or an iron circle, it lays its hand upon its mouth. So with the arts. Painting, ruefully comparing sunshine and flake-white, gives up truth of colour, as it had already given up relief and movement; and instead of vying with nature, arranges a scheme of harmonious tints. Literature, above all in its most typical mood, the mood of narrative, similarly flees the direct challenge and pursues instead an independent and creative aim. So far as it imitates at all, it imitates not life but speech: not the facts of human destiny, but the emphasis and the suppressions with which the human actor tells of them. The real art that dealt with life directly was that of the first men who told their stories round the savage camp-fire. Our art is occupied, and bound to be occupied, not so much in making stories true as in making them typical; not so much in capturing the lineaments of each fact, as in marshalling all of them towards a common end. For the welter of impressions, all forcible but all discreet, which life presents, it substitutes a certain artificial series of impressions, all indeed most feebly represented, but all aiming at the same effect, all eloquent of the same idea, all chiming together like consonant notes in music or like the graduated tints in a good picture. From all its chapters, from all its pages, from all its sentences, the well-written novel echoes and re-echoes its one creative and controlling thought; to this must every incident and character contribute; the style must have been pitched in unison with this; and if there is anywhere a word that looks another way, the book would be stronger, clearer, and (I had almost said) fuller without it. Life is mon-

349

strous, infinite, illogical, abrupt and poignant; a work of art, in comparison, is neat, finite, self-contained, rational, flowing and emasculate. Life imposes by brute energy, like inarticulate thunder; art catches the ear, among the far louder noises of experience, like an air artificially made by a discreet musician. A proposition of geometry does not compete with life; and a proposition of geometry is a fair and luminous parallel for a work of art. Both are reasonable, both untrue to the crude fact; both inhere in nature, neither represents it. The novel, which is a work of art, exists, not by its resemblances to life, which are forced and material, as a shoe must still consist of leather, but by its immeasurable difference from life, which is designed and significant, and is both the method and the meaning of the work.

The life of man is not the subject of novels, but the inexhaustible magazine from which subjects are to be selected; the name of these is legion; and with each new subject — for here again I must differ by the whole width of heaven from Mr. James — the true artist will vary his method and change the point of attack. That which was in one case an excellence, will become a defect in another; what was the making of one book, will in the next be impertinent or dull. First each novel, and then each class of novels, exists by and for itself. I will take, for instance, three main classes, which are fairly distinct: first, the novel of adventure, which appeals to certain almost sensual and quite illogical tendencies in man; second, the novel of character, which appeals to our intellectual appreciation of man's foibles and mingled and inconstant motives; and third, the dramatic novel, which deals with the same stuff as the serious theatre, and appeals to our emotional nature and moral judgment.

And first for the novel of adventure. Mr. James refers, with singular generosity of praise, to a little book about a quest for hidden treasure; but he lets fall, by the way, some rather startling words. In this book he misses what he calls the "immense luxury" of being able to quarrel with his author. The luxury, to most of us, is to lay by our judgment, to be submerged by the tale as by a billow, and only to awake, and begin to distinguish and find fault, when the piece is over and the volume laid aside. Still more remarkable is Mr. James's reason. He cannot criticise the author, as he goes, "because," says he, comparing it with another work, " *I have been a child, but I have never been on a quest for buried treasure."* Here is, indeed, a wilful paradox; for if he has never been on a quest for buried treasure, it can be demonstrated that he has never been a child. There never was a child (unless Master James) but has hunted gold, and been a pirate, and a military commander, and a bandit of the mountains; but has fought, and suffered shipwreck and prison, and imbrued its little hands in gore, and gallantly retrieved the lost battle, and triumphantly protected innocence and beauty. Elsewhere in his essay Mr. James has protested with excellent reason against too narrow a conception of experience; for the born artist, he contends, the "faintest hints of life" are converted into revelations; and it will be found true, I believe, in a majority of cases, that the artist writes with more gusto and effect of those things which he has only wished to do, than of those which he has done. Desire is a wonderful telescope, and Pisgah the best observatory. Now, while it is true that neither Mr. James nor the author of the work in question has ever, in the fleshly sense, gone questing after gold, it is probable that both have ardently desired and fondly imagined the details of such a life in youthful day-dreams; and the author, counting upon that, and well aware (cunning and low-minded man!) that this class of interest, having been frequently treated, finds a readily accessible and beaten road to the sympathies of the reader, addressed himself throughout to the building up and circumstantiation of this boyish dream. Character to the boy is a sealed book; for him, a pirate is a beard, a pair of wide trousers and a liberal complement of pistols. The author, for the sake of circumstantiation and because he was himself more or less grown up, admitted character, within certain limits, into his design; but only within certain limits. Had the same puppets figured in a scheme of another sort, they had been drawn to very different purpose; for in this elementary novel of adventure, the characters need to be presented with but one class of qualities — the warlike and formidable. So as they appear insidious in deceit and fatal in the combat, they have served their end. Danger is the matter with which this class of novel deals; fear, the passion with which it idly trifles; and the characters are portrayed only so far as they realise the sense of danger and provoke the sympathy of fear. To add more traits, to be too clever, to start the hare of moral or intellectual interest while we are running the fox of material interest, is not to enrich but to stultify your tale. The stupid reader will only be offended, and the clever reader lose the scent.

The novel of character has this difference from all others: that it requires no coherency of plot, and for this reason, as in the case of *Gil Blas,* it is sometimes called the novel of adventure. It turns on the humours of the persons represented; these are, to be sure, embodied in incidents, but the incidents themselves, being tributary, need not march in a progression; and the characters may be statically shown. As they enter, so they may go out; they must be consistent, but they need not grow. Here Mr. James will recognise the note of much of his own work: he treats, for the most part, the statics of character, studying it at rest or only gently moved; and, with his usual delicate and just artistic instinct, he avoids those stronger passions which would deform the attitudes he loves to study, and change his sitters from the humourists of ordinary life to the brute forces and bare types of more emotional moments. In his recent *Author of Beltraffio,* so just in conception, so nimble and neat in workmanship, strong passion is indeed employed; but observe that it is not displayed. Even in the heroine the working of the passion is suppressed; and the great struggle, the true tragedy, the *scène-à-faire,* passes unseen behind the panels of a locked door. The delectable invention of the young visitor is introduced, consciously or not, to this end: that Mr. James, true to his method, might avoid the scene of passion. I trust no reader will suppose me guilty of undervaluing this little masterpiece. I mean merely that it belongs to one marked class of novel, and that it would have been very differently conceived and treated had it belonged to that other marked class, of which I now proceed to speak.

I take pleasure in calling the dramatic novel by that name, because it enables me to point out by the way a strange and peculiarly English misconception. It is sometimes supposed that the drama consists of incident. It consists of passion, which gives the actor his opportunity; and that passion must progressively increase, or the actor, as the piece proceeded, would be unable to carry the audience from a lower to a higher pitch of interest and emotion. A good serious play must therefore be founded on one of the passionate *cruces* of life, where duty and inclination come nobly to the grapple; and the same is true of what I call, for that reason, the dramatic novel. I will instance a few worthy specimens, all of our own day and language; Meredith's *Rhoda Fleming,* that wonderful and painful book, long out of print,[1] and hunted for at book-stalls like an Aldine; Hardy's *Pair of Blue Eyes;* and two of Charles Reade's, *Griffith Gaunt* and *The Double Marriage,* originally called *White Lies,* and founded (by an an accident quaintly favourable to my nomenclature) on a play by Maquet, the partner of the great Dumas. In this kind of novel the closed door of *The Author of Beltraffio* must be broken open; passion must appear upon the scene and utter its last word; passion is the be-all and the end-all, the plot and the solution, the protagonist and the *deus ex machina* in one. The characters may come anyhow upon the stage: we do not care; the point is, that, before they leave it, they shall become transfigured and raised out of themselves by passion. It may be part of the design to draw them with detail; to depict a full-length character, and then

[1] Now no longer so, thank Heaven!

behold it melt and change in the furnace of emotion. But there is no obligation of the sort; nice portraiture is not required; and we are content to accept mere abstract types, so they be strongly and sincerely moved. A novel of this class may be even great, and yet contain no individual figure; it may be great, because it displays the workings of the perturbed heart and the impersonal utterance of passion; and with an artist of the second class it is, indeed, even more likely to be great, when the issue has thus been narrowed and the whole force of the writer's mind directed to passion alone. Cleverness again, which has its fair field in the novel of character, is debarred all entry upon this more solemn theatre. A far-fetched motive, an ingenious evasion of the issue, a witty instead of a passionate turn, offend us like an insincerity. All should be plain, all straightforward to the end. Hence it is that, in *Rhoda Fleming,* Mrs. Lovel raises such resentment in the reader; her motives are too flimsy, her ways are too equivocal, for the weight and strength of her surroundings. Hence the hot indignation of the reader when Balzac, after having begun the *Duchesse de Langeais* in terms of strong if somewhat swollen passion, cuts the knot by the derangement of the hero's clock. Such personages and incidents belong to the novel of character; they are out of place in the high society of the passions; when the passions are introduced in art at their full height, we look to see them, not baffled and impotently striving, as in life, but towering above circumstance and acting substitutes for fate.

And here I can imagine Mr. James, with his lucid sense, to intervene. To much of what I have said he would apparently demur; in much he would, somewhat impatiently, acquiesce. It may be true; but it is not what he desired to say or to hear said. He spoke of the finished picture and its worth when done; I, of the brushes, the palette, and the north light. He uttered his views in the tone and for the ear of good society; I, with the emphasis and technicalities of the obtrusive student. But the point, I may reply, is not merely to amuse the public, but to offer helpful advice to the young writer. And the young writer will not so much be helped by genial pictures of what an art may aspire to at its highest, as by a true idea of what it must be on the lowest terms. The best that we can say to him is this: Let him choose a motive, whether of character or passion; carefully construct his plot so that every incident is an illustration of the motive, and every property employed shall bear to it a near relation of congruity or contrast; avoid a sub-plot, unless, as sometimes in Shakespeare, the sub-plot be a reversion or complement of the main intrigue; suffer not his style to flag below the level of the argument; pitch the key of conversation, not with any thought of how men talk in parlours, but with a single eye to the degree of passion he may be called on to express; and allow neither himself in the narrative nor any character in the course of the dialogue, to utter one sentence that is not part and parcel of the business of the story or the discussion of the problem involved. Let him not regret if this shortens his book; it will be better so; for to add irrelevant matter is not to lengthen but to bury. Let him not mind if he miss a thousand qualities, so that he keeps unflaggingly in pursuit of the one he has chosen.